The Atlas of the Later Zulu Wars

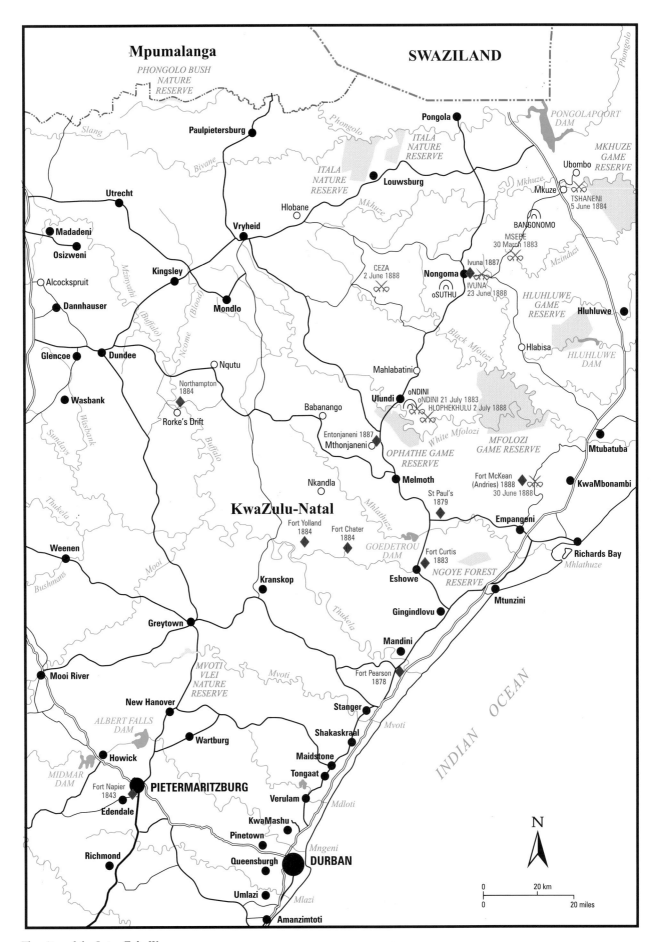

The sites of the Later Zulu Wars.

The Atlas of the
Later Zulu Wars
1883–1888

by

John Laband

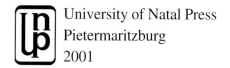

University of Natal Press
Pietermaritzburg
2001

ISBN 0 86980 998 9

Cartography: M Design

Cover design: Brett Armstrong

The cover picture showing the battle of oNdini on 21 July 1883 is a watercolour by Olive Anderson, with DTP by Anthony Cuerden, on an engraving from the *Pictorial World* in the Rai England Collection.

Typeset by the University of Natal Press, Pietermaritzburg, South Africa
Printed and bound by Interpak Books, Pietermaritzburg

Contents

Part VI: Conclusion

Acknowledgements

It must go without saying that an atlas would not be an atlas without maps. That is why my deepest debt of gratitude is to my cartographers, Di Matheson and Marise Bauer. We started on these maps in 1996, and then laid them aside for a year or two to prepare *The Illustrated Guide to the Anglo-Zulu War*. Once that was published in 2000, we resumed work. I imposed the military features and troop movements on the bases drawn by Di and Marise, and they then transformed these into the elegant finished product. Throughout the process they proffered skilled and welcome advice which helped me to express my intentions with greater clarity and precision. This has been a most productive and amiable partnership which I greatly value.

I am also much beholden to Glenn Cowley, the Publisher at the University of Natal Press, for giving this protracted project his support and encouragement, and to the University of Natal Research Fund for granting the necessary funding to defray cartographic and research costs.

During the course of research I received unfailing professional assistance from a number of archives, libraries and museums, and I wish to register my appreciation to the staff of the following institutions: the Pietermaritzburg Archives Repository; the Natal Society Library, Pietermaritzburg; the Cecil Renaud Library, University of Natal, Pietermaritzburg; the KwaZulu-Natal Museum Service, Pietermaritzburg; the Killie Campbell Africana Library, Campbell Collections, Durban; the Local History Museum, Durban; the South African Library, Cape Town; MuseuMAfrica, Johannesburg; the National Army Museum, London; and the Public Record Office, Kew.

I am indebted to Ian Knight who most generously made his own extensive photographic collection available and secured permissions from several other private collections in the United Kingdom. For many years now we have communicated regularly concerning our mutual interest in warfare in Zululand and have shared information and ideas. Lt-Col Ian van der Waag of the Military History Department at the South African Military Academy attentively read through this atlas when it was in draft form, and made many constructive and invaluable suggestions which I have appreciatively adopted. Thanks are also due to Gilbert Torlage of KwaZulu-Natal Provincial Museum Services for his helpful comments.

Sally Hines, my unruffled editor at the University of Natal Press, deserves especial thanks. Not only has she efficiently combed the text and made many improvements in style and format, but the effective page design is also hers. Andrea Nattrass cast the last discriminating eye over the book.

It is over twenty years since first I brought out a book. Then, as now, Fenella has unfailingly sustained and encouraged me even though research and writing are all too often introverted pursuits which exact their toll on those closest to an author.

John Laband
University of Natal, Pietermaritzburg

Key to Symbols

Colour identification of military units and works

uSuthu

Mandlakazi

British

colonial and imperial (raised locally)

Boer

Classification of military units

Zulu

military concentration

military unit

Boer

Boer commando

British and Colonial

headquarters

cavalry

artillery

infantry

Size of military units

squad

section

infantry platoon, or division of artillery battery

infantry company, cavalry troop or artillery battery

infantry battalion or cavalry squadron

Weapons

gun

Gatling gun

Military commander

Zibhebhu

Military works

Zulu fastness

British fort

British camp or Boer laager

Engagement

battle

Members of a chiefdom

abaQulusi

Features

umuzi (Zulu homestead)

destroyed *umuzi*

civilian encampment

British magistracy

trading store

Anglican mission station

Hermannsburg mission station

Norwegian mission station

Swedish mission station

town

track

international boundary

magisterial boundary

Key to British and
Colonial Units in Zululand
1883–1888

British
Cavalry
6th (Inniskilling) Dragoons   **6ID**

Artillery
H Battery, 4th Brigade, Royal Field Artillery   **H, 4RFA**

Infantry
1st Bn, Princess Louise's (Argyll and Sutherland Highlanders)   **1/ASH**
2nd Bn, The Northamptonshire Regiment   **2/NR**
1st Bn, The Prince of Wales's (North Staffordshire Regiment)   **1/NSR**
1st Bn, The Royal Inniskilling Fusiliers   **1/RIF**
1st Bn, The Royal Scots (Lothian Regiment)   **1/RS**
2nd Bn, The Prince of Wales's Volunteers (South Lancashire Regiment)   **2/SLR**
1st Bn, The Welsh Regiment   **1/WR**

Mounted Infantry
Drawn from infantry units above   **MI**

Colonial
Mounted
Addison's Horse   **AH**
Basuto Special Police   **BSP**
Mounted Basutos   **MB**

Foot
Carrington's Levy   **CL**
Dunn's Levy   **DL**
Eshowe Levy   **EL**
Knight's (Entonjaneni) Levy   **KL**
Mnyamana's Auxiliaries   **MA**

Mounted and Foot
Basutos   **B**
Reserve Territory Carbineers   **RTC**
Zululand Police   **ZP**

PART I

The Framework

'During his boyhood [Dinuzulu] did not experience the full happiness of boys who are still growing up, for he was born in very bad times. The great men (*izikulu*) of the Zulu country were at war, and the king himself [Cetshwayo] had been made to cast down his shield. The *izikulu* had begun to dispute and to fight among themselves, and to seize cattle from one another. In particular they seized many of the king's cattle . . . In the end they attacked the king and killed him . . . soon after the white people had brought him back . . . The king did not know that . . . his son [Dinuzulu] would soon be an outcast . . . He was caught up in the great bloodshed of the men when he was still young.'

(Dr Pixley ka Isaac Seme, lawyer and political activist, 12 May 1925)

'Godide ka Ndhlela was killed by Zibebu at oNdini [battle in 1883], after Cetshwayo had returned from across the sea. After he was killed his body was not carried away; it was eaten by birds, by vultures . . . If you were victorious in fighting, you would return to the bodies and "bury" (*lahla*) them by covering them with their shields . . . This was not done to Godide, for our side was defeated.'

(Ntshelele ka Godide, 27 February 1922)

Introduction

For the Zulu living at the time, and in the people's memory today, it was not the Anglo-Zulu War of 1879 which spelt the end of their kingdom and transformed their way of life. Rather, it was during the wars of the 1880s that, in the words of Magema M. Fuze, the Zulu historian writing at the very beginning of the twentieth century, 'the calabash and its contents were shattered'.

Certainly, the Anglo-Zulu War still holds pride of place amongst those with an interest in Victorian colonial campaigns, and there seems no end to the quite enormous literature that is still burgeoning around it. Yet this was not the final war the British fought against the Zulu. Indeed, the last time the British Army ever went on campaign still wearing scarlet was in Zululand in 1888.

The Zulu wars of the 1880s were smaller in scale than the Anglo-Zulu War, and fewer British and colonial troops were deployed. Yet the level and geographical extent of devastation among homes, crops and livestock was perceptibly greater, and casualties among the Zulu – civilians as well as fighting-men – comparable. What made the fighting all the more terrible and unforgiving was the dominating strand of civil war between the uSuthu and Mandlakazi that ran through it all, even when some among the Zulu were combatting the land-grabbing Boers or resisting the newly-imposed British colonial administration. Indeed, civil war poisoned Zululand in these years and delivered the Zulu people into the hands of its future colonial rulers.

Important as the civil wars and rebellion of the 1880s undoubtedly were for the people of Zululand in the years to come, they are also of interest from a more purely military perspective. They took place at a time of transition in fighting-methods and tactics for both the British and the Zulu.

The complex campaigns that were waged the length and breadth of Zululand (encompassing a far wider theatre than that of the more famous war of 1879) are intriguing in their own right; while the variety in style and intensity of the many battles fought exemplifies the changes then occurring in colonial warfare.

No convenient phrase, like the 'Seven Years War' or the 'Bhambatha Rebellion', has achieved popular currency for encompassing this interrelated series of conflicts in Zululand between the Anglo-Zulu War of 1879 and the Anglo-Boer War of 1899–1902, so in this atlas the term the 'Later Zulu Wars' has been coined for the sake of expedience. However, even if it should gain some acceptance in future, it can hardly be doubted that it is likely to prove as contentious as any of the labels for wars mentioned above.

This book sets out to describe and analyse the Zulu wars and battles of the 1880s, while at the same time explaining the political context in which they took place. As is appropriate in an historical atlas, pride of place goes to Parts II to V and the maps and accompanying explanatory text embracing political developments, military campaigns and individual battles. Taken in chronological order, these maps lay out the history of Zululand from the abortive British political settlement of September 1879 to the final collapse in October 1888 of Zulu resistance to British rule. The maps are preceded in Part I by some elucidatory reflections on the nature of the diverse military forces fighting in Zululand at that time, and on the ways in which colonial control was imposed and divisions among the Zulu exploited to that end. The overall significance and implications of the conflicts of the 1880s are considered in Part VI.

The uSuthu and Mandlakazi

The uSuthu

When King Mpande kaSenzangakhona sent an army against the Pedi in 1851, they brought back as booty 'Suthu'-type cattle which were greatly admired because they were so much larger than the Zulu variety. Indeed, they were said to be able to drink in one gulp enough water to satisfy a whole herd of the smaller breed. So when the adolescent Prince Cetshwayo kaMpande and his boon companions wished to boast, they would say, 'We are the Suthu cattle! See how we drink our beer!' Soon the Prince and his entourage adopted the word 'uSuthu' as their distinguishing cry.

Later, when Cetshwayo, now in his early twenties, used to regularly visit his mother Ngqumbazi at her kwaGqikazi *ikhanda* (military homestead) in the Vuna River valley in northern Zululand, the *amabutho* (members of the age-set regiments) stationed there and at the associated ekuBazeni *ikhanda* developed strong bonds with him. They too took up the cry of 'uSuthu!' as their own. It consequently became the war-cry and collective name of all of Cetshwayo's followers in the civil war of 1856 when he destroyed his brother Mbuyazi and his supporters, known as the iziGqoza, thus securing his succession to the Zulu throne. When Cetshwayo became king in 1872, 'uSuthu!' became the national cry since all the Zulu people now belonged to him, and was uttered by the *amabutho* at the great festivals and in battle.

After the Zulu defeat by the British in 1879 and Cetshwayo's exile, the term 'uSuthu' came to denote all those who still adhered to the royalist cause. It most especially applied to those who dwelt in the vicinity of the old kwaGqikazi *ikhanda*, for they came directly under the chieftainship of Cetshwayo's brothers whose *imizi* (homesteads) were clustered nearby along the Vuna River. Their most bitter enemies were those who benefited best from Sir Garnet Wolseley's settlement of Zululand of September 1879, particularly the Mandlakazi.

The Mandlakazi

In 1819 King Shaka kaSenzangakhona defeated Zwide kaLanga of the Ndwandwe people and drove them north across the Phongolo River. Since Shaka lacked the resources to bring the chiefdoms north of the Black Mfolozi – which had been Zwide's tributaries – under his direct control, he permitted his authority in these new north-eastern territories of his growing kingdom to be exercised through a viceroy. This viceroy was Maphitha kaSojiyisa of the Mandlakazi people who was closely related to the Zulu kings through descent from their common ancestor, Jama kaNdaba. The wily and ruthless Maphitha ruled his chiefdom with a considerable degree of autonomy, dying only in the final days of King Mpande's reign.

His very able son, Zibhebhu, continued his father's quest for greater political independence, and eagerly grasped the opportunity Wolseley offered him in 1879 to set up as a sovereign ruler in north-eastern Zululand. His newly-won position was threatened, however, by the aspirations of the uSuthu, particularly after Cetshwayo's restoration in 1883. Consequently, Zibhebhu led his Mandlakazi and whatever allies they could find in a relentless struggle against the uSuthu. This political rivalry between the two factions was made more inflammable through disputes over land, for uSuthu and Mandlakazi *imizi* were inextricably and explosively intermingled in many parts of northern Zululand.

Zulu Military Organisation and Fighting Techniques during the 1880s

'The [military] system has, during a period of more than half a century, taken deep root in the Zulu nation. It is part and parcel of the Zulu life, and its extinction would be the work of many years. The organisation is there, the material is there, the machinery is there [though it] has been suffered to run down and lies in disuse.'

(Sir Henry Bulwer, Governor of Natal and Special Commissioner for Zulu Affairs, August 1882)

The suppression of the *ibutho* system

The fully functioning Zulu military system which, ever since the reign of King Shaka, had formed the basis of the king's power and authority, came to an abrupt end with defeat in the Anglo-Zulu War of 1879 and the subsequent deposition of King Cetshwayo. The members of the age-set regiments, or *amabutho* (singular – *ibutho*), who were only a militia and not professional soldiers, scattered to their homes and resumed their civilian roles. Only the king had the authority to call them up again, and in the political settlement which the British imposed on the vanquished Zulu, Gen Sir Garnet Wolseley tried to make sure that there would in future be no monarch or central authority available to revive the military system. He divided the former kingdom into thirteen fragments under appointed chiefs who could be depended upon to ensure that the aspirations of Cetshwayo's family and supporters were kept firmly in check. In the conflicts which rapidly broke out after the withdrawal of the British forces among the appointed chiefs and the royalist faction, known as the uSuthu, all sides deployed fighting-men whose organisation and loyalties were regional and personal to them, rather than to the king, as was previously the case when mustered in their *amabutho*.

The partial and short-lived revitalisation of the *ibutho* system

When in late 1882 the British agreed to restore Cetshwayo to the central portion of his former kingdom in order to limit the mounting violence in Zululand, it was on condition that he would not attempt to revitalise or even permit the existence of the military system in his territory. His colonial neighbours in Natal were particularly firm on this point since they still entertained a healthy fear of Zulu military potential. But this prohibition made it difficult for Cetshwayo to reassert his authority over his former subjects, and jeopardised his ability to defend himself against the enemies of the royal house in Zululand whose short-lived power had been curtailed or threatened by his return.

Consequently, despite his undertaking to the British government not to do so, Cetshwayo did make a half-hearted attempt to revitalise the military system. He exercised his former authority to reconstitute and rename a young *ibutho*, apparently formed just before the Anglo-Zulu War, though it had taken no part in that campaign. Yet the uFalaza, as this *ibutho* was called, bore only a limited resemblance to the *amabutho* of the old kingdom. These had provided the vehicle through which the king had exercised his power over the manpower of every particular age-group in Zululand, thereby denying the regional chiefs ultimate control over the young men of their chiefdoms. However, the uFalaza *ibutho*, since it was raised only from young men in Cetshwayo's truncated territory, and not throughout the kingdom as was formerly the case, did not perform this essential politically cohesive function, and was thus nothing more than a military unit of the uSuthu faction.

Indeed, the great chiefs of Zululand, once freed in 1879 from the rule of the House of Shaka, had resumed their ancient prerogative of raising their own *amabutho*. Notable among these was the ambitious Chief Zibhebhu kaMaphitha of the Mandlakazi, whom the British raised up as their chief instrument in foiling the

In June 1883 uSuthu amabutho *mustered at King Cetshwayo kaMpande's oNdini* ikhanda *in the Mahlabathini plain to confront the threat posed by the king's cousin and mortal enemy, Chief Zibhebhu kaMaphitha of the Mandlakazi. As part of the ritual preparations for a campaign, men of rival* amabutho *would* giya, *or perform a war dance before the king, shouting ritual challenges at each other. Note Cetshwayo on the right of the picture wrapped in his blanket, and the dancing* amabutho *stripped for action of their festival finery and carrying an assortment of spears, knobkerries and modern rifles. This engraving is done from a drawing by William A. Walton, the special artist and correspondent of the* Pictorial World, *who arrived at oNdini on 13 June 1883. He left again on 27 July when he accompanied Cetshwayo's family into the Reserve Territory where they were seeking refuge after the king's devastating defeat at Zibhebhu's hands six days previously.*   Ian Knight Collection

aspirations of the royal house. His *ama-butho*, the ekuVukeni, iNyonemhlope and Bangonomo, would face the uSuthu *amabutho* on many occasions during the 1880s.

Two of these *amabutho* of Zibhebhu, the ekuVukeni and Bangonomo, were named after two of his principle home-steads, and this was in accordance with the custom of barracking each *ibutho* in its own military homestead, or *ikhanda* (plural – *amakhanda*). All Cetshwayo's royal *amakhanda* had been destroyed by the British in the war of 1879. Here too, he circumvented his undertaking to the British not to re-establish the military sys-tem by building a new oNdini close to his principal royal homestead of the same name which had been burned by the Brit-

ish, and several other *amakhanda* in the Mahlabathini plain, such as kwaNodwen-gu. They were all on a smaller scale than previously, for they were to accommodate his *amabutho* whose continued existence was, in any case, more notional than real, and whose numbers were greatly depleted. This was not only because of the casual-ties they had sustained in 1879, but because many of their members no longer remained loyal to the royal cause and had instead given their allegiance to their local chiefs.

Thus, when open war duly broke out in 1883 between Cetshwayo and his enemies, and he attempted to muster his supporters in their old *amabutho,* only a limited number heeded his summons. At the bat-tle of oNdini on 21 July 1883, Zibhebhu's forces scattered these partially reconstituted *amabutho* for the last time, and killed most of their now elderly commanders who had remained loyal to their king. Zibhebhu's army also destroyed all the partially rebuilt *amakhanda* in the Mahlabathini plain, thus once and for all erasing the locus of royal power in the valley of the White Mfolozi where it had been situated ever since the founding of the Zulu kingdom.

Small units of irregulars increasingly replace the *amabutho*

In the continuing struggle against Zibhebhu, Dinuzulu, Cetshwayo's successor, employed his royal prerogative to form a new *ibutho*, the imBokodwebomvu. But, exactly like the uFalaza *ibutho*, it was really nothing more than a military formation of the uSuthu faction. And although the uFalaza and the imBokodwebomvu fought as discrete units at Ceza on 2 June 1888 and again at Ivuna on 23 June 1888, it was only as the smaller part of uSuthu forces which were more than half made up of territorially based irregulars such as the abaQulusi and emGazini people who were drawn from specific chiefdoms. Indeed, as early as the battle of Msebe on 30 March 1883, the uSuthu had mustered into territorial divisions under their chiefs, rather than into *amabutho*. This fact, and the practice of operating in the field during the 1880s with tactical units at the level of companies, or *amaviyo* (singular – *iviyo*), which consisted of between 50 and 60 men each, rather than, as in 1879, with the much larger *amabutho* several thousands strong, underlined the real changes that had taken place in Zulu military organisation and scale since the defeat of the royal armies in the Anglo-Zulu War.

The diminished scale of military operations

During the war of 1879 the Zulu had repeatedly fielded an army of between 15 000 and 20 000. By contrast, the forces deployed during the wars of the 1880s reflected the considerably smaller scale of military operations. Thus, during the civil war of 1883–1884, the uSuthu put an army of only about 5 000 men into the field at Msebe against some 1 500 Mandlakazi; while at oNdini 3 600 uSuthu (with another 2 000 men uncommitted in the vicinity) were routed by a combined force of 3 000 Mandlakazi and Ngenetsheni. On 10 May 1884, only some 1 000 uSuthu unsuccessfully attacked the British camp near the Nkandla forest. At Tshaneni, 6 000 uSuthu confronted 3 000 Mandlakazi. During the uSuthu Rebellion of 1888, Dinuzulu drove back the British on Ceza Mountain with about 2 000 men, and at Ivuna defeated Zibhebhu's 700 or 800 Mandlakazi with a force of some 4 000. Between 1 500 and 2 000 uSuthu were driven off when they attacked Fort Andries on 30 June 1888. The action at Hlophekhulu was even smaller with the British dispersing just over 1 000 uSuthu.

Tactical innovations

At first glance, the Zulu way of war and battle tactics during the 1880s seem to have remained remarkably unaffected by the sharp defeats administered by the British in 1879. When the uSuthu marched at a leisurely pace against Zibhebhu in the campaign that culminated with the battle of Msebe, they were accompanied as was customary by their unarmed *izindibi* (singular – *udibi*) boys of fourteen years or older, who carried their baggage. The traditional chest and horns attacking formation, through which the Zulu (since the time of Shaka, if not before) attempted to envelop the opposing force, and then to destroy it through hand-to-hand combat waged with spear and shield, was still adopted unswervingly in all the major engagements of the 1880s by the uSuthu and their Mandlakazi opponents alike, and by the uSuthu against the British on Ceza.

However, other familiar elements in the Zulu tactical repertoire began to be given greater prominence. At Msebe the advancing uSuthu fell into a trap laid by the Mandlakazi and were outflanked and enveloped before they could deploy into battle order. At Tshaneni Zibhebhu again attempted to make use of the lay of the

'The Usutu army [at the battle of Tshaneni] advanced in the usual Zulu way, with breast and two arms . . . The left wing of my force closed with the right arm of the enemy, and drove it back in confusion on to the breast.'

(Chief Zibhebhu kaMaphitha, 13 June 1884)

ground and natural cover to ambush the numerically superior uSuthu, though on this occasion premature action by some of the Mandlakazi units ruined the element of surprise. Although both the battles of oNdini and Ivuna developed more conventionally with units formed up and facing each other, the uSuthu in the former encounter and the Mandlakazi in the latter were disadvantaged and in some disarray after being taken by surprise in a dawn attack after a long night-march by their foe.

Besides employing ambush and surprise to better effect than in the 1879 campaign, both the uSuthu and Mandlakazi made far greater use than before of the two instruments of modern war in Africa: the horse and gun. In this the Zulu were latecomers, for other African people like the Sotho and Pedi had long adopted them with considerable success in their wars against both the Boers and the British. The Zulu continued to place their greatest emphasis on the mass, frontal attack but, at Msebe and oNdini, Zibhebhu fielded a few mounted riflemen (including a handful of white mercenaries), where they were particularly effective against the uSuthu flanks, and in transforming retreat into rout. The uSuthu, while also raising mounted riflemen, failed to learn from Zibhebhu's tactical lesson. Consequently, when at Ivuna Dinuzulu unimaginatively led his crack force of mounted riflemen straight at the Mandlakazi centre, rather than around their flanks, they were ignominiously thrown back in confusion. At Tshaneni, by contrast, it was the effect of the repeated fusillades by the uSuthus' allies, the mounted Boers, fired over their heads into the Mandlakazi centre, which proved decisive in shattering its advance and turning the tide of battle.

On occasion, and possibly because with the attenuation of the *ibutho* system its ethos had also faded, all the Zulu forces of the 1880s were more prepared than previously to adopt flexible skirmishing tactics, making better use of cover and putting a premium on mobility. A feature of operations in the 1880s was the repeated use the

> 'We, Zibepu's men, were attacked at the Unduna hill [battle of Ivuna] by Dinizulu's impi wearing the chokabezi badge, cowtails; they called out "Usutu" as they chased us . . . We saw the mounted men coming towards us, and we ran to meet them: on seeing us approach the mounted men . . . drew us on to the force approaching from behind, on foot, which, as it came near us, fired at us. Then they came to close quarters and stabbed us with assegais, and overpowered us, back and front, and we had to retreat.'
> (Mhlupeqi, son of Mnimba, 31 January 1889)

Zulu made of natural fastnesses (whether the Nkandla and Dukuduku forests, or mountains such as Ceza, Hlophekhulu or Bende), not only as strongholds to be held against attack, but as secure bases for small parties raiding widely for cattle and supplies from the surrounding countryside.

Weapons

In these engagements of the 1880s the Zulu employed a variety of weapons. The majority still wielded the traditional cow-hide shield and long-bladed stabbing-spear, or *iklwa* (plural – *amaklwa*), though firearms were increasingly in evidence, especially among the militarily more innovative Mandlakazi who had gained greater familiarity with firearms through their contacts with white hunters, traders and adventurers in north-eastern Zululand. Effective, modern breech-loading rifles were still in the minority on both sides, however, and most firearms in Zulu hands were still the obsolete muzzle-loaders such as the uSuthu used so ineffectively against the British on Hlophekhulu.

> '[At the battle of Ceza] we rushed on to the English, firing as we went, we three companies . . . We were armed with guns, war-shields, assegais, and we wore the chokabezi. We could not reach the English, because their fire was too hot, and we had to take shelter behind rocks: every time we rose up from our hiding place, we had to sit down again: eventually we rested: we told those who had guns to keep up firing, as it was impossible for those with assegais only to get near the English.'
> (Umhlalo, son of Mqapai, uFalaza *ibutho*, 4 February 1889)

'Forces from Undini marched towards Ntukwini stream washed themselves [ritually] and marched back to Undini and Ncinda [purification ceremony] again, black bull, three men seriously injured in seizing the bull, to dislocate its joints [killing of a black bull and the ritual eating of strips of its flesh was also a part of these pre-battle ceremonies].'

(Henry Francis Fynn, Jnr, British Resident in Zululand, 18 July 1883)

Ritual

All the Zulu factions still complied when possible with the age-old ritual preparation before battle, for it was necessary to be strengthened by the war-doctors, or *izinyang*a (singular – *inyanga*) against the dark, mystical force of *umnyama*, whose evil influence was especially called up through the shedding of human blood, and also to be ritually purified by them again after combat. When doctoring their men, *izinyanga* attempted at the same time to weaken their enemies. Thus, before the battle of Ivuna, the famous war-doctor, Mathanga of the Mthethwa people, who was engaged by Dinuzulu, stuck into the ground a Mandlakazi spear-blade which had been picked up after Zibhebhu's victory at oNdini, and which he had bent and tied with ritual medicines. The uSuthu warriors filed past it, all touching it and shouting incantations. The magical intention was to blunt the Mandlakazi spears in the coming battle.

Dress

Zulu dress on campaign also reflected this uneasy period of transition from the traditional to the more westernised. Gone for most was the showy full regalia of precious feathers and skins flaunted formerly by the *amabutho* on ceremonial occasions, though there is evidence that elements of the traditional finery were still worn during the rituals and dances that preceded going to war. It seems, though, that the distinctive and intricate uniform attire once adopted by each individual *ibutho* was scarcely any longer attempted, although Zibhebhu's iNyonemhlope *ibutho* all wore black feathers, for example. One particular item of apparel symbolised better than anything else the conditions of civil strife that prevailed in the Zululand of the 1880s. The *imishokobezi*, or white cow-tail decorations, tied below the knees or above the elbows, became the emblem of the uSuthu and were worn in battle to distinguish them from their foes. To *shokobeza* meant to rebel, and referred originally to those Zulu who crossed out of the Reserve Territory and the white man's jurisdiction in 1883 to

serve Cetshwayo, their restored king. To these royalists the other Zulu who, like the Mandlakazi, opposed the king, were the *amambuka*, the renegades.

A badge of allegiance such as the *imishokobezi* was necessary, for on campaign the warriors of all Zulu factions still stripped down as they had during the Anglo-Zulu War to their sparse everyday dress of loin-cover (a bunch of animal tails in front and an oblong of cowskin behind) and little else, spruced up with a few feathers and ornaments denoting rank or, sometimes, identifying membership of an *ibutho*. Those who were entitled could not resist wearing the *iziqu* despite their inconvenience, for these amulet necklaces or bracelets of small pieces of willow-wood, which possessed the ritual power of warding off the evil effects of homicide, advertised that the wearer had already performed great deeds in battle.

These traditional ingredients of dress jostled with articles of western apparel like tweed jackets. Prince Dabulamanzi, for example, evinced a preference for braided coats and wide-awake hats. The latter head-dress did not sit well with the *isicoco*, or headring, the circlet of tendons or fibres sewn into the hair, coated with beeswax or gum and then greased and polished. In the past, it was the king's prerogative to permit his *amabutho* to assume the *isicoco*, denoting the attainment of ritual manhood and the right to marry. And though the *ibutho* system was fading away, no Zulu male in the 1880s was yet prepared to jettison this prized and visible indication of his mature status in the community. Even as westernised a Zulu as Zibhebhu kept his famous, lop-sided little *isicoco*, as well as the long finger-nails of the Zulu aristocrat. But, appropriately enough for a practised horseman, he habitually wore jacket, trousers and gaiters – though no shoes. In riding barefoot he was no different from other Zulu who had taken increasingly to the saddle, nor from many of the mounted African auxiliaries in British service.

British, Colonial and Boer Forces in Zululand during the 1880s

Colonial defence and army reform

Since the 1840s, British governments had been attempting to make the colonies militarily more self-reliant. Colonies, by raising and training volunteer units from the local settlers, supported by auxiliaries drawn from the indigenous population, would, it was hoped, bear more of the cost of their own defence and so reduce the need for garrisons of British troops to be stationed overseas.

The army reforms carried out under Edward Cardwell, Secretary of State for War (1868–1874), were aimed at withdrawing troops from colonies of settlement and scaling down garrisons elsewhere, except for India. The introduction of short service in 1870, whereby recruits spent six years in the regular army and six more in the reserve, was designed to create a large pool of trained reservists. The Localisation Bill of 1872 established 66 territorial districts in Britain with two linked battalions attached to each brigade depot. The intention was that the battalions would alternate in recruiting at home and serving abroad, so ensuring that the Empire would be guarded only by seasoned troops. However, mounting demands during the 1870s and 1880s for imperial defence, of which the Anglo-Zulu War of 1879 was a notable instance, required a stronger military presence overseas than Cardwell had envisaged. This demand upset the balance between battalions stationed at home and those serving overseas, and resulted in imperfectly trained battalions being posted to the colonies.

Cardwell's territorial brigade districts usually conformed to existing counties in Britain, for it was his intention to tie infantry battalions to particular geographical regions in order to foster local loyalties and to encourage recruitment. In 1881 Hugh Childers, Secretary of State for War (1880–1882), took Cardwell's plan to its logical conclusion by permanently linking regular battalions within specific geographical areas. The first 25 numbered line regiments were each given two battalions, while the remainder were amalgamated in pairs to form the two battalions of the new regiments. The old regimental numbers and county affiliations, which had previously characterised individual battalions, were changed to territorial titles. Thus, to take as an example a battalion that served in the Anglo-Zulu War and again in Zululand in the 1880s, the 58th (Rutlandshire) Regiment became the 2nd Battalion, The Northamptonshire Regiment.

The 1st Bn, Princess Louise's (Argyll and Sutherland Highlanders) photographed on parade in full ceremonial dress at Fort Napier in Pietermaritzburg, the headquarters of the British garrison in Natal, on some date between 1883 and 1885. The battalion had been stationed in South Africa since February 1879 and had seen service in the Anglo-Zulu War with the Eshowe Relief Column and the 1st Division, fighting in the battle of Gingindlovu on 2 April 1879. In November 1885 it embarked for Ceylon, its next station abroad.

Killie Campbell Africana Library (B4/044)

'Because two Inniskilling regiments happen to be quartered in the same place [Fort Napier], is that any excuse for the young officers of the Garrison to show their good fellowship for one another by nightly turning the camp into a pandemonium? . . . Night after night these young gentlemen have been galloping and hallooing about the camp and country, awaking by their uproar unfortunate non-commissioned officers and their families.'

('Discipline' in *Natal Witness*, 11 August 1887)

However, these changes failed to raise either the quantity or quality of recruits. Economising governments neglected to make pay competitive, and conditions of service life (though improved) remained harsh. Although the purchase of commissions had been abolished in 1871, the elite social composition of the officer corps remained essentially unchanged and its ethos generally conservative.

Nonetheless, there were officers concerned with reforming and modernising the British Army. The late Victorian army was engaged primarily in colonial campaigns in which improvisation, initiative and flair were required of officers. Frequent experience under fire in small wars against diverse kinds of enemy employing very different tactics and levels of military skill ensured the attainment of the required competence. The challenge of regularly campaigning over difficult terrain led steadily towards improvements in transport and supply arrangements in the field which sometimes, as in the case of the Anglo-Zulu War, had proved decidedly inadequate. These services were finally reformed and amalgamated in December 1888 with the formation of the Army Services Corps.

The lessons learned by the British in fighting small wars naturally differed greatly from those taught in the full-scale campaigns of the American Civil War and the Austro-Prussian and Franco-Prussian Wars. Nevertheless, they served to confirm the general (but by no means universal) shift in the British Army away from the dense formations employed as late as the Crimean War towards a greater emphasis on open-order tactics and flexibility. Of course, what made this possible was the extensive re-armament of the British Army during the last three decades of the nineteenth century. The introduction of breech-loading rifles increased the rate of fire and allowed soldiers to fire from a kneeling or prone position. Early forms of machine-guns were experimented with in action, and the Royal Artillery finally adopted breech-loading ordnance. Regular colonial campaigns provided the opportunities for testing and improving this weaponry.

The Natal garrison and army organisation

The headquarters and supply and remount centre of the British garrison in the Colony of Natal was at Fort Napier, overlooking Pietermaritzburg, the colonial capital. The garrison was the local strategic reserve, to be deployed in order to maintain internal security, to defend Natal from attack, or to secure wider imperial interests in the region when these obligations proved beyond the capability of the locally raised colonial forces. The colonial government contributed about ten per cent of the total imperial expenditure to maintaining the garrison. The recent experiences of the Anglo-Zulu War of 1879 and the First Anglo-Boer War of 1880–1881 proved that the colonial forces remained insufficient for Natal's self-defence, so the establishment of the garrison was substantially increased after 1881 to make it the largest peacetime concentration of imperial troops in South Africa at that time. Throughout much of the 1880s its strength consisted of a regiment of cavalry, a battery of Royal Field Artillery and three battalions of infantry, though the imperial system of troop reliefs meant that the garrison could temporarily be weaker or stronger than normal. There were also support units such as the Royal Engineers and Royal Army Medical Corps, as well as commissariat and ordnance personnel. Zululand was in the sphere of responsibility for the garrison so, when required, units were deployed there to garrison military posts or to undertake operations.

In the 1880s a cavalry regiment on overseas service normally consisted of eight troops grouped into four squadrons. The cavalry troop, which was the standard tactical unit, nominally consisted of 75 men of all ranks, including a farrier and a trumpeter, so that a cavalry regiment's strength hovered around 600 men. A battery of Royal Field Artillery was made up of six guns and 174 men. The battery was the usual tactical unit, but was often

The Natal Garrison
1879–1891

Cavalry:
1881–1890   6th (Inniskilling) Dragoons

Artillery:
1884–1893   H Battery, 4th Brigade, Royal Field Artillery

Infantry:
1879–1880	3/60th Regiment (The King's Royal Rifle Corps)
1880–1884	58th (Rutlandshire) Regiment; *re-titled* 2nd Bn, The Northamptonshire Regiment
1881–1886	1st Bn, The Welsh Regiment
1883–1885	1st Bn, Princess Louise's (Argyll and Sutherland Highlanders)
1884–1887	2nd Bn, The Prince of Wales's Volunteers (South Lancashire Regiment)
1886–1888	1st Bn, The Royal Inniskilling Fusiliers
1888–1891	1st Bn, The Royal Scots (Lothian Regiment)
1887–1890	1st Bn, The Prince of Wales's (North Staffordshire Regiment)

broken up if necessary into three divisions of two guns each. The standard infantry tactical unit was the battalion. On service, the battalion was made up of a headquarters and eight companies, with a nominal complement of three officers and 110 ranks in each, or about 900 men.

Colonial warfare had taught the British of the need to combine the speed of cavalry with the infantry's firepower for scouting and fighting, a combination basic to the Boer commando. Mounted infantry were therefore regularly raised from volunteers among the infantry battalions. During the 1880s mounted infantry units drawn from the Natal garrison were regularly deployed in Zululand. A squadron of mounted infantry usually consisted of three officers and 110 men.

The supply and transport of troops operating in Zululand from Natal were in the not necessarily efficient hands of the personnel of the Commissariat and Transport Staff and the Commissariat and Transport Corps, known respectively before the overhaul of 1880–1881 as the Commissariat and Transport Department and the Army Service Corps. In mitigation, though, it should be noted that the rutted dirt tracks across Zululand's broken and hilly terrain were extremely poor, and often impassable during the rainy season

The imperial garrison stationed at Fort Napier played a prominent part in the social life of Pietermaritzburg, the capital of the Colony of Natal, and was inevitably represented at ceremonial occasions. Its participation was never more appropriate than on 11 October 1883 when the Governor of Natal and Special Commissioner for Zulu Affairs, Sir Henry Bulwer, unveiled the Anglo-Zulu War Memorial in the gardens abutting the large public building erected in 1871, which then housed both the Supreme Court and the Legislative Assembly of Natal. In the foreground of the photograph, a contingent of the 2nd Bn, The Northampstonshire Regiment is drawn up with their backs to the camera. Until 1881 the battalion was titled the 58th (Rutlandshire) Regiment, and as such had fought in the Zulu campaign of 1879 as part of the 2nd Division, South African Field Force, and had been present at the battle of Ulundi. Not caught in the photograph, but also present honouring comrades who had fallen in the war of 1879, were colonial mounted troops, namely, the Natal Mounted Police, the Natal Carbineers and the Edendale Horse. The Maritzburg Rifles, who as a volunteer infantry unit had not proceeded to the front in 1879 but had remained home to guard their city, are shown in the photograph arrayed at right angles to the British troops.   Pietermaritzburg Archives Repository (C. 111)

'Since 1886 a road has been constructed from Fort Yolland in the Eshowe district along the eastern spurs of the Nkandhla range to the seat of the magistracy at Empandhleni and thence on to Rorke's Drift but . . . the gradients are so excessive . . . as to render it impracticable for mule transport, and only available for ox transport with half loads and double spanning at the steep places.'
(Intelligence Division of the War Office, 1895)

'D' Company, Mounted Infantry, drawn from the 1st Bn, Princess Louise's (Argyll and Sutherland Highlanders), photographed in February 1884 while on parade in Fort Napier. Note that they are wearing cork sun helmets and corduroy trousers with riding boots.

Killie Campbell Africana Library (C55/015)

from September to March. There were no bridges across the many dongas and considerable rivers, which were liable to sudden floods, rendering the drifts impassable. In such conditions, transport persistently broke down or was delayed for days, making it very difficult to bring up supplies.

Communication between magisterial and military posts and headquarters was equally tenuous. The telegraph line from Pietermaritzburg ended in Eshowe, though in 1888 the British laid down a field telegraph to headquarters when it advanced to Nkonjeni. Otherwise, orders and despatches were relayed by helio-

Lt-Gen H.A. Smyth was appointed the General Officer Commanding in South Africa on 23 January 1888. He took personal command of the British forces operating in Zululand in late June 1888, and was photographed emerging from the hut in which he had sent off a telegraphic message to Sir Arthur Havelock, the Governor of Natal and Zululand, who was in Pietermaritzburg. Havelock insisted on being in regular communication with Smyth in order, in the General's opinion, to interfere unwarrantably in his military planning. Smyth was knighted (KCMG) in 1890 when he was appointed Governor of Malta.

South African Library (INIL 929)

graph, which was at the mercy of cloudy weather, or by mounted orderlies and post-runners, who were often held up by flooded rivers.

Colonial forces

During the Anglo-Zulu War of 1879, the white Natal Mounted Police and Natal Volunteer Corps, as well as African levies raised in the Natal Native Reserves and the Christian community at Edendale outside Pietermaritzburg, had taken an active part in the invasion of Zululand. The involvement of Natal colonial forces in Zululand during the military operations of the1880s was much smaller, however. Col Friend Addison found in July 1888 that he could raise barely 20 volunteers from among the reluctant white settlers of Victoria County and the local Natal

Mounted Volunteers unit, the Victoria Mounted Rifles (which he commanded), to join Major McKean's Coastal Column in Zululand as mounted levies. Addison consequently abandoned the attempt, and no other was made to persuade white volunteer units to serve in Zululand. It was otherwise, though, with the men of Eden-dale, who had distinguished themselves in 1879 as the Edendale Troop of the Natal Native Horse. Some 150 were raised in July 1888 under the command of Capt C.B. Addison, issued with carbines, and sent to Zululand as Addison's Horse.

In 1883, soon after the southern third of Zululand was placed under colonial administration as the Reserve Territory, Cmdt George Mansel raised a paramilit-ary police force recruited from among the Zulu themselves to maintain law and

Men of the Reserve Territory Carbineers photographed in c.1885 with their commander, Cmdt George Mansel, standing in the centre. This para-military police force was created in April 1883 to maintain order in the southern third of Zululand which was administered by colonial officials. When Zululand was annexed as a British colony in May 1887, the Reserve Territory Carbineers were renamed the Zululand Police and Mansel confirmed as their commander. On Zululand being incorporated into the Colony of Natal in December 1897, Mansel was made Assistant Commissioner of the Natal Police, eventually becoming Chief Commissioner. His second-in-command in the Reserve Territory Carbineers, Richard Addison (called 'Dick' by the Zulu), stands on the far left with his dog. Addison was subsequently appointed Assistant Commissioner and Resident Magistrate of the Ndwandwe District in Zululand in June 1887. His career suffered an eclipse as a result of his perceived mishandling of the uSuthu in his district which helped drive them into open rebellion in 1888, and he spent many lonely subsequent years as magistrate of quiet districts out of harm's way. However, his services as a political adviser to the Natal forces during the 1906 Rebellion restored him fully to favour, and his revitalised career was capped in 1913 with his appointment as Chief Native Commissioner for Natal and Zululand. He retired in 1916 with the Imperial Service Order.

Pietermaritzburg Archives Repository (C. 5055)

Hlubi's contingent of Mounted Basutos photographed when part of the Eshowe Column in Zululand during July 1888. Chief Hlubi kaMota Molife himself sits in the centre with his men drawn up behind him, his sergeant at his right hand. Hlubi was chief of the Tlokwa, Sotho-speakers from the Harrismith district who migrated in 1867 to the Weenen–Estcourt area in Natal. During the Anglo-Zulu War Hlubi commanded a troop of Tlokwa in the Natal Native Horse, when they served with No. 2 Column, and subsequently with No. 4 Column. As part of the settlement that ended the war, Gen Sir Garnet Wolseley appointed him chief over the strategic territory abutting Natal at the junction of the Thukela and Mzinyathi (Buffalo) rivers. Many stalwart uSuthu supporters lived there, and they greatly resented the alien Tlokwa presence. To Hlubi's left, with the terrier, is Maj Alexander McKean, 6th (Inniskilling) Dragoons, the commander of the column and Assistant Commissioner and Resident Magistrate of the Nqutu District.

South African Library (INIL 932)

order. Known as the Reserve Territory Carbineers, about a third of its complement was mounted. Its headquarters were at Eshowe. With the British annexation of Zululand as a colony in May 1887, the Reserve Territory Carbineers were restyled the Zululand Police and enlarged. Under the continued command of Mansel, assisted by three white sub-inspectors, the Zululand Police were posted to the six newly-established magisterial posts with the object of protecting the white magistrates and enforcing their authority.

As early as 1884, the Reserve Territory Carbineers had proved insufficient for maintaining colonial authority, and the officials in the Reserve Territory were forced to call on Chief Hlubi kaMota Molife and his Tlokwa for assistance. Hlubi and his Sotho-speaking followers originally came from over the Drakensberg and had fought for the British during the Anglo-Zulu War as Hlubi's Troop in the Natal Native Horse. In the settlement that ended the war, the pro-British Hlubi was made one of the appointed chiefs and given the strategic territory at the

Walton's illustration for the Pictorial World *of African levies raised in May 1884 by Melmoth Osborn, the Resident Commissioner of the Reserve Territory, for action against the uSuthu concentrated in the Nkandla forest. Note that almost all the levies carry traditional weapons, even when they have a firearm. A number have the distinguishing red rag tied around their head, and others wear European-style hats. The levy leaders are mounted.*

Ian Castle Collection

confluence of the Thukela and Mzinyathi rivers. In 1884 Hlubi rallied again to the British call, and over the next four years his Mounted Basutos (and some infantry as well) played a vital part in helping to assert British authority.

In addition to calling out the Tlokwa in 1884, the British officials also raised temporary unmounted and untrained levies under white levy-leaders from among the Zulu of the Reserve Territory. Although they proved most unreliable, during the 1888 rebellion a number of levies were raised once again throughout the Colony of Zululand among those Zulu who were threatened by, or who opposed Dinuzulu and the uSuthu resisting British rule. Some, like Mnyamana's Auxiliaries, were organised and fought in entirely traditional style under their own leaders; but others, like the Eshowe Levy, were under levy-leaders and were subject to some military discipline.

The Mounted Basutos, like the Zululand Police, Addison's Horse and other levies employed in Zululand were paid for out of the funds of the Colony of Zululand.

During the military operations of 1888, in which regular British troops of the Natal garrison were engaged side-by-side with African forces raised in Zululand and (to a much lesser extent) in Natal, it became necessary to define the parameters of civil and military authority. It was agreed that the General would have command over the British troops, the Mounted Basutos and any other African levies raised along military lines. The Resident Commissioner would retain control over the Zululand Police and any chiefs and their adherents employed as auxiliaries.

Boer commandos
The Boers from the South African Republic neighbouring Zululand took frequent advantage of the civil strife of the 1880s to raid Zulu livestock and, in 1884, to intervene militarily on Dinuzulu's side in return for the cession of vast tracts of territory. The Boers, who were all volunteers and supplied all their own equipment, fought as mounted infantry in the traditional commando style originally developed on the Cape eastern frontier. They often dismounted in action for better firepower, and retired in alternating ranks if it became necessary to disengage. In hostile territory, as in Zululand in 1884, the lightly encumbered and mobile Boer commando would operate from the secure base provided by a laager, or improvised fortification of wagons drawn up in all-round defensive position.

Dress
The British Army made few concessions to suitability when it issued its men with uniforms to wear in the field in Zululand during the 1880s. The standard overseas issue undress remained the five-buttoned unlined frock which was scarlet for infantry and Engineers, and blue for all others except the Rifles, who wore green. With the organisational changes of 1881, the traditional facing colours of the old regiments were replaced by national ones worn on cuffs and on the collar: white for English and Welsh regiments, yellow for Scottish and green for Irish. Trousers were dark blue with a red welt for infantry and a wide red stripe for artillery. Highland regiments wore kilts and their officers trews. Officers wore either a frock of the plain tunic colour (except those in

The men and officers of 'C' Company of the 1st Bn, Princess Louise's (Argyll and Sutherland Highlanders) photographed in Pietermaritzburg during May 1885. In front of them, and ranged to the side, are the men of the battalion band, including pipers in kilts. Normally, a battalion had sixteen 'trumpeters' on its establishment but this, being a Highland battalion, had permission to employ five men as pipers. Killie Campbell Africana Library (C55/019)

Highland regiments whose frocks, like those of their men, had rounded skirts in the front and gauntlet cuffs), or blue patrol jackets, introduced in 1866. Mounted infantry wore their regimental frocks with dark buff corduroy trousers and carried ammunition in leather bandoliers. Accoutrements for infantry, including ammunition pouches, were of the Valise pattern, introduced in 1871. Headgear was the light cork sun helmet, adopted for overseas service in 1877. The brass shako-plate badge was usually removed on active service, and the white helmet (and equipment straps) stained light brown.

The widespread use of khaki by the British began in India during the Mutiny of 1857, though its adoption throughout the army was slow and often reluctant. By the mid-1880s, however, after disasters like the 1881 campaign against the Boer marksmen of the Transvaal, the army was committed in practice to fighting in khaki, though operations in Zululand proved an exception. With the memory of the Anglo-Zulu War still so fresh in Zulu minds, the moral effect of again wearing scarlet was thought to outweigh the negligible danger from indifferent Zulu marksmen. As it turned out, the troops skirmishing in Zululand in 1888 were the last in the British Army to fight in scarlet. In 1897 khaki was adopted as service wear on all overseas postings.

Only some of the colonial forces in Zululand were uniformed. The Zululand Police wore khaki frocks and white trousers with khaki puttees above bare feet. However, those police who were mounted also wore boots. Headgear was a khaki glengarry. Officers wore a blue frock, light-coloured breeches and riding-boots. The Mounted Basutos and Addison's Horse were dressed in an assortment of blue or khaki frocks, usually with buff trousers and riding-boots or puttees. They wore brown slouch hats with a red puggaree around the hatband and carried their ammunition in leather bandoliers. The various African levies and auxiliaries wore usual Zulu dress of the time. To distinguish them from their

similarly arrayed Zulu foes they wore (as had previously been the practice in the Anglo-Zulu War) a red cloth tied around the head. Boers on commando likewise wore their everyday clothes with bandoliers.

Weapons

British infantry in Zululand throughout the 1880s were armed with the Martini-Henry Mark II rifle, introduced in 1874. It was a single-shot, centre fire weapon with a falling block mechanism operated by a lever. It weighed 9 lbs (4.08 kg), and fired a .450 calibre lead bullet. It was sighted up to 1 200 yards (1 097 m), but was most effective at less than 400 yards (366 m). The original Boxer pattern cartridge with its thin rolled brass case had a tendency to tear and jam, and from 1885 it was replaced by a cartridge of stronger drawn brass. The Martini-Henry was fitted with a triangular socket bayonet, 22 inches (0.56 m) long, known as the 'lunger'. In 1888 the Martini-Henry was replaced by the bolt-action Lee-Metford Mark I, the first magazine rifle adopted by the British Army. It was not until 1900 that the Army insisted that officers carry the .455 Webley revolver, and until then they chose their own pattern.

The Dragoons in Zululand in the 1880s carried the slightly curved, single-edged 1864-pattern sword, with modifications dating from 1882 to the guard and scabbard design, and with a stronger blade introduced in 1885. Although the British cavalry remained wedded to the concept of close-quarter shock action with the sword or lance, the carbine had long been accepted as a secondary weapon. In 1877 the cavalry adopted the Martini-Henry carbine, which was sighted up to 1 000 yards (914 m). It was then replaced by the Martini-Metford carbine in 1892. Mounted infantry also carried the carbine.

The artillery deployed in Zululand in the 1880s were light 7-pounder Rifled Muzzle Loader (RML) Mark IV steel mountain guns, mounted on light carriages. With a maximum range of 3 100 yards (2 835 m) for explosive shells and a low muzzle-

'Zibepu's men wore the Government red badge, tied round the head, the forehead; those badges are served out at the Magistrate's Office.'

(Matuta, son of Ketagili, Zululand Police, 31 Janaury 1889)

velocity, they were not very effective. Nevertheless, they were considered suitable for transport across the broken Zululand terrain. In the event, they were never actually fired in action during operations in Zululand. Nor were the machine-operated guns which were available. These hand-cranked Gatling guns, which had come into service in 1871, could fire 200 Boxer .450 rounds a minute with an effective range of up to 1 000 yards (914 m).

The Zululand Police, Mounted Basutos and Addison's Horse carried rifles and carbines, though not necessarily of the latest model. Levies and auxiliaries were armed with their traditional spears and shields, though a few would have carried obsolete muzzle-loading firearms. The Boers on commando were armed with a number of different types of rifle ranging from Snider breech-loaders to British Martini-Henrys. Particularly favoured during the 1880s was the Westley-Richards falling-block rifle.

Colonial warfare

As early as the North American campaigns of the eighteenth century, the British had learned that in fighting highly mobile enemies over broken ground they could no longer rely on their well-tried dense column and line formations. Rather, individual soldiers had to be self-reliant and well motivated, and prepared to be deployed in open rather than mass formations in order to make better use of the terrain. Moreover, the focus of operations shifted from pitched engagements to reconnaissance, ambushes, patrols and skirmishes. These North American lessons tended to be forgotten, however, for lack of practical reminders, and had to be relearned through culminating experience in the colonial 'small wars' of the nineteenth century.

By the late 1870s emphasis was placed on attacking in depth, with a battalion deploying two companies as skirmishers, two further companies in line some distance behind in support, and the remaining four companies in line behind

Two Gatling guns in Eshowe manned by men of the 2nd Bn, The Prince of Wales's Volunteers (South Lancashire Regiment), stationed in South Africa since June 1884. In November 1884 the detachment in Eshowe was redeployed to Fort Northampton across the Mzinyathi (Buffalo) River from the mission station at Rorke's Drift, so the photograph must have been taken between these two dates. In February 1887 the battalion embarked for Singapore, its next station abroad.
Killie Campbell Africana Library (B41/038)

them. However, firepower in such extended formation could prove insufficient to stem a determined attack – as the British discovered to their cost at Isandlwana in 1879. Against rapidly moving, enveloping mass attacks as practised by the Zulu, all-round defensive formations such as the infantry square, or prepared defensive positions like forts and laagers, prove much more effective than the extended firing-line.

When in September 1883 a British column again advanced into Zululand, it was accordingly ordered to laager at every halt and to concentrate if attacked in a defensive formation. However, it soon became apparent to the British in the Zululand operations of the 1880s that they were no longer confronted, as they had been in 1879, by dense masses of Zulu *amabutho*. Rather, encounters took more the form of running skirmishes in which

'Sanitary Precautions. – On the march, when the heat is oppressive, the men should be allowed greater freedom around the neck by opening the tunic and shirt. Exposure to a hot sun without a helmet should be checked. The men should, when practicable, sleep under cover; on no account omitting to wear their cholera belts, the evil effects from any chill to the stomach or bowels being found to exceed all other risks in this climate . . . The men should be cautioned against drinking from stagnant pools or eating wild fruits.'
(Intelligence Division of the War Office, 1895)

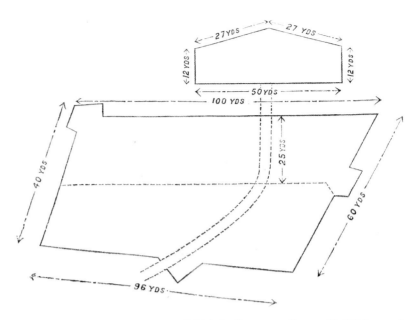

British Parliamentary Papers (C. 3864): enc. in no. 137

Fort Curtis was constructed in October 1883 under the superintendence of Lt W. Yolland of the Royal Engineers and named after Col F.G.S. Curtis, CMG, Deputy Adjutant- and Quartermaster-General in South Africa. It was sited on rising ground near a good supply of water to the right of the road leading into the interior of Zululand, about 0.8 km (0.5 miles) beyond the turn-off to the Eshowe Mission Station. A small lunette, large enough for a garrison of 150 men, with an earthwork parapet 2.46 m (8 feet) high, revetted with hurdles, was intended as a permanent work. The rest of the fort, which was meant to shelter a much larger force, consisted of a timber stockade revetted with sods which, at 1.85 m (6 feet) or so was commanded by the lunette. It was possible to reduce the perimeter of this lower part of the fort by bisecting it with a stockade to allow a smaller garrison to maintain the same concentration of fire-power. The ditches surrounding these works were V-shaped and from 3.65 m (12 feet) to 4.26 m (14 feet) wide, with barbed-wire trip-wires beyond. In the photograph troops of the garrison are seen manning the defences and one of the division of two 7-pounder guns deployed at the fort. The diagram of the fort was sent by Lt-Col R.J. Hawthorn on 24 October 1883 to the Royal Engineer Office, Fort Napier. South African Library (INIL 7583)

the British attempted to dislodge the Zulu from their mountain fastnesses without being enveloped as they attacked. In these circumstances, the contemporary trend towards even more flexible attack formations proved suitable. Ideally, attacks were supposed to be in depth and in open order. The first line was meant to dominate the enemy with its firepower while the second advanced in support, charging through the first line with the bayonet. The third line was either to pursue the broken enemy, or cover the retreat of the first two if repulsed. The successful British assault on Hlophekhulu Mountain on 2 July 1888 exemplified many of these tactical principles. A variant on that occasion was the use of swiftly-moving African levies and auxiliaries to outflank the Zulu defending the mountain, and to cut off their retreat. In general, such troops were used in support to follow up the flying enemy and to round up their abandoned livestock.

Fortified depots and laagers along the British lines of communication had played an important part in the Zululand campaign of 1879. During the 1880s the British built the earthwork Forts Curtis, Yolland, Chater and Entonjaneni and the stone-walled Fort Northampton as strategic strong-points in southern and central Zululand. They could be garrisoned in case of emergency, and troops could concentrate and supplies be stored under their protection. During the uSuthu Rebellion the British also established forward and less permanent bases like Nkonjeni and the Aivuna Camp. The civil authorities built small earthwork fortifications for the protection of some of their more vulnerable magistracies, such as at Ivuna in the Ndwandwe District. In the Lower Umfolosi District the magistrate and his garrison of Zululand Police in Fort Andries successfully resisted an uSuthu assault on 30 June 1888.

Cavalry in Zululand in the 1880s generally operated as mounted infantry. The mounted Zululand Police, the Mounted Basutos, Addison's Horse and the Boer commandos did likewise, scouting and skirmishing and dismounting in action to make more effective use of their firearms. However, at Ceza on 2 June 1888 the withdrawing Dragoons and Zululand Police charged the uSuthu, and their traditional cavalry shock action deterred their pursuers.

Zulu and British Military Strategy in Zululand during the 1880s

The common strategy employed by both the uSuthu and Mandlakazi against each other

Throughout the wars of the 1880s there was little real change in Zulu strategy from the established practices of the past. During the civil wars both the uSuthu and the Mandlakazi concentrated their forces at a major *ikhanda* or chiefly homestead preparatory to marching into the heart of the enemy's territory, living off the countryside as they advanced. The primary objective of such operations was to drive out the enemy from the territory he occupied.

The preferred way of doing so remained the crushing of the enemy's forces in battle, though (as in the case of the Zulu civil wars) where opposing forces are similarly armed, it was often difficult for the attacking force to bring an unwilling foe to battle. In such circumstances a combat strategy would have had to be replaced with a logistic one, and the enemy compelled to evacuate his lands by destroying his means of survival through burning his homesteads and fields, plundering his grain stores and driving off his livestock. If the enemy both avoided battle and succeeded in taking refuge with families and livestock in impregnable strongholds, then the invaders might have to be content with their plunder only, and eventually have to withdraw. For although considerable hardship beset those sheltering in caves, on mountain tops or in deep forests, it was even more difficult for the invaders to maintain themselves in countryside they had comprehensively ravaged. Thus stalemate was often the outcome of a campaign. The minor skirmishing that went on between full-scale operations, with small raiding parties making forays into enemy territory, were enough to irritate the enemy, but inevitably also fell far short of the primary objective of driving the foe from his lands.

Only a pitched battle, therefore, could have any conclusive effect. And certainly, where the enemy army was surprised or otherwise brought successfully to battle, as at Msebe, oNdini, Tshaneni and even Ivuna, the strategic consequences were dramatic, resulting in the entire collapse of the enemy's forces, the flight of his leaders and the abandoning of great tracts of territory to the victors.

The dearth of uSuthu strategic options against British and colonial forces

Yet if Zulu fighting Zulu in the 1880s were able to attain their objectives employing strategies that would have been familiar 50 years before, it was quite another matter when confronting colonial and British troops in the Reserve Territory, and later in the Colony of Zululand, intent on repressing armed resistance to their administration.

In mounting such resistance, the uSuthu lacked coherent or viable strategic objectives. They had learned from terrible experience during the Anglo-Zulu War that they could not hope to win a conventional battle against the overwhelming firepower the British could bring against them. Accordingly, during the 1888 campaign, for example, although it was feasible to sweep down with success against the Mandlakazi allies of the British, the uSuthu never contemplated attacking British forces in the same way. The Anglo-Zulu War should also have taught them the futility of attacking prepared defences.

'Usibepu says he is not afraid of encountering his black enemies, but what chance of success has he got when they are joined by white men as the Boers have done[?] He and his people are not armed as white men are. He fears that with this help given by the Boers he will be beaten by the Usutu who will spare none.'
(Rozana, messenger of Zibhebhu, 2 May 1884)

Walton of the Pictorial World*'s dramatic representation of Chief Zibhebhu and his forces withdrawing in triumph after sacking oNdini on 21 July 1883 and scattering King Cetshwayo's army. (Note the horseman wearing a top hat and shirt rifled from Cetshwayo's boxes of European clothes acquired during his exile in Cape Town and London. Walton, by his own statement, took a lion's share of this loot.) A decisive victory such as this was achieved through a combination of speed, surprise and discipline, as well as the effective use of firepower. Zibhebhu's Mandlakazi* amabutho *carry a combination of traditional weapons and firearms; though it was those who used modern firearms and were mounted who were the most potent in battle. They would operate in concert with Zibhebhu's hardened white mercenaries and military advisers, two of whom are portrayed riding directly behind the chief.*

Rai England Collection

In the main it did so, though in 1888 the Mphukunyoni foolhardily tried to storm Fort Andries and were easily repulsed.

If the Zulu dared not confront the British in the open field and could not capture their posts and bases, what were they to do? In the event, they concentrated in 1884 in the depths of the Nkandla forest, or in 1888 on mountain fastnesses like Ceza and Hlophekhulu. From strongholds such as these they raided the surrounding countryside, targeting British collaborators like the Tlokwa or Buthelezi people, white traders and storekeepers, and the British lines of communication. Their immediate intention, it would seem, in both 1884 and 1888, was to establish their ascendancy in the regions around their strongholds and to deny them to the British. But the scattered

and limited nature of these uprisings meant that the British were soon able to isolate the uSuthu in their strongholds and then drive them from them one by one. Small successes against the British, like that on Ceza in 1888, were only temporary. And in that same campaign, any forlorn option of trying to raise more of Zululand in guerrilla-style resistance was scotched by the swift and ruthless passage of British flying columns.

No longer-term strategic objectives seem to have been devised by the uSuthu in the 1880s against the British occupying forces, most likely because there were none possible. The uSuthu simply could not muster enough forces against the British and their Zulu collaborators to cause more than a temporary and localised

'The Boers, having taken up a favourable position, opened a heavy flank fire on my men [the Mandlakazi], and it soon became impossible for them to stand it, and they gave way.'
(Zibhebhu, 13 June 1884)

embarrassment. Some uSuthu in 1888 supposed that if they managed to forge an alliance with the Boers of the New Republic they might prevail more conclusively against the British. But it was one thing for the Vryheid Boers to have meddled to their considerable personal gain in the civil wars between the uSuthu and Mandlakazi; it was quite another to fall foul of Britain. Certainly, the ill-policed territory of the New Republic afforded sanctuary to the uSuthu, and when under attack by the British they were able to move back and forth to their advantage over the border. However, Boer support went no further than turning a blind eye to uSuthu movements and condoning the armed participation of a few white mercenaries.

The reality was that in strategic terms uSuthu resistance in 1884 and 1888 to British rule never had any chance of success. As similar circumstances in 1906 were to confirm, Bhambatha's Rebellion would prove an identical strategic dead-end.

British strategy against the uSuthu

In normal circumstances, the civil authorities in the Reserve Territory, and subsequently the Colony of Zululand, depended on the locally raised African paramilitary police to enforce their administration. However, when the police proved unequal to the task, the soldiers of the Natal garrison were called upon to help protect the civil authorities against Zulu resisting their administration, and to quell any insurrection.

Considering the size of Zululand, its difficult terrain and the inadequacy of its communications, there were strategic limitations to the form such operations could take. The prime objective was to establish fortified bases that could be held against any attack, and from which offensives could be mounted against hostile elements. The next was to secure the safety of the lines of communication between these posts. The British consequently established Fort Curtis at Eshowe as their headquarters, with Forts Yolland and Chater protecting the eastern approaches

to the Nkandla forest where uSuthu resistance was concentrated in 1884. Fort Northampton at Rorke's Drift provided a military point of entry for operations in the Reserve Territory to the west of the Nkandla forest.

With the annexation of Zululand in 1887, posts at St Paul's, Entonjaneni and Nkonjeni were established along the track to the Ndwandwe District north-west of Eshowe to allow for the quick intervention of troops should the uSuthu, who were concentrated there, resist the new resident magistrate. On a number of occasions in late 1887 and early 1888 troops were pushed forward from Nkonjeni to an advanced post in the vicinity of the Ivuna magistracy, where their mere presence had the desired effect of cowing nascent uSuthu opposition.

However, this strategy broke down when the uSuthu took up arms in 1888 and concentrated on their mountain strongholds. The military underestimated Dinuzulu's men, and their inadequate intervention when the uSuthu defied the civil authorities contributed to the débâcle on Ceza Mountain. When the military then decided that the Ivuna magistracy was too distant and exposed to protect and evacuated the magistrate and his Zulu collaborators to Nkonjeni, they thereby abandoned all of Zululand north of the Black Mfolozi River to the uSuthu.

After this ignominious setback, the British rethought their strategy. They first reinforced the troops concentrated at Nkonjeni, and then secured their line of communication and supply by clearing the uSuthu from their stronghold on Hlophekhulu Mountain in central Zululand. Meanwhile, the troops concentrated at Eshowe were sent forward to relieve and reinforce the Lower Umfolosi District magistracy which was under threat of attack.

Having thus stabilised the situation, the British set about restoring their authority in the northern districts they had relinquished. Troops were moved forward from Nkonjeni to advanced posts east of Ceza Mountain, thereby masking Dinuzulu's last stronghold and forcing him to abandon it. Meanwhile, in pacification operations reminiscent of those that marked the closing stages of the Anglo-Zulu War, a column moved up the coast towards Ivuna, burning homesteads, overawing the inhabitants, forcing submissions and fragmenting any further organised resistance. At Ivuna, where the magistrate was restored to his post, this coastal column was joined by troops from Nkonjeni, who marched back with it to the coast, eliminating on the way what small pockets of resistance still existed.

With the suppression of the rebellion, the responsibility for maintaining law and order was placed back in the hands of the civil authorities. The greatly reduced garrison was strategically concentrated at Eshowe in the south and at Entonjaneni in central Zululand, thus positioning it to act effectively if called upon to do so again by the civil authorities.

'Shingana has taken up a strong position in [the] Hlopekulu mountains, from which he is raiding and terrorising the loyal inhabitants of this district . . . It would be most injudicious to make any forward movement towards the Ceza bush and leave so serious a danger in our rear; such an advance would not only expose the whole of that neighbourhood to be raided by Shingana's followers, but would enable them in the wooded valley of the two Umfoloosi's [Mfolozi rivers] to interrupt our communications and cut off our supplies. I submit, therefore, that before an advance to the Ceza bush takes place, Shingana's following must be dispersed . . . . from the Hlopekulu. Following on the success of these operations, I propose an immediate advance on the Ceza bush, leaving garrisons at N'konjeni and Entonjanini. Seven days' provisions should be taken with the force, and a post formed at the Insugazi kraal, with a sufficient detachment to ensure its safety. From the Insugazi kraal an advance would be made to Peter Louw's store, about four miles from the Ceza bush, where a laager should be formed.'

(Col H. Sparke Stabb, Colonel on the Staff Commanding Troops Natal and Zululand, 17 June 1888)

Boundaries and Colonial Control in Zululand

Chiefdoms and boundaries

At the heart of the continuing civil strife in Zululand during the 1880s was the manner in which the British in 1879, 1883, 1887 and twice in 1888 imposed territorial boundaries on the Zulu which either disregarded existing political and social realities, or deliberately exploited them to keep alive local divisions in order to serve the colonial power's interests.

Chiefdoms in the Zulu kingdom before its overthrow by the British in the war of 1879 were not territorially discrete units with clear-cut boundaries. Rather, the area of each one was defined by those individuals who tendered their allegiance and loyalty to a particular chief. Even if, strictly speaking, the land in Zululand belonged to the king, he delegated his royal prerogative to allocate it to his subjects through a descending hierarchy of greater chiefs to those of lesser degree. It was consequently these chiefs who actually parcelled out land to the people in the districts they administered through their own subordinate headmen or *izinduna* (singular – *induna*). Each head of an individual homestead or *umuzi* (plural – *imizi*) who accepted his chief's ultimate authority, was designated an area by his *induna* roughly defined by natural features such as rivers or hills. There the homestead head or *umnumzane* (plural – *abanumzane*) was permitted to build his *umuzi*, graze his cattle and grow his crops in return for his allegiance.

A chief's adherents would present a fairly solid core clustering around his own principle *imizi*, but those living towards the fringes of his sphere of influence would be increasingly dispersed, and their *imizi* would gradually become intermingled with those of people recognising the authority of other chiefs. Inevitably, the allegiance of such adherents was more uncertain than that of those living closer to the heart of the chiefdom.

British territorial boundaries

When laying down their boundaries in Zululand, the British habitually disregarded these existing territorially complex patterns of authority and loyalty. This was not because succeeding teams of boundary commissioners fell in with the desire often expressed by high colonial officials for compact abstract shapes, like triangles, that would look neat on maps. Rather, all commissioners showed a preference for natural boundaries which followed easily recognisable topographical features like streams and mountains, and which could therefore be depicted with a better claim to precision on the defective, if not positively misleading, maps of Zululand available at that time.

But, as we have seen, the distribution of *imizi* adhering to a particular chief did not comply with tidy topographical-based boundaries. Sir Garnet Wolseley, in his instructions in September 1879 to the Zululand boundary commissioners beaconing off the thirteen chiefdoms into which he had divided the former kingdom, admitted that no boundaries could be satisfactorily fixed because, in far too many instances, the *imizi* of the various chiefdoms were so mixed up. Wolseley's solution was to rule that where people were excluded by the new, fixed boundaries from their former chiefs, they were to be given the option either of moving across the line to place themselves back under their authority, or of staying where they were and tendering their allegiance to their new rulers. Thus Wolseley concocted a recipe for an infinite number of disputes and bitter future conflicts, especially since the British redrew the boundaries on several occasions, each

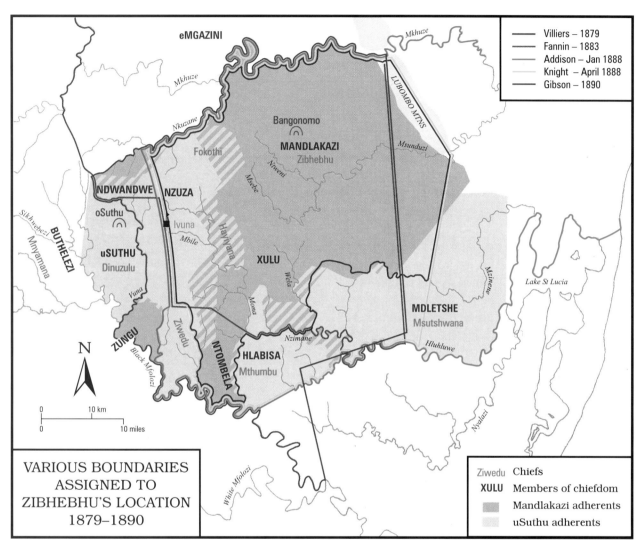

VARIOUS BOUNDARIES ASSIGNED TO ZIBHEBHU'S LOCATION 1879–1890

The five different boundaries, startlingly at variance with each other, which a series of Zululand officials assigned to Zibhebhu's location between 1879 and 1890, reflected the fluctuations in policy regarding the Mandlakazi chief, and the degree of favour in which the British held their arch-collaborator in Zululand. Thus Addison's boundary of January 1888 was drawn expressly to curb the recalcitrant uSuthu by placing many of them under Zibhebhu's authority; while Gibson's demarcation of 1890 succeeded Zibhebhu's fall from official grace, and heralded the new attempt by the Zululand administration to conciliate the uSuthu by releasing many of them (such as the Mdletshe and Hlabisa people and Ziwedu's adherents) from their enemy's rule.

'I cannot but come to the conclusion that this want of a properly defined boundary line between the two tribes [uSuthu and Mandlakazi] is not one of the least causes which have tended to bring about the unfortunate intertribal wars and disturbances of the past, and which keeps alive the animosity which exists between the two peoples in the present.'

(Col F. Cardew, Acting Resident Commissioner
of Zululand, 16 April 1891)

time forcing many Zulu to reconsider their allegiances.

The perpetuation of local divisions

What made these defective boundaries even more divisive than necessary was the way in which the British deliberately manipulated them as an instrument of control in Zululand. By favouring the territorial claims of loyal collaborators at the expense of those chiefs who were considered uncooperative, the British believed they could weaken opponents to their various settlements of Zululand through the consequent perpetuation of local divisions.

The most notorious example of this practice occurred in 1888 in the northern parts of the recently annexed Colony of Zululand. British officials assigned a greatly enlarged location to Chief Zibhebhu kaMaphitha of the Mandlakazi, a leading collaborator, in order to cow the neighbouring uSuthu adherents of Dinuzulu, the heir to the Zulu throne, who was adopting a recalcitrant stance towards the new colonial administration. Zibhebhu insisted on the wholesale eviction from within his new boundaries of all the uSuthu found living there and, with the support of the local magistrate, nearly 5 000 people were accordingly removed. Not surprisingly, this action greatly embittered the uSuthu and brought on their open rebellion against the British, during which they took their revenge on the Mandlakazi, temporarily driving them from their location.

It was only in the 1890s, when at last the British administration in Zululand genuinely set about creating a peaceful settlement, that its officials took full cognisance of the actual position on the ground of the *imizi* adhering to the various chiefs, and drew the boundaries of their locations accordingly.

Collaborators and Colonial Officials

Collaborators and colonial rule

The employment of collaborators was essential in a political settlement (such as the one Sir Garnet Wolseley imposed on Zululand in 1879) which aimed simultaneously at avoiding the responsibility of direct annexation while maintaining a measure of control. Nor was this practice unusual. In fact, the use of collaborators in a colonial situation to counter-balance the influence of recalcitrant elements was a common device among imperial administrators. It also had the financial advantage of minimising the need to deploy expensive colonial or imperial troops to maintain order.

Shepstone and indirect rule

What gave such a policy consistency in the context of Zululand between 1879 and 1888 was the abiding influence of Sir Theophilus Shepstone, who had framed and administered 'Native Affairs' in the Colony of Natal from 1845–1877. His was an expedient system of indirect rule. Shepstone was always conscious of the dangers inherent in a precipitate transition from an African to a colonial administration. He believed that hereditary chiefs should be left in 'native locations' with the exercise of a modicum of their former powers under the supervision of white officials. The ultimate objective of this arrangement, as had proved effective in Natal, was to bring the chiefs' adherents to the realisation that the real source of authority and patronage had passed from their traditional rulers into the hands of the white officials. And once the people understood this, the chiefs' authority naturally but inexorably withered away to the advantage of the colonial administration.

Shepstone envisaged this administrative system being eventually extended to Zululand. However, in the short term, since in 1879 Wolseley wished to implement a set-tlement that fell short of direct annexation, Shepstone advised the appointment of thirteen independent chiefs who owed their elevation to the British, and who could thus be counted on to collaborate in ensuring that the abolished Zulu monarchy did not re-emerge. In the longer term, through

> 'It may be accepted as an axiom, that it is impossible to govern effectively a Zulu population, such as either that of Natal or Zululand, without the aid of their own institutions, at the head of which are their Chiefs or Headmen ... The Magistrate represents the Government to the Native population in his district, but that population is governed by its Chiefs and Headmen, whom the Magistrate holds responsible to him ...'
>
> (Sir Theophilus Shepstone, former Secretary for Native Affairs in Natal, 23 April 1887)

Sir Theophilus Shepstone, KCMG, called 'Somtsewu', or 'father of the white man' (pioneer) by the Zulu. Diplomatic Agent to the Native Tribes, 1845–1855; Secretary for Native Affairs, Natal, 1856–1876; Administrator of the Transvaal, 1877–1879. As the acknowledged expert in colonial circles on 'native affairs', his opinions were repeatedly solicited even in retirement by imperial officials; while his influence lived on and his policies continued to be implemented through his protégés and members of his family who served as colonial officials in Natal and Zululand. He was brought temporarily out of retirement in January 1883 to supervise King Cetshwayo's restoration to the central portion of his former kingdom. He was photographed in the centre of a group of his staff and officers of the escort of 6th (Inniskilling) Dragoons accompanying Cetshwayo from Port Durnford to Mthonjaneni where the king's installation was to take place.

Pietermaritzburg Archives Repository (C. 378)

a loyal school of Natal officials who looked to him as their mentor, Shepstone was able to ensure that his political philosophy of indirect rule would continue to form the basis of the various settlements the British imposed on Zululand over the following decade. Indeed, Shepstone's system was finally implemented in Zululand with the annexation of the territory as a British colony in 1887, and confirmed with that territory's ultimate absorption into the Colony of Natal in 1897.

The unequal relationship between collaborators and colonial officials

In practice, this adherence to the principles of indirect rule meant that the Shepstonian officials in Zululand persisted in favouring and supporting those chiefs most opposed to the restoration of the authority of the deposed royal house. They regarded the politically adroit and militarily successful Chief Zibhebhu of the Mandlakazi as their principal and most effective instrument for counter-weighing royalist uSuthu influence.

Zibhebhu kaMaphitha, Chief of the Mandlakazi in north-eastern Zululand, standing centre, was one of the most able and ambitious men in the kingdom. As King Cetshwayo's cousin, he resisted royal interference in the affairs of his chiefdom and forged strong trading contacts with the colonial world. During the Anglo-Zulu War he was too young to hold the highest command, yet proved himself one of the most resourceful and successful of the Zulu generals. Appointed one of the thirteen chiefs in 1879, Zibhebhu remained the staunchest ally the British had in Zululand, collaborating with them through thick and thin to suppress the aspirations of the royal house. In 1883 he utterly routed the uSuthu and forced Cetshwayo into renewed exile, pursuing his vendetta against his heir, Dinuzulu, after the king's death. Himself defeated and exiled in 1884 by the alliance forged between the uSuthu and the Boers, he returned to his chiefdom in 1887 at the behest of the British who wished to use him as a counter-weight against the uSuthu resisting their administration. His harsh treatment of the uSuthu was a crucial factor in setting off their rebellion in 1888. Defeated once again by the uSuthu in 1888, Zibhebhu and his followers were resettled in southern Zululand. In 1898 the colonial authorities allowed him to return to his chiefdom as part of the British attempt to settle the affairs of Zululand, and he died in 1904 at Bangonomo, his chief umuzi. Pietermaritzburg Archives Repository (C. 740)

Naturally, ambitious collaborators, such as Zibhebhu or Sokwetshatha ka-Mlandela of the Mthethwa, had their own political and economic agendas to pursue, but these had to be adapted to conform with the requirements of the colonial manipulators who had placed them in authority and were maintaining them there. Thus the 'loyalty' of collaborators was ensured, especially when (as in the case of Zibhebhu) military setbacks dealt out by their resentful enemies made them more than ever dependent for survival on the goodwill of the colonial officials. Yet the reverse side of this coin meant that the tribulations experienced by their loyal clients at the hands of their common adversaries obliged officials to lend their unswerving support, even when it drew them into increasingly untenable policies.

Thus, in the case of Zululand, the uSuthu Rebellion of 1888 was brought on in large part by the Zululand officials' blatantly partisan support of Zibhebhu's interests. Yet when they eventually sought a genuinely lasting and equitable settlement of Zululand, these same officials cynically accepted that they could only finally achieve it at the price of jettisoning their longstanding ally. For it was also axiomatic to the expedient and essentially unequal relationship between colonial officials and collaborators that the latter would be dropped without compunction the moment they had ceased to serve their purpose, and had become an embarrassment to their masters.

> 'The Zulus in Central Zululand appear to be far from satisfied with the recent settlement of their country . . . As a matter of policy I would suggest the return of Usibebu and his people to their old country. We know their loyalty, and can depend upon them in case of any disturbances there, and by sending them back we would have a strong loyal body at the extreme end of the country, and the Zulus would thus be between it and us, and would feel the difficulty and danger of their position should they contemplate any rising.'
>
> (Henrique Shepstone [son of Sir Theophilus and called by the Zulu 'Gebuza', or one who paws the ground impatiently], Secretary for Native Affairs in Natal, 26 April 1887)

Many uSuthu were subsequently to believe that the civil war with the Mandlakazi began on 31 August 1881 at the foot of Nhlazatshe Mountain in central Zululand. On that fateful day Maj-Gen Sir Evelyn Wood, Acting High Commissioner for South East Africa, met representatives from the contending Zulu factions. During the meeting, which he conducted in full uniform and with as much military music and glitter as he could summon, Wood made it unequivocally clear that the British authorities intended to uphold Sir Garnet Wolseley's Zulu settlement of September 1879, and that they would throw their full support behind the thirteen chiefs Wolseley had appointed. The uSuthu leadership present – which included Cetshwayo's son, Dinuzulu, five of the exiled king's brothers and many other leading chiefs – realised with considerable consternation that they could hope for no redress from the British; while their adversaries, the six appointed chiefs present, gloatingly welcomed Wood's pronouncement.

Lady Florence Dixie, daughter of the ninth Marquess of Queensbury, writer, explorer and big game hunter, sympathised with Cetshwayo and the royalist cause, and recorded her Zululand experiences in her book, In the Land of Misfortune. She attended the Nhlazatshe meeting, and the engraving is from this work. She described the proceedings as follows:

> In the centre of the half circle, squatting on mats, were five of the reigning [appointed] chiefs and several representatives of those unable to attend; while on a chair close to them was seated John Dunn. On either side of the chiefs two lines deep of indunas and great men were clustered together; and behind these again was a long row of petty chiefs and men of rank and importance. Around these ran a horse-shoe circle, in lines ten or twelve deep, of Zulus, who were all arranged in complete order and at a respectful distance from their superiors . . . Opposite the chiefs were placed a row of chairs and benches, Sir Evelyn [Wood] occupying the centre, having on his right Mr Osborne [sic], the British Resident in Zululand, and two interpreters . . . while on his left I was seated. Behind us stood his aides-de-camp, military and private secretaries, and a large group of officers and men . . . Behind us the troops were drawn up in line; and as the three squadrons [of 6th (Inniskilling) Dragoons] simultaneously unsheathed their swords, there was a momentary movement of panic amongst the horse-shoe circle, which, however, quickly subsided . . . [At the end of the meeting] the troops formed up and marched away, and the slopes of the Inhslazatye re-echoed for the last time with a triumphant march which seemed to exult in a victory whose gain could produce no good result. Amidst that native crowd murmurs of discontent waxed loud. Was it for this that many had come long and weary distances?

Lady Florence Dixie, *In the Land of Misfortune*, 1882, opp. p. 380

PART II

The Partition of Zululand

1879 and 1882

'I did not land in a dry place. I landed in the mud . . . I came and found
long-standing feuds and bitterly opposed enemies.'

(King Cetshwayo kaMpande, mid-1883)

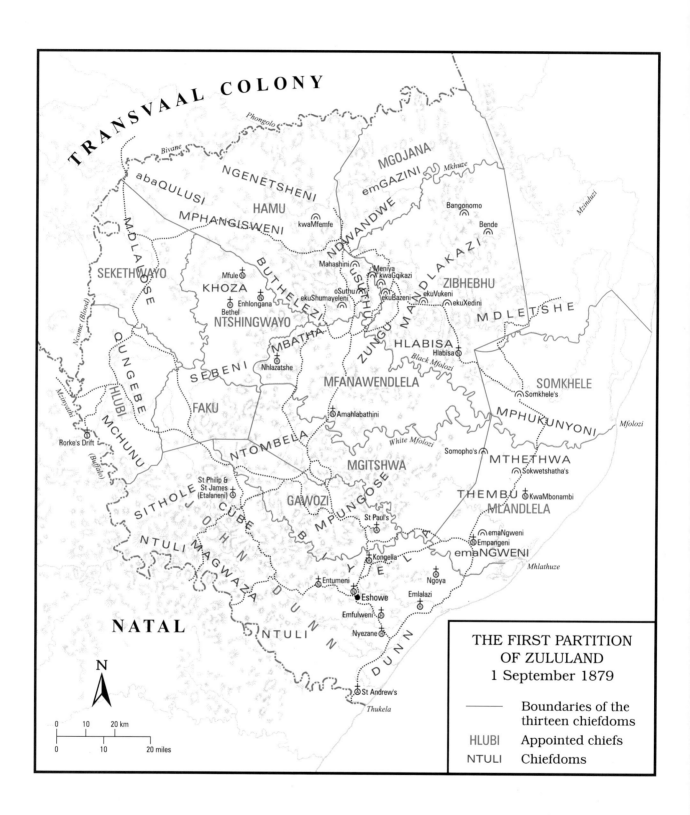

TRANSVAAL COLONY

Phongolo

Bivane

NGENETSHENI

MGOJANA

emGAZINI

Mkhuze

Mzinduzi

abaQULUSI

HAMU

MPHANGISWENI

kwaMfemfe

NDWANDWE

Bangonomo

Bende

MDLAKOSE

SEKETHWAYO

KHOZA

BUTHELEZI

Mfule

Mahashini

Meniya
kwaGqikazi

oSuthu
ekuShumayeleni

ekuVukeni

ZIBHEBHU

MDLETSHE

Enhlongana
Bethel

ekuBazeni

ekuXedini

Ncome (Blood)

NTSHINGWAYO

MBATHA

ZUNGU MANDLAKAZI

HLABISA

Hlabisa

Black Mfolozi

QUNGEBE

SEBENI

Nhlazatshe

MFANAWENDLELA

SOMKHELE

Somkhele's

HLUBI

FAKU

Amahlabathini

White Mfolozi

MPHUKUNYONI

Mfolozi

Mzinyathi

MCHUNU

NTOMBELA

Somopho's

MTHETHWA

Sokwetshatha's

Rorke's Drift

MGITSHWA

(Buffalo)

St Philip &
St James
(Etalaneni)

GAWOZI

MPUNGOSE

St Paul's

THEMBU

KwaMbonambi

MLANDLELA

SITHOLE

CUBE

emaNgweni

Empangeni

NTULI MAGWAZA

Kongella

emaNGWENI

Mhlathuze

J O H N

B Y E L A

NATAL

Entumeni

Ngoya

N

Eshowe

Emlalazi

DUNN

Emfulweni

Nyezane

NTULI

DUNN

0   10   20 km

0   10   20 miles

St Andrew's

Thukela

THE FIRST PARTITION
OF ZULULAND
1 September 1879

———— Boundaries of the
thirteen chiefdoms

HLUBI   Appointed chiefs

NTULI   Chiefdoms

The Partition of the
Zulu Kingdom

1879

Zulu defeat in the Anglo-Zulu War

The British invasion of the Zulu king-dom in 1879 culminated after a pro-tracted and hard-fought campaign in the final and crushing defeat on 4 July of the Zulu army at the battle of Ulundi. The worsted Zulu army dispersed, never again to reassemble, and the Zulu king, Cetshwayo kaMpande, fled into the broken terrain of the northern reaches of Zululand. Although the great Zulu chiefs rapidly began to submit and make their peace with the British, Gen Sir Garnet Wolseley (the Commander-in-Chief of the

Cmdr Crawford Caffin, RN, sketched the captive King Cetshwayo on 4 September 1879 embarking on a surf-boat at Port Durnford before being rowed out to the steam-transport HMS Natal *which was to carry him into exile in Cape Town. Cetshwayo is wearing a red and green table-cloth as a shawl, and is determinedly maintaining his dignity despite his deep dismay at leaving Zululand. A small party of attendants prepare to follow him up the plank to share his captivity. They include Mkhosana kaSangqana, a longstanding companion and adviser, who stands in front of a group of four young women of the royal household and a female servant. The three other men of the king's suite are also shown, one of whom was his hairdresser. The men of No. 3 Troop, Natal Horse (Bettington's Horse), who had escorted him to the coast from Gen Sir Garnet Wolseley's camp at kwaSishwili near oNdini, are drawn up on the shore, flanked on either side by a company of the 91st Regiment (Princess Louise's Argyllshire Highlanders) who, later renamed the 1st Bn, Princess Louise's (Argyll and Sutherland Highlanders), would again take part in operations in Zululand during the 1880s. In the background, with flag flying, is the signal station, while the ambulance wagon drawn by ten mules, which had transported the king from kwaSishwili, stands between the ranks of troops.* Illustrated London News, *18 October 1879*

'The Chiefs who had been assembling here for some days past assembled this afternoon in front of my tent & I made them a long speech . . . I believe that what I said gave general satisfaction & that the Chiefs are very glad of the turn affairs have taken and as grateful as Zulus can be for the leniency with which they have been treated.'
(Gen Sir Garnet Wolseley, High Commissioner in South Eastern Africa, 1 September 1879)

British forces in South Africa and High Commissioner in South Eastern Africa), who had been entrusted by the British government with the final pacification of Zululand, realised that a lasting settlement was impossible until the king had been captured. Until he was in British hands, he would remain a rallying-point for all those Zulu who contemplated further resistance. Patrols were sent out, and on 28 August Cetshwayo was captured in the Ngome forest and immediately escorted to exile in Cape Town.

Wolseley's settlement
With Cetshwayo removed from the scene, the leading Zulu chiefs agreed on 1 September to the peace terms Wolseley laid down. The Zulu monarchy was suppressed, and the former kingdom fragmented into thirteen chiefdoms, each under a chief appointed by Wolseley. Although these little chiefdoms were left formally independent, they agreed to submit to the arbitration of a British Resident.

In devising this partition of Zululand, Wolseley was following his government's instructions to come up with a settlement that avoided the expense and responsibility of direct annexation, but which ensured the security of Zululand's British-ruled neighbours. Wolseley understood that the Zulu monarchy and the Zulu military, or *ibutho*, system, so feared throughout the region, were synonymous. For the king's power and political authority rested upon his ability, through this institution (formalised 60 years before by King Shaka), to monopolise and direct the military and economic potential of his subjects. By deposing Cetshwayo and abolishing the monarchy, the *ibutho* system would lose

its meaning and coherence and disappear. None of the thirteen independent chiefs appointed in Cetshwayo's stead would consequently command anything like the military power previously deployed by the Zulu kings, and would cease to pose any military threat to their neighbours. In addition, the newly raised up chiefs would be insecure and in fear of any attempt by the Zulu royal house to regain its lost authority. Therefore, Wolseley calculated, in order to preserve their new-found power, the 'kinglets' could be counted on to collaborate with the British to stifle any revival of royalist influence, and Zululand would be kept as divided and weak as the British government desired.

The thirteen chiefs
With the interests of security in mind, Wolseley deliberately apportioned the two strategic chiefdoms along the southern border of Zululand with Natal to chiefs considered particularly reliable. They were John Dunn, the white hunter and who had once been Cetshwayo's confidant and to whom he had apportioned a chiefdom in south-eastern Zululand; and Hlubi ka-Mota Molife, chief of the Sotho-speaking Tlokwa people from Weenen County in Natal. Both these aliens had fought energetically with their followers on the British side during the Anglo-Zulu War. Their chiefdoms would act as a buffer between Natal and other possibly less amenable chiefs to the north of them.

In northern Zululand, the appointment of two powerful and ambitious Zulu magnates, Prince Hamu kaNzibe of the Ngenetsheni and Chief Zibhebhu ka-Maphitha of the Mandlakazi, to rule over precisely the area where the royalist supporters (or uSuthu) were particularly strong, was calculated to ensure the suppression of the aspirations of the royal house at its territorial core.

Sandwiched between these four chiefs at the southern and northern ends of Zululand upon whom the success of the settlement depended, were nine others. They owed their appointment to the degree of trust Wolseley believed he could place

Prince Hamu was King Mpande's first-born son. But, through the ukuvuza *custom, he was heir not to his biological father but to Nzibe, Mpande's dead brother, for whose spirit the king was 'raising seed'. Hamu ruled over the Ngenethseni people in north-western Zululand from his great* umuzi, *kwaMfemfe, where he maintained royal state. Hamu resented that he was kept from the royal succession, and coveted the throne. During the Anglo-Zulu War he soon defected to the British in the hope that they would recognise him as king in Cetshwayo's stead. However, he was made no more than one of the thirteen appointed chiefs. Allied with Zibhebhu, he bore down as hard as he could on the uSuthu during the civil war that followed on the restoration of Cetshwayo, whom he had hoped to supplant.*

Ian Knight Collection

in them, either on account of their record of actual collaboration with the British, or because during the war they had abandoned the royal cause early. A number, however, had no hereditary status in the territories they were apportioned, and would find it difficult to make themselves obeyed by their new subjects.

Wolseley's pragmatic attempt to neutralise Zululand by dividing it against itself exploited long-standing conflicts between the Zulu monarchy and the more powerful chiefs. It consequently provided a recipe for internecine conflict, especially since the settlement made no provision for containing conflict should it erupt.

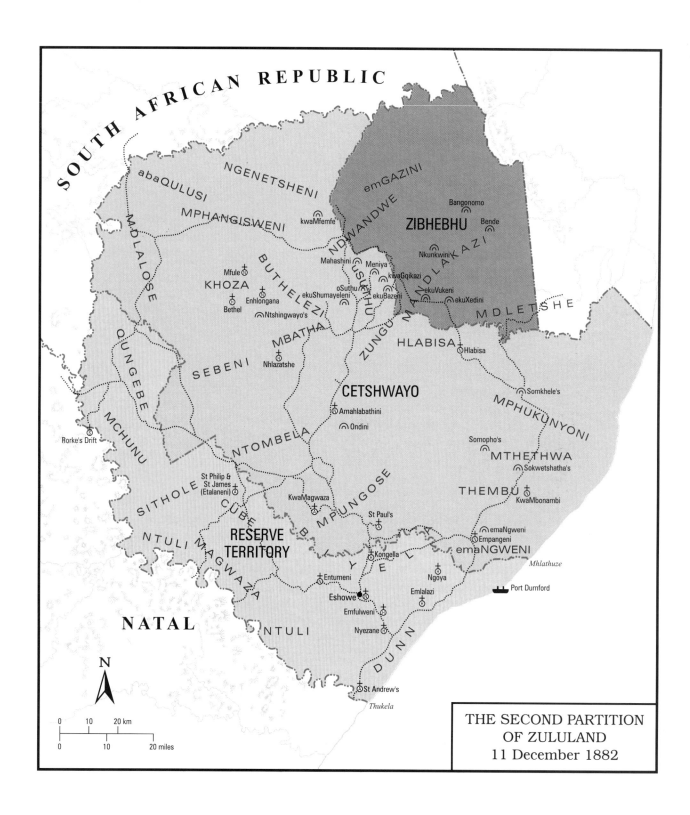

THE SECOND PARTITION
OF ZULULAND
11 December 1882

The Partition of Zululand
1882

The uSuthu negotiate fruitlessly for Cetshwayo's restoration to Zululand

The uSuthu in the Zululand left fragmented by Wolseley soon began to suffer ill-treatment at the hands of Zibhebhu and Hamu, and drew together with other victims of the settlement of 1879 to resist their oppressors. They first took the route of negotiation. Two of Cetshwayo's brothers, Princes Ndabuko and Shingana, with others of the uSuthu leadership, went in deputation to Pietermaritzburg in late May 1880. There they pleaded with Natal colonial officials for the king's return from exile in the Cape in order to restore unity and peace in Zululand. They were rebuffed. A second uSuthu deputation to Pietermaritzburg in late April 1882 received no more satisfaction than the first.

Meanwhile, the British Resident in Zululand, Melmoth Osborn, was throwing his influence behind the anti-uSuthu faction to counteract Ndabuko's and Shingana's initiatives. At Nhlazatshe on 31 August 1881 his policy was thoroughly endorsed by the Acting High Commissioner for South East Africa and Administrator for Natal, Maj-Gen Sir Evelyn Wood, when he met representatives from the two factions. Wood left the uSuthu in no doubt that the British authorities intended to uphold Wolseley's settlement to their detriment.

The outbreak of violence

However, Osborn had no armed forces at his disposal with which to intervene in the looming confrontation which he and other British officials had effectively fanned,

The first uSuthu deputation, which came to plead with the British authorities for King Cetshwayo's restoration to his kingdom, walked to Natal in May 1880. Prince Ndabuko kaMpande stands in the centre of the group with his hands crossed over his staff. To his right is his half-brother, Prince Shingana kaMpande, and to his left Ngcongcwana kaMgundane, Cetshwayo's uncle, who later travelled to London in August 1882 with the king as his inceku *(personal attendant and adviser), and who would be killed in the rout at the battle of oNdini in July 1883.*   Pietermaritzburg Archives Repository (C. 868)

'Had we left Cetywayo on the throne, or annexed the country, we should in either case have taken an intelligible course. As it is, we neither control the affairs of Zululand, nor are we free from responsibilities for them.'

(Earl of Kimberley, Colonial Secretary, 6 September 1881)

rather than quenched, and Zululand began to slip into sporadic conflict. During September 1881 Hamu determined to expel the royalist abaQulusi and Mphangisweni people from his chiefdom. Under armed threat from the Ngenetsheni, they began to take refuge in their mountain fastness or to move across the Bivane River into the South African Republic which, by the Pretoria convention of 3 August 1881, had regained its independence from Britain. On 2 October Hamu's forces attacked the abaQulusi in the Bivane valley and scattered them with considerable slaughter. Ndabuko and Chief Mnyamana ka-Ngqengelele of the Buthelezi, who had been King Cetshwayo's chief *induna* at the time of the Anglo-Zulu War, mobilised

in retaliation, and Zibhebhu advanced threateningly in their direction in support of Hamu.

This time, both sides drew back from the brink of a major military clash, and Osborn was able to persuade all the belligerents to withdraw their forces. Whether he would be able to do so in the future remained to be seen, especially since the reasons for the narrowly averted conflict remained unchanged.

The British Colonial Office decides on a fresh Zululand settlement

For his part, the exiled Cetshwayo, made desperate by the reported state of affairs in Zululand, was using what influence he could muster to negotiate his restoration. His efforts bore fruit only once the officials of the British Colonial Office in London came to the unwelcome but inescapable conclusion that the Wolseley settlement was breaking down. Since in the circumstances they could envisage no alternative to the direct annexation of Zululand (which they wished to avoid) but the expedient of sending Cetshwayo back to calm the situation, they permitted the king to come to England in August 1882 to plead his cause in person.

The Colonial Secretary was not certain, however, whether Cetshwayo's restoration would serve to return stability. Lord Kimberley was under pressure from Natal officials who feared the military potential of a reunited Zululand, and he also felt obliged to protect those of the thirteen appointed chiefs who had actively collaborated with the British to the detriment of the uSuthu. Consequently, although Kimberley finally decided to allow Cetshwayo to return to Zululand, it was not to be as ruler of the kingdom as it had existed before the Anglo-Zulu War.

'But even today in bringing him [Cetshwayo] back you are killing him, killing him, I say, as you have done all along . . . We thought that this King was now a child of the Queen. Do you mock us in saying you are restoring him? . . . We thought you would inquire how these 13 Chiefs came to do as they have done, killing our people, and seizing our daughters, and eating up our cattle. What sort of settlement is this, Sir! We do not call it a settlement at all.'

(Hemulana kaMbangezeli, Buthelezi *induna*, 29 January 1883)

King Cetshwayo was photographed in London in August 1882 by Alex. Bassano of Old Bond Street while negotiating his restoration to Zululand. Dressed impeccably in British style and displaying his natural royal ease of manner, he was lionised by fashionable society and granted an audience at Osborne by Queen Victoria.
Pietermaritzburg Archives Repository (C. 683)

The terms of Cetshwayo's restoration and the new partition of Zululand

Cetshwayo's authority was confined to the central portion of the old Zulu kingdom (including Hamu's former chiefdom) under the supervision of a Resident, Henry Francis Fynn, Jnr. He was hemmed in to the north-east by Zibhebhu, who was awarded an enlarged independent chiefdom that encompassed the uSuthu heartland and many of Cetshwayo's staunchest supporters. To the south, as a further check against Cetshwayo's ambitions, the Reserve Territory was created out of Dunn's and Hlubi's chiefdoms to act as a military buffer for Natal, and as a place of sanctuary for those Zulu who wished to avoid the king's re-imposed rule. Although still an independent territory, it was to be administered by officials recruited from Natal, consisting of a Resident Commissioner assisted by various sub-commissioners, ruling through Zulu chiefs and paid for by a hut tax. In practice, this implied the extension of Natal's control over the southern third of Zululand.

Although deeply disappointed with these conditions placed on his restoration to Zululand, Cetshwayo realised he had no alternative but to assent to them, which he did on 11 December 1882. On 10 January 1883 he set foot once again in Zululand at Port Durnford (in what was now the Reserve Territory) and proceeded directly to the territory assigned to him.

Henry Francis Fynn, Jnr, son of one of the early pioneers in Natal and a fluent Zulu linguist, photographed at the end of the Anglo-Zulu War with members of the Border Guard he had raised for the defence of the Natal border against Zulu invasion. Since 1876 he had been Resident Magistrate of the Umsinga Division, having risen through the ranks of the Natal colonial administration. On 12 January 1883 Sir Henry Bulwer, as Special Commissioner for Zulu Affairs, appointed him 'British Resident with Cetywayo'. Fynn had known Cetshwayo since 1873 and enjoyed a close friendship with him. He was called 'Gwalagwala' by the Zulu after the red feather of the lourie which he wore in his hat, and which had associations with heroic qualities in battle. Fynn took up station as Resident in his camp on the hills overlooking oNdini, and was able to empathise with the restored king's difficulties. But as the representative of the British government he was required to keep the peace between Cetshwayo and his foes, and his neutrality was not always appreciated by the king. Not that Fynn was much able to sway events. He had no armed forces at his disposal, and moral suasion usually proved insufficient in a time of civil war. He stayed with the king until 16 October 1883 when Cetshwayo finally took refuge with the British authorities in Eshowe. Fynn then resumed his post at Umsinga, retiring in 1897. Ian Knight Collection

The detachment of British troops, which met the restored King Cetshwayo at Port Durnford on 10 January 1883, served both as a guard of honour and as an unmistakable indication that he was being restored under British protection. The escort was composed mainly of a detachment of the 6th (Inniskilling) Dragoons under Col F.G.S. Curtis. An anonymous officer of the regiment sketched the Dragoons crossing the lower Thukela River on 29 December 1882 on their way to Port Durnford. He described how they were sent over the drift in two troops of 70 each, the men in their shirts with legs bare. Note Fort Pearson, built in November 1878, crowning the hill commanding the drift. The tree under which the British ultimatum was delivered to the Zulu on 11 December 1878 prior to the Anglo-Zulu War can be seen on the riverbank to the left. Graphic, 10 February 1883

PART III
The Civil War
1883–1884

'Zibhebhu is the Napoleon of North Zululand, and his army have named him
Matshetshe or "one quick in his movements".'

(Herbert J. Nunn, Prince Hamu kaNzibe's resident trader and adviser,
and *Natal Mercury* correspondent, 1 April 1883)

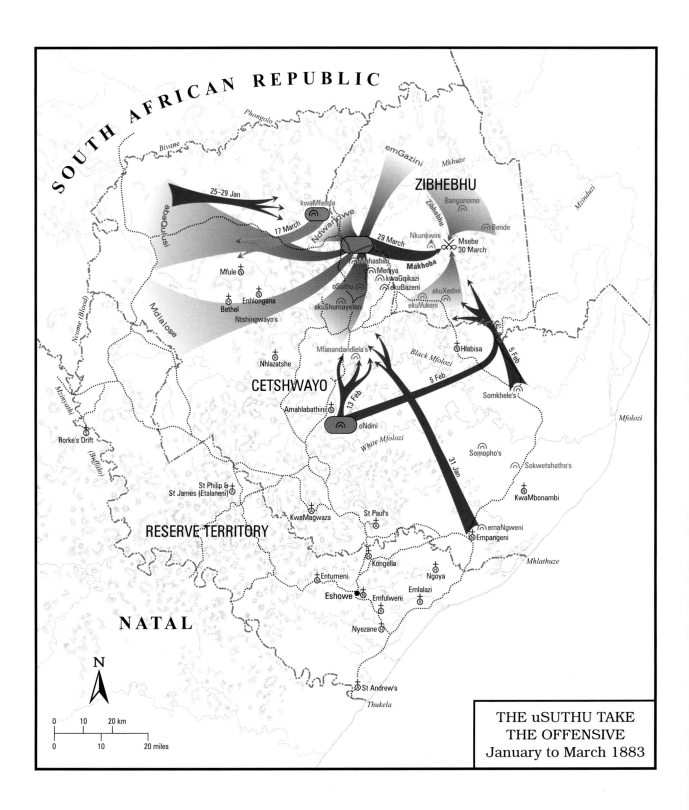

THE uSUTHU TAKE
THE OFFENSIVE
January to March 1883

The Msebe Campaign

January – March 1883

Lt M.F. Rimington, 6th (Inniskilling) Dragoons, sketched King Cetshwayo for the Graphic *receiving a delegation of his relatives on the Mthonjaneni heights a few days before his installation as king on 29 January 1883. The king's enemy, Zibhebhu, had started a rumour that what the British had brought with them was only a waxwork doll dressed up (or an* isithombe) *and his followers were joyful to see that it was indeed he. The sketch shows a few chiefs sitting at the king's feet in conversation with him, while the people dance and sing Cetshwayo's praises, or intently watch him, as Rimington described, talking to each other in awed whispers.*

Graphic, 10 March 1883

Obstacles to stability in Cetshwayo's territory

Cetshwayo's return in January 1883 to the territory in central Zululand assigned to him by the British only succeeded in intensifying the already simmering conflict. Ten of the formerly independent chiefs appointed by Wolseley in 1879 now fell within his reduced kingdom and under his rule. He faced their inevitable resentment and hostility, most especially that of Hamu, the Ngenetsheni chief and close associate of Zibhebhu of the Mandlakazi, whom the settlement of 1883 had left as an independent chief and bulwark against Cetshwayo's ambitions. At the same time, those uSuthu who had suffered under the oppression of these chiefs, naturally looked on Cetshwayo's restoration as the moment to exact revenge.

Raid and counter-raid in central and northern Zululand

Cetshwayo was no sooner back on the Mahlabathini plain and building oNdini, a new royal homestead to replace the previous one burned by the British in 1879, when the royalists started raiding some of these deposed anti-uSuthu chiefs. The abaQulusi struck at Hamu's Ngenetsheni on 25–29 January, and the emaNgweni attacked those elements of the Zungu people nearby who adhered to Mfana-wendlela kaThanga on 31 January. On 5 February three companies or *amaviyo* (singular – *iviyo*) of uSuthu from oNdini

> 'Cetshwayo, much excited [said] Zibhebhu was his Cetshwayo's dog and now land of the Zulus had been given to him and he was bragging over Cetshwayo, how could this continue, the people could not stand all this, nothing could have been done more likely to cause bloodshed, than to deprive the Zulus of their king their own land and give it to the king's dog, now his bitterest enemy.'
>
> (Fynn, 20 February 1883)

Immediately after his installation as the ruler of central Zululand on 29 January 1883, Cetshwayo's adherents set about building him a new royal residence just to the east of the previous oNdini, which had been destroyed in the war of 1879. It was about two-thirds the size of its predecessor with a diameter of 461 m (504 yards) and consisted of about a thousand huts. Walton's drawing of women carrying supplies to the amabutho *who were concentrating at oNdini in mid-1883 was subsequently published in the* Pictorial World.*

Rai England Collection

At the old oNdini, burned in 1879, Cetshwayo had possessed a special house of audience in the isigodlo, *or royal enclosure, built in the European style. When Walton of the* Pictorial World *made this pencil drawing in July 1883, Cetshwayo, for want of a similar house at the new oNdini, had pitched a British tent in the* isigodlo *from which he conducted his official business. He is depicted seated behind a European table with turned legs receiving a visit from the British Resident in Zululand, Henry Francis Fynn, Jnr. The attendant at the tent-flap is observing the correct Zulu protocol in the presence of his superiors by crouching low.*

MuseuMAfrica (W81)

joined the uSuthu-aligned Mphukunyoni of Chief Somkhele kaMalanda in a raid across the Hluhluwe River against Zibhebhu's Mandlakazi; while on 13 February the uSuthu at oNdini plundered Mfanawendlela again. In the far north-west, between 10 and 17 March, there were raids and counter-raids between the royalist abaQulusi and those among their own people who were aligned with Hamu. The Ngenetsheni chose that moment to retaliate against the abaQulusi who had raided them in January, and to pillage the pro-uSuthu Zungu under Chief Mkhosana kaSangqana.

The uSuthu muster for war against Zibhebhu

Yet it was Zibhebhu who precipitated full-scale war by ruthlessly expelling the uSuthu from their own heartland which had been assigned to his enlarged chiefdom by the 1882 settlement. The displaced uSuthu were determined to fight back. By late March they and their allies were concentrating along the Sikhwebezi River in the territory of Mnyamana, the Buthelezi chief.

This uSuthu force of about 5 000 was mustered on Prince Ndabuko's orders in territorial units under their various chiefs, rather than by age-grades in *amabutho*, as would have been the case in a royal army up to 1879. The assembled force was made up of Ndabuko's uSuthu, the Buthelezi under Tshanibezwe kaMnyamana, the eGazini under their chief, Hlezibane, the emGazini under Chief Mabokho kaMasiphula, the Ndwandwe under Chief Mgojana kaSomaphunga, the abaQulusi and Mphangisweni under

> 'Sent to Cetshwayo to say . . . he bound himself to respect the boundaries of the 3 districts of the Zulu country . . . which I have so constantly explained to him . . . I have done so and continue to urge upon him to adhere to all the terms of his restoration, and I am doing my duty as his friend – and I tell him again and again the Government hold him personally responsible for any breach or breaking of the laws of his restoration, including any disturbance committed in or beyond his district by his adherents.'
>
> (Fynn, 30 March 1883)

Prince Mahanana kaMpande and the Mdlalose people. Makhoba kaMaphitha, a half-brother of Zibhebhu's who was aligned with the uSuthu, was in command.

Zibhebhu's victory over the uSuthu at Msebe

In the last days of March the uSuthu army began its advance east, deep into Mandlakazi territory, its objective being Bangonomo, Zibhebhu's main *umuzi*. Zibhebhu, who had only some 1 500 men and a handful of white mercenaries under Johan Colenbrander ('Tozana') available to defend his territory, fell back as far as the Msebe valley. There he prepared an ambush into which the uSuthu blundered unprepared on 30 March. The Mandlakazi swiftly broke the uSuthu army which fled in helpless rout as far as the Nongoma hills to the west. Only ten Mandlakazi were killed, compared to well over a thousand royalists. Msebe was a stunning victory for Zibhebhu and a fatal setback for Cetshwayo's attempt to reassert royal authority over his former subjects. As such, it also doomed Britain's 1882 settlement of Zululand to failure.

The Battle of Msebe

30 March 1883

The mustering of the uSuthu army

During late March 1883 Prince Ndabuko, Chief Mnyamana and other uSuthu chiefs whose following lived in northern Zululand, left oNdini, where they had been attending King Cetshwayo, to organise an army to deal once and for all with Zibhebhu who had been expelling uSuthu supporters from his territory. It is not clear whether they went with Cetshwayo's explicit sanction, for the king had been warned by Fynn, the British Resident, that any aggressive move against Zibhebhu was certain to antagonise the British.

The uSuthu army began to muster in Buthelezi territory near Mnyamana's homesteads along the Sikhwebezi River. Impatient to come to grips with the Mandlakazi, the hot-headed Ndabuko refused to take Mnyamana's cautious advice not to open the campaign until reinforced by the strong contingent promised by the abaQulusi. Consequently, on 29 March the force of some 5 000 men concentrated at Mnyamana's ekuShumayeleni *umuzi*, loosely organised into divisions according to allegiance to their particular chiefs, rather than by *ibutho*, which was the usual practice on campaign. Ndabuko placed the army under the command of Makhoba.

The uSuthu advance into Mandlakazi territory

Makhoba led the army east across the Vuna River into Mandlakazi territory, and advanced between the Msebe and Mkhuze rivers towards Bangonomo, Zibhebhu's principal *umuzi*.

The uSuthu marched in a great column 30 men wide and several kilometres long, their numbers swollen by the numerous unarmed *izindibi* (singular – *udibi*) or

---

uSuthu forces

Some 100 *amaviyo* (or about 5 000 men) assembled at ekuShumayeleni loosely organised as follows into three divisions by chief, rather than by *ibutho*: the uSuthu under Prince Ndabuko kaMpande; the Buthelezi under Tshanibezwe kaMnyamana; and the emGazini under Chief Mabokho kaMasiphula. Ndabuko placed the army under the command of Makhoba kaMaphitha.

During the battle the emGazini were on the left flank and the Buthelezi on the right. The uSuthu contingent was to their rear.

Mandlakazi forces

Chief Zibhebhu kaMaphitha commanded 30 *amaviyo* (about 1 500 Mandlakazi), some of whom were mounted and armed with rifles. Five or six mounted white mercenaries were with them under the command of Johan Colenbrander.

uSuthu casualties

Well over 1 000 were killed, mainly in the prolonged pursuit. Many prominent uSuthu were slain including their general, Makhoba kaMaphitha, and Mgwazeni kaMbhonde, Cetshwayo's maternal uncle. Ten sons of Mnyamana's and five of Ndabuko's were reportedly among the dead. Cetshwayo's brother, Prince Sitheku kaMpande was captured, as was Ndulunga, another son of Mnyamana's.

Mandlakazi casualties

Ten killed.

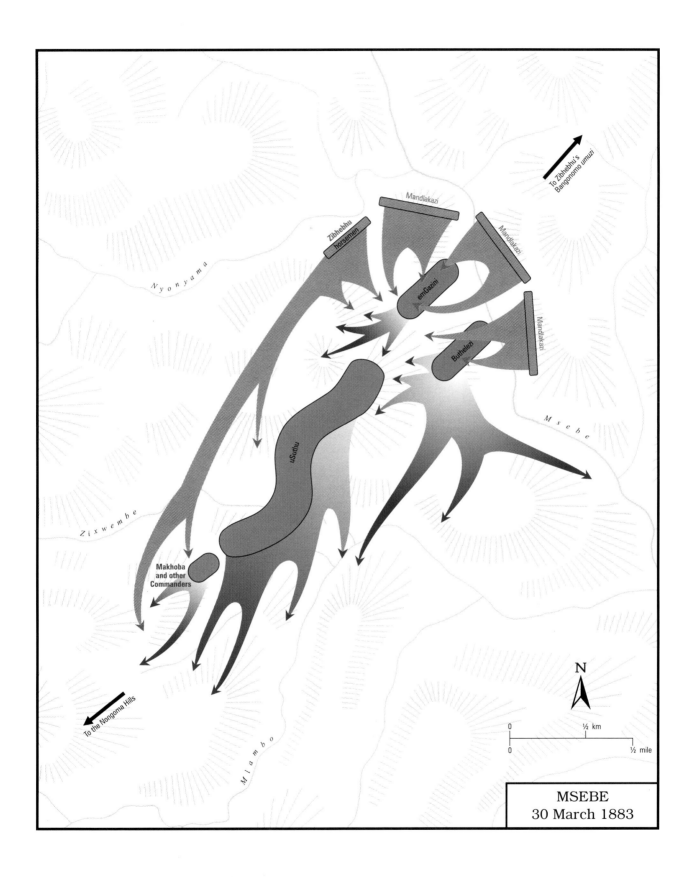

To Zibhebhu's Bangonomo *umuzi*

Mandlakazi

Zibhebhu horsemen

Mandlakazi

Nyonyama

emGazini

Mandlakazi

Buthelezi

Msebe

uSuthu

Zixwembe

Makhoba and other Commanders

To the Nongoma Hills

N

0   ½ km

0   ½ mile

Mlambo

MSEBE
30 March 1883

baggage boys who accompanied them. As they advanced the uSuthu burned and plundered the Mandlakazi *imizi*, especially those belonging to Zibhebhu and members of his family. But uSuthu morale was fairly low because it was rumoured that Cetshwayo had not sanctioned their campaign and, perhaps more crucially, because they were distinctly wary of Zibhebhu and his record of military prowess.

Zibhebhu sets his ambush

Zibhebhu was in need of all the military skill he could summon, for to face the uSuthu host he only had 1 500 men. But they were well-disciplined, and were bolstered by five or six white mercenaries under Johan Colenbrander, the white trader from whom Zibhebhu had obtained his essential firearms.

Zibhebhu fell back before the advancing uSuthu, drawing them on into the bush-country at the heart of his territory. There, in the valley of the Msebe stream, it was his intention to ambush them. The site was well chosen. There are no nearby hills from which his position could be spied, while the gently sloping sides of the shallow valley are ribbed by water-

courses, making it impossible to see any great distance; moreover, the long grass, scrub and mimosa trees were sufficient to conceal the crouching Mandlakazi, stretched north to south across the path along which Zibhebhu planned to lure the uSuthu.

The uSuthu are drawn into the ambush

Soon after sunrise on 30 March six of Zibhebhu's mounted men fired on the uSuthu who were eating mealies near his Nkunkwini homestead, which they had torched. The horsemen then fell back to the north-east, as if in flight, drawing the disorderly and unsuspecting uSuthu into the trap. Made over-confident by their unopposed progress through Zibhebhu's territory, the uSuthu advanced carelessly as if out on a hunting-party, their poorly marshalled ranks crowded with the non-combatant *izindibi*. Two contingents led the way, the emGazini on the left, and the Buthelezi on the right. The uSuthu straggled after them with the commanders in the very rear, as was often customary with an advancing army.

The trap is sprung

Zibhebhu had posted his men in three divisions in the traditional fighting formation, and positioned himself and his mounted riflemen on the right flank. To overcome their numerical inferiority, Zibhebhu boldly unleashed both his centre and right divisions against the emGazini contingent on the uSuthu left. The Mandlakazi 'chest' thus cut straight between the Buthelezi and emGazini and, in a co-ordinated manoeuvre with the right wing, completed the envelopment of the emGazini, supported by Zibhebhu's horsemen. Surprised and outflanked, the emGazini immediately broke and fled. Because of the nature of the terrain, the uSuthu could not see what was happening to units other than their own, and panic rapidly set in. The Buthelezi contingent, which was attacked by the Mandlakazi left wing, almost immediately followed the emGazini in their rout. The uSuthu contingent to their rear only put up a token resistance before joining the others in desperate flight, in which the different units became hopelessly intermingled. Most fled back the way they had come, towards the Nongoma hills, while a few escaped down the Msebe valley. Some of the emGazini tried to break away to the north towards their homes.

The pursuit

The pursuit lasted until sunset, the uSuthu only occasionally attempting a stand. The open country offered them little cover in their flight, and the bones of the slaughtered uSuthu littered the plain for years to come. Zibhebhu and his horsemen ranged at will among their stampeding foes. They made especially for the uSuthu leadership who had been to the rear of their forces, and picked off particular enemies with their rifles. Most of the prominent uSuthu nevertheless managed to escape, but Makhoba, the uSuthu general, was sought out in the rout and killed, as were other uSuthu of high lineage. Many believed that in no other battle had the Zulu ever suffered greater loss of life than the uSuthu had that day. By contrast, losses among the victorious Mandlakazi were minimal.

> 'We got mixed up in the flight, and were pursued and stabbed and shot down, only one company of the Sutu made any resistance . . . I joined in with Zibebu's forces as if one of them and so eventually escaped from them that night . . . We fled because when on our way we got to understand Ndabuko had for his own purposes mustered us and we had not courage to fight, as we were not sent by Cetshwayo. Both forces had large numbers of guns and Zibebu got possession of the guns and assegais of the fallen men of our force.'
>
> (Ntangweni, son of Nobengula, 4 April 1883)

> 'Zibebu fell by accident from his horse and was assisted in soon remounting and came in again amongst our forces shooting us down . . . Zibebu prevented a son of Mnyamana's from being killed and protected him himself and allowed him to escape.'
>
> (Ntangweni, 4 April 1883)

From Msebe to oNdini
1 April – 21 July 1883

The Ngenetsheni and Mandlakazi ravage the northern uSuthu

Following the rout of the uSuthu at Msebe on 30 March 1883, Hamu's Ngenetsheni systematically raided their royalist neighbours: on 5 April six *amaviyo* attacked the Mdlalose; the abaQulusi were struck the following day; and on 11 April the Ngenetsheni followed up when twelve *amaviyo* raided Prince Mahanana of the Mphangisweni. Zibhebhu likewise was pressing his advantage against the uSuthu. On 16 April he concentrated his forces near the Mona River, and on 18 April raided up both sides of the Black Mfolozi as far as the Nongoma range. Then, between 6 and 8 May, he turned north and attacked the emGazini of Masiphula.

The uSuthu strike back inconclusively in northern Zululand

Meanwhile, from the beginning of April, Mnyamana, Ndabuko and Ziwedu had been concentrating their scattered forces of

Buthelezi, abaQulusi, eGazini and Mdlalose in the Ngome forest and along the upper Sikhwebezi River. On 8 May they began an advance on Hamu, who withdrew to two strongholds either side of the Phongolo River. From there the Ngenetsheni counter-attacked, four *amaviyo* and some Mandlakazi raiding the eGazini and Ntombela in the vicinity of the sources of the Black Mfolozi, though they lost the cattle they had seized when abaQulusi and Mdlalose forces pursued them. During these encounters Zibhebhu created a diversion in favour of the Ngenetsheni by raiding across the Black Mfolozi on 13 May in the direction of oNdini. The uSuthu resumed the offensive when Mnyamana's forces of about 100 *amaviyo*, supported by about ten Boers, attempted to surround Hamu in his two fastnesses. However, on 25 May 20 *amaviyo* of Ngenetsheni successfully counter-attacked, and drove the uSuthu back across the Phongolo. Mnyamana fell back on the Ngome forest and began mustering his diminished forces for a new attack on Hamu.

At the very beginning of June the uSuthu had some success against a few of Hamu's lesser strongholds and his abaQulusi ally, Msebe kaMadaka. On 24 June Mnyamana's forces, supported by the uFalaza *ibutho* from oNdini, raided Hamu's stronghold on Ngotshe Mountain, but were beaten back by the Ngenetsheni and ten *amaviyo* of Mandlakazi in support.

The uSuthu take on Zibhebhu again, but with mixed results

While these inconclusive hostilities were taking place in the north, the uSuthu leadership around King Cetshwayo decided on a fresh offensive to eliminate Zibhebhu. On 25–26 June 50 *amaviyo* of uSuthu at oNdini began to ready themselves to link up with Mnyamana's forces. But in late

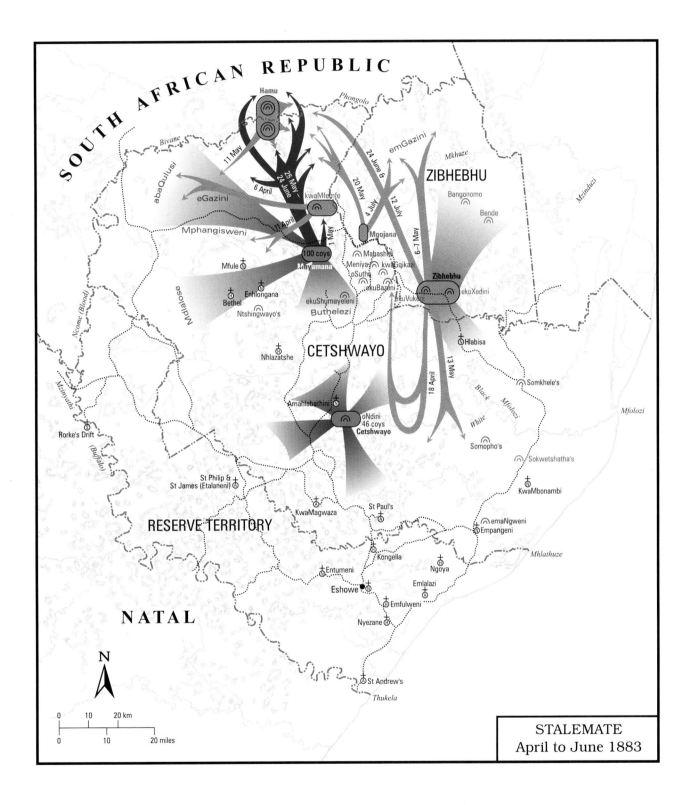

STALEMATE
April to June 1883

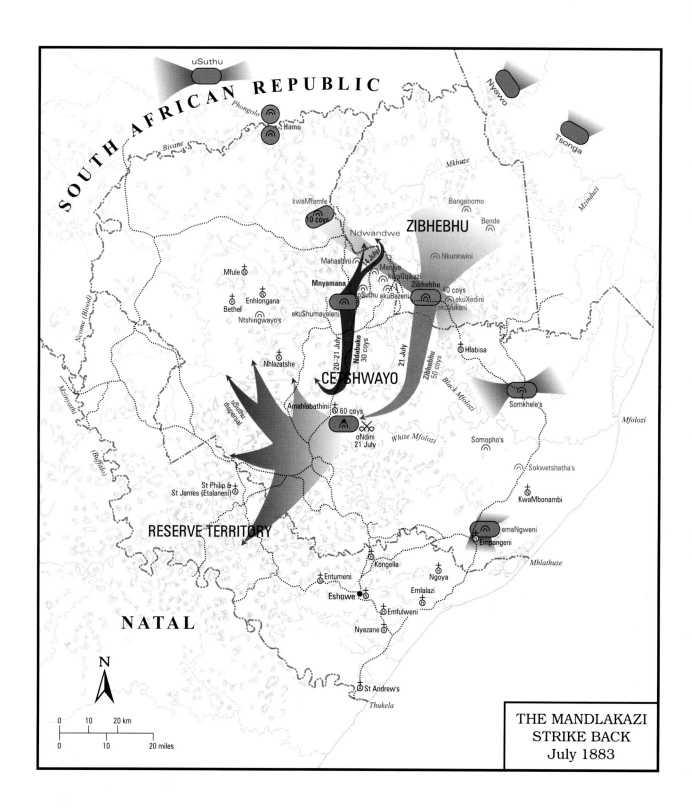

uSuthu

SOUTH AFRICAN REPUBLIC

Nyawo

Phongolo

Hamu

Tsonga

Bivane

Mkhuze

Mzinduzi

kwaMfemfe

Bangonomo

Bende

10 coys

Ndwandwe

ZIBHEBHU

Nkunkwini

Ncome (Blood)

Mfule

Mahashini

Menya

kwaGqikazi

Mnyamana

oSuthu ekuBazeni

Zibhebhu

40 coys

ekuXedini

ekuVukeni

Enhlongana

Bethel

ekuShumayeleni

Ntshingwayo's

CETSHWAYO

Nhlazatshe

Ndabuko

30 coys

Zibhebhu

50 coys

Hlabisa

Somkhele's

Mfolozi

Mzinyathi

uSuthu dispersal

Amahlabathini

60 coys

oNdini

21 July

White Mfolozi

Somopho's

Sokwetshatha's

(Buffalo)

Black Mfolozi

KwaMbonambi

St Philip &
St James (Etalaneni)

RESERVE TERRITORY

emaNgweni

Empangeni

Mhlathuze

Kongella

Ngoya

Entumeni

Emlalazi

Eshowe

NATAL

Emfulweni

Nyezane

N

St Andrew's

Thukela

| 0 | 10 | 20 km |
| 0 | 10 | 20 miles |

**THE MANDLAKAZI
STRIKE BACK
July 1883**

June a preparatory advance of three *amaviyo* of uSuthu under Prince Dabula-manzi kaMpande were compelled to beat an ignominious retreat at the Black Mfolo-zi when they encountered ten *amaviyo* of Mandlakazi. This débâcle was balanced when on 4 July five *amaviyo* of Mandlaka-zi were repulsed at the Dlomodlomo hills by three *amaviyo* of the uFalaza and iNgo-bamakhosi *amabutho*.

The Mandlakazi began to move up on 12 July to relieve Hamu's strongholds, which were again under pressure from the northern uSuthu. As it happened, the Ma-ndlakazi advance coincided with a major thrust by two columns of Mnyamana's men who had concentrated at the Sikhwe-bezi River. The left column consisted of abaQulusi and Mdlalose, and the right column of Buthelezi and uSuthu. First raiding Mgojana kaSomaphunga's and Mswazi's Ndwandwe, they joined at Tokazi Mountain before sweeping back for fear that Hamu would attack their base in their absence.

The uSuthu mobilise for a conclusive offensive against Zibhebhu

At much the same time as these relatively low-key operations were taking place, Cetshwayo was calling on his allies for an all-out and concerted offensive against Zi-bhebhu. The strategy the king devised envisaged attacks by the fully mobilised uSuthu from all points against the Mandla-kazi: the army of 60 *amaviyo* currently being 'doctored' for war at oNdini would advance from the south; Mnyamana's army would close in from the west; the Mphukunyoni and emaNgweni would move up from the south-east; those uSuthu who had taken refuge across the Phongo-lo would strike back from the north-east; and the Nyawo and Tsonga in the north-east would block any Mandlakazi attempt to withdraw through the Lubombo Moun-tains.

Zibhebhu steals a march and annihilates the uSuthu at oNdini

Threatened thus from all sides, Zibhebhu resolved to pre-empt the uSuthu. On 20

Prince Dabulamanzi kaMpande, Cetshwayo's half-brother, was next to him in age and particularly trusted by the king. During the Anglo-Zulu War he proved an impetuous general, commanding unsuccessfully at the battle of Rorke's Drift. He stood close by Cetshwayo during his restoration, and after the king's death vigorously carried on the struggle against the Mandlakazi from the Nkandla forest. Dabulamanzi was shot down in cold blood by a party of Boers on 22 September 1886, possibly at the instigation of his brothers, jealous of his influence over the young king, Dinuzulu. Pietermaritzburg Archives Repository (C. 873)

July he concentrated forty *amaviyo* of Ma-ndlakazi and ten *amaviyo* of the Mfemfe contingent of the Ngenetsheni (about 3 000 men in all) at his ekuVukeni *umuzi*, sup-ported by between ten and twelve mounted white mercenaries. The uSuthu mistakenly believed this concentration was aimed at Mnyamana to the west. But Zibhebhu's objective was oNdini itself, and he bril-liantly took the uSuthu by surprise with a night march. He caught the king's army of more than 4 000 men at oNdini entirely unprepared on 21 July and easily scattered it, killing most of the uSuthu leadership which had been gathered around the king. Cetshwayo escaped wounded to the Nkandla forest far to the south in the Re-serve Territory. A force of ten *amaviyo* of Buthelezi, ten *amaviyo* of abaQulusi and ten *amaviyo* of northern uSuthu under Ndabuko, which had been advancing from the Black Mfolozi in support of the king, turned back on learning of the utter rout of Cetshwayo's forces.

> 'The truth of information . . . regarding Zibebu coming to fight Cetshwayo probably has been invented, to give apparent foundation for Cetshwayo to assemble as he is doing from everywhere for the purpose of fighting Zibebu, and I hear the Ncinda (war charm ceremony) will take place today or tomorrow at Undini.'
> (Fynn, 26 June 1883)

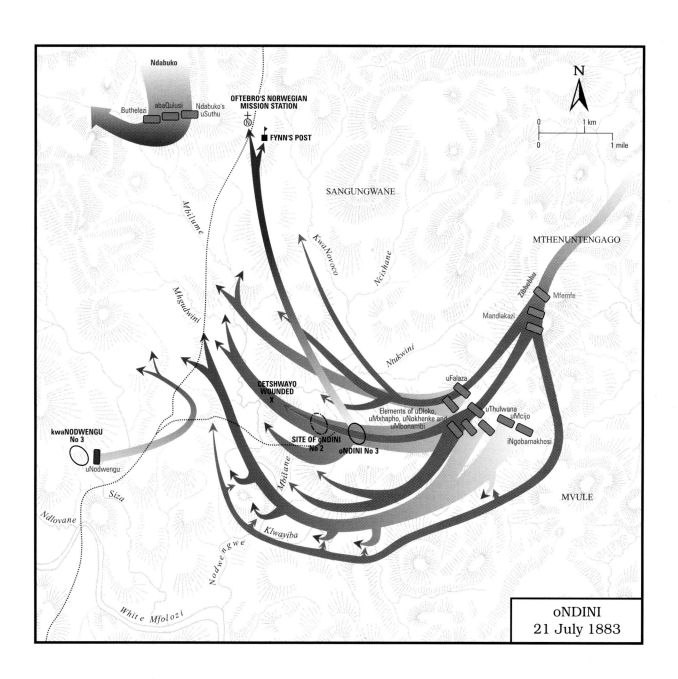

Ndabuko

Buthelezi   abaQulusi   Ndabuko's
uSuthu

OFTEBRO'S NORWEGIAN
MISSION STATION

■ FYNN'S POST

SANGUNGWANE

MTHENUNTENGAGO

Mbilume

KwaNovoco

Ncishane

Mhgudwini

Mfemfe

Mandlakazi

Ntukwini

uFalaza

CETSHWAYO
WOUNDED
X

Elements of uDloko,
uMxhapho, uNokhenke and
uMbonambi

uThulwana
uMcijo

kwaNODWENGU
No 3

SITE OF oNDINI
No 2

oNDINI No 3

iNgobamakhosi

uNodwengu

Mbilane

MVULE

Siza

Ndlovane

Nodwengwe

Klwayiba

White Mfolozi

oNDINI
21 July 1883

The Battle of oNdini
21 July 1883

Zibhebhu prepares a pre-emptive strike against the uSuthu at oNdini

Aware that King Cetshwayo was concentrating his uSuthu forces at oNdini for a fresh offensive against the Mandlakazi, Zibhebhu decided on a pre-emptive strike. On 20 July Zibhebhu mustered about 3 000 of his adherents and allies at his ekuVukeni homestead. His force consisted of 40 *amaviyo* of Manlakazi and ten *amaviyo* of Ngenetsheni, as well as between ten and twelve mounted white mercenaries. The uSuthu leadership at oNdini learned of these preparations. However, they believed that Zibhebhu's

> 'I don't like to name him,
> If I named him there would be an outburst of wailing.
> He who stalked forth in broad daylight,
> For he entered oNdini not when it was dark,
> But when it was clear and they saw him,
> He finished them off entirely,
> Destroyer of the enemy assembly.'
>
> (*From* Zibhebhu's praises)

uSuthu forces

At oNdini:

Sixty *amaviyo* (3 600 men) under the command of Ntuzwa kaNhlaka with Prince Sitheku kaMpande, Prince Dabulumanzi kaMpande and Prince Shingana kaMpande as his lieutenants.

Their battle deployment was as follows:
Left horn: uFalaza *ibutho* under Bhejana kaNomagaje.
Centre: uThulwana *ibutho* under Hayiyana kaMaphitha (killed); uDloko *ibutho* under Chief Ntshingwayo kaMahole (killed); uMxhapho *ibutho* under Chief Godide kaNdlela (killed); uMbonambi *ibutho* under Ntuzwa kaNhlaka; uNokhenke *ibutho* under Nzwakali (killed).
Right horn: uMcijo *ibutho* under Nquga (killed); iNgobamakhosi *ibutho* under Lurulurulu (killed).

At kwaNodwengu:
uDududu, iSangqu and iMbube *amabutho* under Chief Sekethwayo kaNhlaka (killed).

Advancing from the Ngome forest:
Ten *amaviyo* each of abaQulusi, Buthelezi and northern uSuthu (1 800 men) under Prince Ndabuko kaMpande.

Mandlakazi and Ngenetsheni forces
Forty *amaviyo* of Mandlakazi (2 400 men) and ten *amaviyo* of the Mfemfe contingent of the Ngenetsheni (600 men) under Chief Zibhebhu kaMaphitha. Ten or twelve mounted white mercenaries, including J. Eckersley, J. McAlister and G. Darke.

uSuthu casualties
More than 500 killed, including 59 of the leading men of the old Zulu order and the core of the uSuthu leadership, as well as three royal wives, three royal widows and Nyoniyentaba, a son of Cetshwayo.

Mandlakazi and Ngenetsheni casualties
Seven killed.

Walton witnessed Zibhebhu's victory at oNdini on 21 July 1883, and made this pencil sketch of the uSuthu débâcle. It vividly bears out Fynn's description that night in his diary of what he had seen: 'About 8.30 they [the uSuthu] became scattered like a swarm of bees and were running westward and passed the entrance of Undini in full flight . . . when I observed the huts on the right side of the entrance of Undini on fire, and could hear guns firing amongst the scattered people running and covering the country westwards of Undini.' MuseuMAfrica (W83)

The finished engraving of Walton's sketch of the battle of oNdini as it appeared in the Pictorial World *after redrawing by the paper's team of staff artists. Note the degree of license taken with the original sketch.* Rai England Collection

mobilisation was aimed at supporting his ally Hamu of the Ngenetsheni in operations to the west against Mnyamana and the uSuthu forces concentrated in the Ngome forest, and took no precautions against attack.

Zibhebhu's night march catches the uSuthu unprepared

During the night of 20 July Zibhebhu's men marched nearly 50 km (32 miles) south-west over the difficult terrain of the Black Mfolozi valley towards oNdini. Shortly before sunrise on 21 July word reached Cetshwayo that Zibhebhu's force was only 5 km (3 miles) away. Consternation seized the uSuthu leadership. Many of the fighting men were still asleep or were dispersed cutting wood, washing in the river, or fetching water. oNdini itself was thronged with elderly chiefs summoned by Cetshwayo for consultation, and with women who were engaged in thatching the partially built royal homestead. Consequently, the unprepared *amabutho* hurried to regroup and moved out from the front and rear of oNdini in irregular order to take up position alongside the already raggedly drawn up uFalaza *ibutho* (they were up early, escorting home women who had brought supplies the previous day).

The uSuthu dispositions

At about 08h00 the uSuthu (who numbered about 60 *amaviyo* – or 3 600 men) drew themselves up in disjoined battle-order 1.5 km (0.9 miles) east of oNdini under the command of Ntuzwa kaNhlaka. The uFalaza were on the left wing and the uMcijo and iNgobamakhosi *amabutho* on the right. The rest of the *amabutho* were jumbled up in the centre. A further uSuthu force, consisting of the uDududu, iSangqu and iMbube *amabutho*, was stationed at the new kwaNodwengu *ikhanda* 5 km (3 miles) north-west of oNdini, and was too far away to join the battle-line in time.

Zibhebhu routs the uSuthu

The uSuthu dispositions were still incomplete when the Mandlakazi left horn came in menacing sight over the Mthanunte-ngwayo ridge. Disregarding the ineffective fire from the uSuthu right wing, the Mandlakazi left swept past in an outflanking movement. Fearful of being cut off, the uSuthu right stampeded south-west of oNdini into the broken and bushy terrain of the valley of the White Mfolozi River, pursued by the Mandlakazi left horn and most of their centre.

The uSuthu centre and left (where the commanders were stationed) initially made a stand, firing on the Mandlakazi right and the Ngenetsheni contingent which was in support. But the resolute advance of Zibhebhu's men unnerved the uSuthu, and at about 08h30 they broke and fled west before their enemy could come to grips with them. Some of the uThulwana *ibutho* attempted to make a stand in oNdini, but were cut off and killed.

The pursuit

When the fugitives from the uSuthu centre and left got beyond oNdini, they attempted to turn south towards the White Mfolozi. However, the Mandlakazi right and centre, who had already pursued the broken uSuthu right horn up the river valley, cut off their retreat, forcing them in a north-westerly direction. The uSuthu contingent from kwaNodwengu, which had been hurrying towards oNdini, now got caught up in the general rout, and broke without attempting to make a stand. The Mandlakazi set oNdini alight and all the other homesteads in the Mahlabathini plain.

The uSuthu relief force turns back

Meanwhile, a mixed force of 30 *amaviyo* of abaQulusi, Buthelezi and northern

> 'All the principal headmen were killed – Seketwayo, Ntshingwayo . . . Mbopa and many others. Being all fat and big-bellied, they had no chance of escape; and one of them was actually run to earth and stabbed to death by my little mat-bearers.'
>
> (Grosvenor Darke, a trader and hunter who fought as one of Zibhebhu's mercenaries at both Msebe and oNdini, 25 July 1883)

> 'Our men rushed out to meet the enemy, not as an *impi*, in fighting array, but just as working people hurrying from their work and all abroad, and there was not time even to marshal those who were there. So the enemy with their horses soon scattered them, and reached the kraal, and burned it, killing Chiefs and old men, women and children, the Royal female attendants, and numbers of the working women, killing the King's own wives and children.'
>
> (Nomalhobodiya and Kukula, 4 August 1883)

uSuthu, which had set out south across the Black Mfolozi River under the command of Ndabuko when Zibhebhu's intention of attacking oNdini had at last become plain, failed to come to Cetshwayo's aid. On learning 8 km (5 miles) short of their objective that oNdini was already sacked and the king's forces dispersed, they turned back to prepare to defend their own base in the Ngome forest.

The massacre of the uSuthu leadership

A number of uSuthu, including women and members of the king's family, managed to find sanctuary in the camp of Fynn, the British Resident, on the hills to the north of oNdini. But other members of the royal family were not so fortunate. In the rout three of King Mpande's widows, as well as three of Cetshwayo's wives and his little son, Nyoniyentaba, were killed. Among the approximately 500 uSuthu dead were 59 or more chiefs and men of influence from every part of the kingdom on whom Cethswayo had depended, who were left defenceless when the uSuthu *amabutho* fled. With their slaughter the old Zulu order ended.

> 'The sons of late Chief Ntyingwayo and a few men with them, arrived here yesterday (31 July) on their way to bury Ntyingwayo; but, owing to the decomposed state of the dead about Undini, they have returned and state they were unable to identify Ntyingwayo's remains.'
>
> (Fynn, 1 August 1883)

> 'Cetshwayo sends Ndungunya to let me know he is alive and has sent to Mr Osborn and is on his way to the reserve. He had two assegai wounds (not very dangerous) between his knee and hip, right leg and did not impede his travelling. Cetshwayo thanks me for my kindness to his wives and children in caring for them and giving them blankets and has heard of my searches amongst the dead . . . Had he Cetshwayo not constantly told me Zibebu was coming to kill him and I had said it was not true, were his words not true now[?]'
>
> (Fynn, 2 August 1883)

Cetshwayo flees to the Nkandla forest

Cetshwayo himself was wounded when he took refuge in a clump of trees near the junction of the Ntukwini and Mbilane streams. He managed nevertheless to make his way to a cave on the left bank of the White Mfolozi, where he stayed until it was safe on 1 August to flee south to refuge in the Nkandla forest in the Reserve Territory.

Zibhebhu withdraws

Zibhebhu, who had lost only seven men in the battle, retired north with his victorious Mandlakazi by way of Nhlazatshe Mountain, while the Ngenetsheni returned to Mfemfe along the Black Mfolozi.

Chief Ntshingwayo kaMahole of the Khoza in north-western Zululand had been a leading member of King Cetshwayo's council before the war of 1879, during which he commanded at the battle of Isandlwana and fought as a senior commander at the battle of Khambula. In September 1879 Wolseley appointed him one of the thirteen chiefs, but Ntshingwayo remained a royalist and rallied to Cetshwayo in 1883. During the battle of oNdini he commanded the uDloko ibutho in the uSuthu centre, when he was killed in the rout. Walton's grisly pencil drawing after the battle of his corpse, stabbed in many places, is the only fully authenticated representation of this influential Zulu general that is known.

MuseuMAfrica (W89)

From the Battle of oNdini to the Death of Cetshwayo

22 July 1883 – 8 February 1884

The triumphant Mandlakazi and Ngenetsheni harry the defeated uSuthu in central Zululand

After Zibhebhu's victory at oNdini, the Ngenetsheni returned home on 22 July 1883 up the Black Mfolozi valley,

The day after the battle of oNdini, on 22 July 1883, Walton sketched in pencil the victorious Zibhebhu in conversation with Fynn, in whose camp in the hills to the north of the Mahlabathini plain several of the defeated Cetshwayo's women and family members had found sanctuary from the Mandlakazi. (These are the people Walton would later escort to safety in the Reserve.) Walton's notes indicate that Zibhebhu was wearing a corduroy jacket and corduroy leggings with a red handkerchief around his neck. He was holding his 'tiger skin' (leopard or genet skin) cap.

MuseuMAfrica (W88)

and the Mandlakazi up the White Mfolozi, both raiding the uSuthu as they went. Mnyamana, Ndabuko and Ziwedu prepared for the defence of the Ngome forest with some 20 *amaviyo* of the Buthelezi and northern uSuthu against their triumphant foes. Those royalists living between the Black Mfolozi and Mhlathuze rivers, as well as the Mdlalose, fled to the Reserve Territory, while the abaQulusi took refuge on Hlobane Mountain or across the Bivane River in the South African Republic. Cetshwayo fled to the eNhlweni *umuzi* deep in the Nkandla forest in the Reserve Territory where, by early August, he was joined by a number of his brothers and other supporters.

Zibhebhu and his allies raid the coastal uSuthu

With the uSuthu in central Zululand in disarray, on 14 August Zibhebhu mustered his forces anew (including his white mercenaries) at his Nkunkwini *umuzi*, and turned his attention to royalists living along the Zululand coast. While Zibhebhu attacked Chief Somkhele of the Mphukunyoni, his ally, Sokwetshatha kaMlandela of the Mthethwa, first raided the emaNgweni of Somopho kaZikhala before lending the Mandlakazi a hand against Somkhele. The Mphukunyoni fled to their stronghold in the Dukuduku forest, and the emaNgweni fell back south towards the Reserve Territory. Hamu was

> 'Usibebu arrived with an impi during the night and surrounded Somkele's own and many of his people's kraals, which the impi attacked about daybreak. Somkele and most of his people escaped into the bush, but their cattle were all seized and the kraals burnt down.'
>
> (Ugaza, adherent of Chief Somkhele, 20 August 1883)

'The general tone of the replies and statements made by Cetywayo is, I regret to say, most unsatisfactory, and in my opinion clearly indicative of an intention on his part to maintain an independent position in the Reserve, and to remain at the Nkandhla as a place of safety for himself . . . Forcible measures should be taken against Cetywayo without delay.'

(Melmoth Osborn, Resident Commissioner of the Reserve Territory, 23 August 1883)

'The families of van Rooyen are occupying Sekethwayo's district [in western Zululand] and a number of other Boer families have built houses and . . . these Boers say the country belongs to them . . . and drive any natives who remain there away and . . . are carrying off wagon loads of grain from the deserted kraals.'

(Fynn, 11 September 1883)

also not idle, and on 20 August his Ngenetsheni swept off the uSuthu and Buthelezi cattle between the Black Mfolozi and Ngome forest.

Troops from the British garrison in Natal move up to the Reserve Territory

Alarmed by these developments in the Reserve Territory, the Governor of Natal, Sir Henry Bulwer, requested that British troops drawn from the Natal garrison be ordered up to the borders of the Reserve Territory, primarily to deter Cetshwayo from regrouping his supporters in the Nkandla forest as a base for operations. Meanwhile, between 31 August and 1 September, 20 *amaviyo* of the Mandlakazi joined the Ngentetsheni to rout the Buthelezi and abaQulusi in the Ngome forest. By 9 September Zibhebhu and Hamu were advancing on the Black Mfolozi as the worsted northern uSuthu fled south-west before them.

The Officer-in-Command of Natal, Col W.D. Bond, in consultation with Bulwer, decided that these deteriorating circumstances made it necessary for the troops concentrated at Fort Pearson at the mouth of the Thukela River (to which the telegraph line from Pietermaritzburg was extended) to advance to Eshowe and entrench. Their objective was not to be drawn into active operations, for which Osborn's levies raised in the Reserve were considered sufficient. Rather, their mere presence at Eshowe was intended to achieve the political goal of imposing Osborn's authority and lending moral support to loyalist Zulu.

The 'Etshowe Column' as it was to be called, was placed under the command of Lt-Col W.G. Montgomery of the Welsh Regiment, and was made up of a squadron of the 6th (Inniskilling) Dragoons (88 men), a division of H Battery, 4th Brigade, Royal Field Artillery (37 men) with two 9-pdr guns and a Gatling gun, and five companies of the 1st Bn, The Welsh Regiment (369 men), one of which was mustered as mounted infantry. Two Royal Engineers and 25 men of the Commissariat

and Transport Department brought the strength of the column up to 529 men. Fifty African levies raised by Osborn were attached to the column for reconnaissance purposes. With the lessons of the recent Anglo-Zulu War in mind, the Etshowe Column was ordered when it began its advance into the Reserve Territory on 20 September, encumbered as it was with two months of supplies, to take the precaution of sending out reconnaissance patrols, posting picquets and laagering the wagons at night. If attacked, especially on the march, the troops were to concentrate into a compact formation like a square, and to act on the defensive.

Boers begin to occupy north-western Zululand

In the days preceding, Boers from the South African Republic under Cornelius van Rooyen, covetous of the rich pasture-land of north-western Zululand, took advantage of the turmoil to occupy the territory of the Mdlalose.

Zibhebhu strikes south toward the Nkandla forest

On 20 September Zibhebhu and his allies embarked on a major new offensive. Ten *amaviyo* of Ngenetsheni moved out on an extensive raid, first striking the eGazini and then the Buthelezi, who fled westwards. Forty *amaviyo* of the Mandlakazi co-operated in this assault, working up both sides of the Black Mfolozi, while two *amaviyo* of Mfanawendlela's Zungu also joined in. Zibhebhu's strategic intention was first to drive Mnyamana into his Ngome strongholds, and then, having contained the northern uSuthu, for his combined force to veer south to strike against Cetshwayo in the Nkandla forest. He knew that the Cube, Magwaza and other uSuthu in the Reserve Territory were mustering around the king, and the ultimate intention of his advance was (as with the earlier strike against oNdini) to pre-empt a move against him by the uSuthu. By 24 September Zibhebhu's army was at Babanango Mountain on the very borders of the Reserve Territory having encoun-

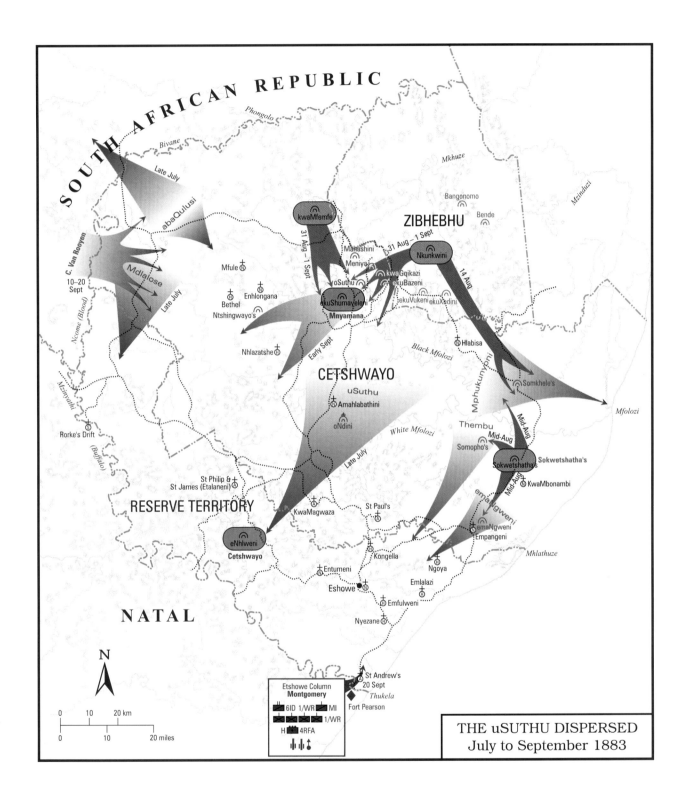

THE uSUTHU DISPERSED
July to September 1883

'You [Melmoth Osborn] will understand that the detachment of troops is intended solely to support by its presence at Etshowe, your position of authority as Resident Commissioner in the Reserve, and to give confidence to the loyal people of the territory, and that it is not to be in any way used for military operations.'

(Bulwer,
14 September 1883)

The 1st Bn, The Welsh Regiment, arrived in South Africa in March 1881 from Gibraltar, their previous station abroad, and proceeded to Fort Napier as part of the Natal garrison. In September 1883 five companies of the battalion (one of which was mustered as mounted infantry) joined the Etshowe Column at Fort Pearson under the command of their colonel, Lt-Col W.G. Montgomery. Unfortunately, Colonel Montgomery was killed by a snakebite, and the command of the column fell to Lt-Col R.J. Hawthorn, RE. During late September the column marched to Eshowe in the Reserve Territory to provide moral support to the civil authorities who were threatened by the turmoil engulfing southern Zululand following Cetshwayo's defeat in July. Several companies of the battalion continued to be stationed in the Reserve Territory until May 1886, when the entire battalion sailed for Egypt, its next station. The photograph was taken while The Welsh Regiment formed part of the garrison at Fort Curtis outside Eshowe. Pietermaritzburg Archives Repository (C. 250)

'Cetywayo hears that Usibebu gives out that he is coming as far as Babanango in pursuit of his prey which escaped him with two wounds, and is now hiding in Nkahndhla . . . Cetywayo says he wants to come to you [Osborn], but he cannot walk all the way, he therefore, asks you to give him a horse to ride, also a pair of trousers, a shirt, and a hat.'

(Zeize, Cetshwayo's messenger,
1 October 1883)

tered little uSuthu resistance on the march, for the demoralised royalists had taken refuge in their fastnesses.

British troops move forward to Eshowe

While Zibhebhu halted at Babanango, pondering whether he should invade the Reserve Territory and risk antagonising the British who were tacitly supporting him, the Etshowe Column advanced from Fort Pearson to reach Eshowe on 29 September. Lt-Col R.J. Hawthorn, commanding the Royal Engineers, Natal, who succeeded Colonel Montgomery in command of the column (Montgomery died on 25 September after being bitten on the leg by a mamba), chose a site for a small redoubt nearby to command the troops' encampment, and named it Fort Curtis after Col F.G.S. Curtis, 6th (Inniskilling) Dragoons. During December a company of the 1st Bn, Princess Louise's (Argyll

and Sutherland Highlanders) relieved one company from the Welsh Regiment.

Cetshwayo places himself under British protection

The British Resident in Zululand, H.F. Fynn, visited Cetshwayo on 13 October in the Nkandla forest. Threatened by Zibhebhu, and feeling his position to be hopeless, Cetshwayo agreed to seek the protection of Melmoth Osborn, the Resident Commissioner, at Eshowe. Escorted by 100 of Hlubi's Mounted Basutos, Cetshwayo reached Eshowe on 15 October. The day before, realising that Cetshwayo posed him no threat and was placing himself out of his reach under British protection, Zibhebhu had retired from Babanango.

The fighting continues across Zululand

Fighting nevertheless continued in central and eastern Zululand. At the end of Octo-

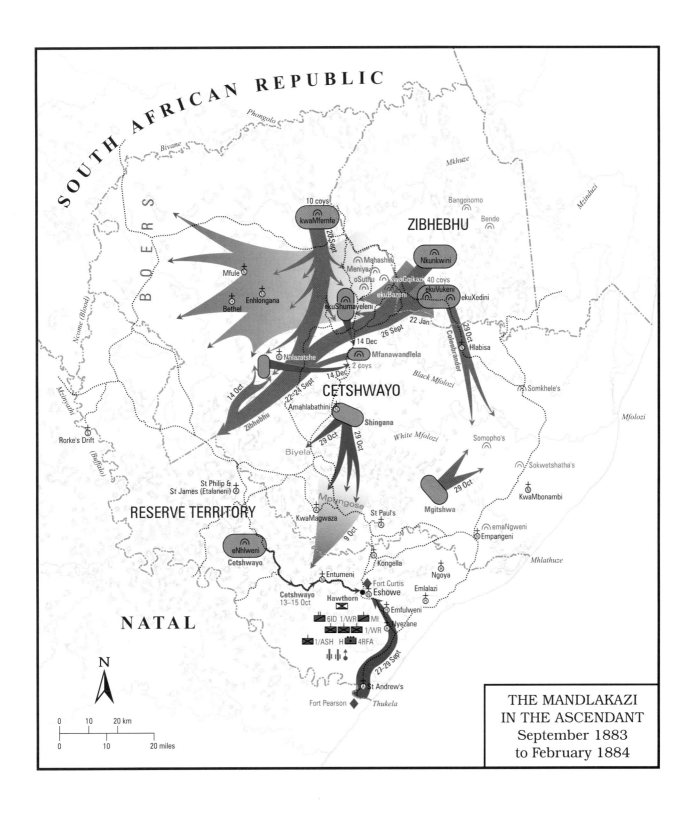

SOUTH AFRICAN REPUBLIC

Phongolo

Bivane

Mkhuze

Bangonomo

Bende

ZIBHEBHU

10 coys

kwaMfemfe

Mahashini

Meniya

oSuthu · kwaGqikazi 40 coys

Mfule

ekuBazeni ekuVukeni ekuXedini

Enhlongana

Bethel

ekuShumayeleni

Nkunkwini

20 Sept

26 Sept

22 Jan

14 Dec

Mfanawandlela

29 Oct

Hlabisa

Somkhele's

2 coys

Black Mfolozi

14 Dec

Nhlazatshe

CETSHWAYO

14 Oct

22–24 Sept

Amahlabathini

Shingana

White Mfolozi

Mfolozi

Zibhebhu

Rorke's Drift

Ncome (Blood)

(Buffalo)

Mzinyathi

29 Oct

29 Oct

Biyela

Somopho's

Sokwetshatha's

29 Oct

Mgitshwa

KwaMbonambi

St Philip & St James (Etalaneni)

RESERVE TERRITORY

Mpungose

KwaMagwaza

St Paul's

9 Oct

emaNgweni

Empangeni

eNhlweni

Cetshwayo

Kongella

Ngoya

Mhlathuze

Entumeni

Emlalazi

NATAL

Cetshwayo
13–15 Oct

Fort Curtis

Eshowe

Hawthorn

Emfulweni

Nyezane

6ID 1/WR MI

1/WR

1/ASH H 4RFA

21–29 Sept

N

0   10   20 km

0   10   20 miles

St Andrew's

Fort Pearson   *Thukela*

**THE MANDLAKAZI
IN THE ASCENDANT
September 1883
to February 1884**

'I, Cetywayo, leave the country to my son Dinuzulu for him to have when I am no longer here . . . The questions about my country are not ended yet. They exist still, and will remain until the Government settle them . . . Take these, my words, to Mr Osborn, and ask him to send them to the Governor, with the request that he would send them to the Queen.'

(Dabulamanzi, Ndabuko, Shingana and Ziwedu, brothers of Cetshwayo, 11 February 1884)

ber the uSuthu of Prince Shingana living along the White Mfolozi raided Siyunguza kaSilwana's Mpungose, who fled on 9 November to the safety of the Reserve Territory. Shingana's men also attacked Mgitshwa kaMvundlana's Biyela on 29 October when four *amaviyo* of the Biyela were absent supporting six *amaviyo* of the Mandlakazi under the white mercenary, Johan Colenbrander, in a raid on Somopho of the emaNgweni. The uSuthu also attacked Mfanawendlela of the Zungu, who fled across the Black Mfolozi on 5 November to take refuge with Zibhebhu. In north-western Zululand, the Boers were still occupying Mdlalose territory. The Mdlaloses' lot was made even harder on account of raids by the Ngenetsheni in late November and early December and their need to retaliate to recover captured livestock.

On 14 December a force of uSuthu led by Mankulumana kaSomaphunga and Ndabazimbi kaTokotoko killed Mfanawendlela at the Momolweni *umuzi*. Believing with this success that they were regaining the ascendancy, the uSuthu began concentrating along the Sikhwebezi River for a thrust against Zibhebhu's ekuVukeni homestead. But Zibhebhu once again forestalled the uSuthu, and dispatched a force of the Mandlakazi (which he did not accompany) to the Sikhwebezi. The Mandlakazi caught the uSuthu unprepared and, for the loss of 60 men, killed 440 uSuthu and scattered the rest.

The death of Cetshwayo
While the fortunes of his cause flickered fitfully, Cetshwayo remained in Eshowe

Dinuzulu was born in 1868 to Cetshwayo and Nomvimbi Msweli. Cetshwayo had captured her at the battle of Ndondakusuka in 1856 when he defeated his brothers to secure the succession to the throne. On Cetshwayo's sudden death in February 1884, his brothers unanimously rallied around the sixteen-year-old Dinuzulu to prevent a disputed succession. This photograph was taken at the time of Dinuzulu's accession when he and the uSuthu were faced by the daunting task of resisting the Mandlakazi who seemed bent on harrying them to complete destruction.
Killie Campbell Africana Library (A42/003)

under Osborn's protection. He died there suddenly on 8 February 1884 (the uSuthu believed that Zibhebhu had him poisoned), leaving his minor son Dinuzulu, who was under the guardianship of Ndabuko and Mnyamana, to carry on the apparently hopeless struggle against Zibhebhu and his allies.

From the Death of Cetshwayo to the Battle of Tshaneni

8 February – 5 June 1884

Growing uSuthu unrest in the Reserve Territory

The funeral ceremonies of King Cetshwayo were completed on 23 April 1884, but not before relations had soured between the uncooperative Resident Commissioner, Melmoth Osborn, and the uSuthu leadership. By the end of April the uSuthu in the Nkandla forest where Cetshwayo was buried were assuming a defiant tone. On 2 May four uSuthu *amaviyo* raided 'loyal' Africans in the Nkandla. In response, Osborn began to build up a force to subdue the uSuthu. He knew that the unrest the uSuthu were stirring up among the inhabitants of the Reserve Territory would make it increasingly difficult to collect the hut tax upon which the functioning of his administration depended.

The abaQulusi threaten Hlubi's territory in the Reserve Territory

Meanwhile, the abaQulusi, unsettled by the Boer presence in north-western Zululand, were moving south towards the south-western part of the Reserve Territory to attack the Sotho-speaking Tlokwa under Hlubi at the confluence of the Thukela and Mzinyathi rivers. The Qungebe (whom the Tlokwa had displaced in the settlement of 1879), and Mdlalose refugees from the Boers, started to leave the Reserve Territory to join the abaQulusi. The Sub-Commissioner of Nqutu, A.L. Pretorius, had to recruit a force of Tlokwa to defend the border. By 20 May 127 horse and 270 foot (known as Basutos) were deployed at two points facing the two concentrations of abaQulusi and their allies who, as it happened, withdrew at this time to take part in the campaign in central Zululand against Zibhebhu.

Osborn's arrangement for the defence of the Reserve Territory

Alarmed by the apparent threat the abaQulusi and their allies posed, Osborn set about perfecting his arrangements for the defence of the Reserve Territory against the uSuthu. Small bodies of Zulu levies totalling 3 000 men were to be stationed along the northern border from the coast to opposite the Nkandla forest. The coastal

Melmoth Osborn (called 'Malemate', a Zulu corruption of Melmoth) entered the Natal Government Service in 1854 and later became Resident Magistrate of Newcastle from 1867 to 1876. He accompanied Sir Theophilus Shepstone to the Transvaal Colony in 1877 as his secretary. He was appointed British Resident in Zululand from March 1880, and held that post until December 1882. Osborn became Resident Commissioner of the Reserve Territory in April 1883, and in June 1887 the Resident Commissioner and Chief Magistrate of the Colony of Zululand. From his first appointment to Zululand in 1880 Osborn proved himself the true disciple of Shepstone, his mentor, doing his best to limit the pretension of the Zulu royal house and to further the establishment of indirect rule through British magistrates. He had a considerable grasp of the Zulu language and customs of the people. However, despite his superficial appearance of judgement and firmness, he was an inefficient bureaucrat with a tendency to let things slide. He retired with a knighthood (KCMG) in 1893.

J.Y. Gibson, *The Story of the Zulus*, 1911, opp. p. 222

forces were to be under John Dunn, who had been one of the thirteen chiefs, and those further inland under Lt R.H. (Dick) Addison of the Reserve Territory Carbineers. To the east of the Nkandla forest, 1 600 levies under Martin Oftebro (a missionary's son and Zulu interpreter to the British troops) were to be concentrated, and a further 1 500 to the south-west under F. Galloway, the superintendent of roads. Galloway's men would protect the Natal border and co-operate with the 1 500 Tlokwa (Basutos) it was optimistically hoped Pretorius would succeed in raising.

The uSuthu repulse Osborn's forces near the Nkandla forest

On 5 May Osborn encamped 9.7 km (6 miles) to the east of the Nkandla forest with a combined force of 3 000 levies under Siyunguza of the Mpungose and Mavumengwana kaNdlela of the Ntuli, and with 50 men of the Reserve Territory Carbineers under Cmdt George Mansel and Lt Dick Addison. After some minor skirmishing, one-third of Osborn's force

Fort Chater, built in May 1884 near the Ntumeni mission station, barred the way to the uSuthu between the Nkandla forest and Eshowe, the seat of the Resident Commissioner of the Reserve Territory. It was an earthwork fortification, big enough to hold a garrison of 200 men. Note the bell tents of the soldiers pitched just outside the fortifications. The huts of African levies and camp servants are in the foreground, at a suitable distance from the British camp.

Killie Campbell Africana Library (D20/104)

deserted. Then, at 02h50 on 10 May, a thousand uSuthu under Dabulamanzi attacked the camp. A firing line 274 m (300 yards) in front of the camp repulsed the uSuthu, killing about a hundred. Two of Mansel's men were killed and three wounded. Believing (erroneously) that another force of uSuthu under Bhejana kaNomageje of the emaNgweni had outflanked him and intended cutting him off from Eshowe, Osborn fell back with 2 000 men on Fort Chater, an earthwork hastily thrown up by men of the 1st Bn, Princess Louise's (Argyll and Sutherland Highlanders), which he reached on 12 May. Dunn and the coastal levies proved unwilling to reinforce Osborn at Fort Chater for fear of attack by uSuthu forces concentrated near the mouth of the Mhlathuze River.

The coastal uSuthu threaten the Reserve Territory

Indeed, while the uSuthu and Osborn's forces were facing each other in the region of the Nkandla forest, military operations had also been occurring outside the Reserve Territory along the Zululand coast, threatening Osborn's defences along the Mhlathuze frontier. In late February 1884, and again in early March, the pro-uSuthu Somkhele of the Mphukunyoni beat off an attack by Sokwetshatha's Mthethwa against his fastness in the Dukuduku forest. On 4 March Somkhele counterattacked, and drove Sokwetshatha temporarily into the Reserve Territory. In a joint offensive on 23–24 March, Somkhele, assisted by Bhejana and Lokothwayo of the emaNgweni, again forced Sokwetshatha across the Mhlathuze, greatly alarming the coastal chiefs of the Reserve Territory.

Hlubi scores some successes against the uSuthu in the Nkandla forest

Meanwhile, the uSuthu in the Nkandla forest were being reinforced from the main uSuthu force under Mnyamana in the Ngome forest. Feeling he was not strong enough to proceed again unassisted against the uSuthu, on 14 May Osborn requested the help of more troops. Now that the abaQulusi threatening Pretorius in

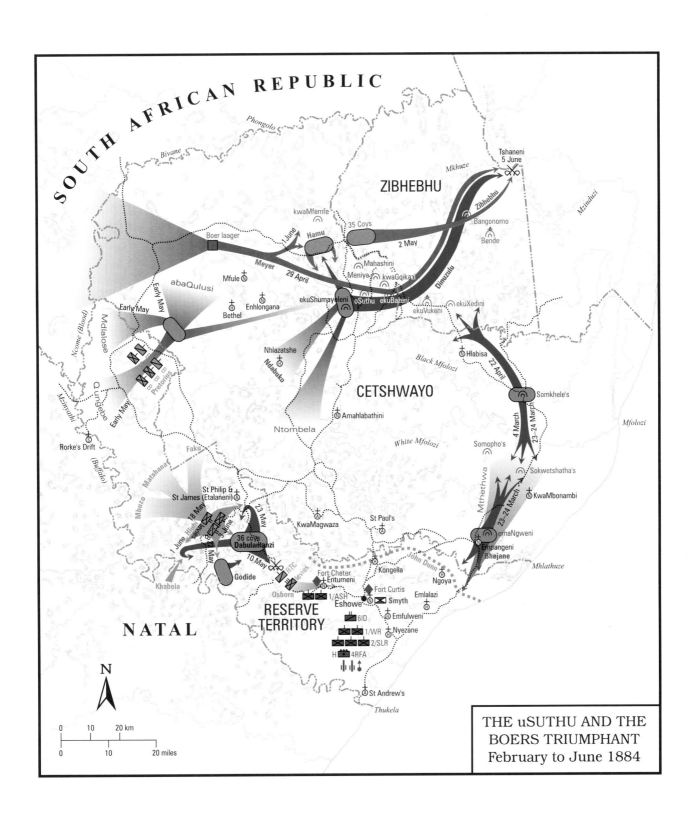

SOUTH AFRICAN REPUBLIC

Phongolo

Bivane

Mkhuze

Tshaneni
5 June

ZIBHEBHU

kwaMfemfe

Bangonomo

Mzinduzi

Boer laager

35 Coys

Bende

1 June

Hamu

2 May

Meyer 29 April

Mahashini

Zibhebhu

Mfule

Meniya kwaGqikazi

Dinuzulu

abaQulusi

ekuShumayeleni oSuthu ekuBazeni

ekuXedini

Early May

Early May

Enhlongana

Bethel

ekuVukeni

Mdlalose

Nhlazatshe

Ndabuko

Ncome (Blood)

Black Mfolozi

Hlabisa

22 April

CETSHWAYO

Qu nGebe

Amahlabathini

Somkhele's

Mfolozi

Early May

Ntombela

White Mfolozi

Somopho's

4 March

23-24 March

Mzinyathi

Rorke's Drift

Sokwetshatha's

(Buffalo)

Mthethwa

KwaMbonambi

Faku

St Philip &
St James (Etalaneni)

23-24 March

23 May

Mbuzo

Matshana

KwaMagwaza

St Paul's

emaNgweni

18 May

1 June

Dabulamanzi

Empangeni

Bhejane

36 coys

10 May

Mhlathuze

RTC

levies

Kongella

Ngoya

John Dunn

Khabela

Godide

Fort Chater Entumeni

Fort Curtis

Osborn

1/ASH

Smyth

Emlalazi

Eshowe

RESERVE
TERRITORY

6ID

Emfulweni

Nyezane

NATAL

1/WR

2/SLR

H 4RFA

N

St Andrew's

Thukela

0   10   20 km

0   10   20 miles

THE uSUTHU AND THE
BOERS TRIUMPHANT
February to June 1884

In May 1884 Lt-Gen the Hon. Sir L. Smyth, KCMG, the British General Officer Commanding in South Africa from 10 November 1880 until 9 November 1885, came from the Cape to inspect the situation in the Reserve Territory. He stationed two companies of the 1st Bn, Princess Louise's (Argyll and Sutherland Highlanders) at Fort Chater to stiffen Melmoth Osborn's African levies who were defending the Reserve Territory against the uSuthu concentrated in the Nkandla forest. The engraving conveys the isolation of the garrison, lost in the vastness of the landscape. Killie Campbell Africana Library (D20/103)

the north-western Reserve Territory were moving off, Hlubi and his force of Basutos were free to proceed towards the Nkandla forest. By 18 May Hlubi was at eNsingabantu in the Qudeni bush with 134 horsemen, 100 foot and about 400 levies drawn from Matshana kaMondisa of the Sithole, Faku kaZiningo of the Ntombela and Mbuzo of the Ntuli. On 22 May Hlubi attacked the Ntuli at their stronghold of oKathongweni (which had been Godide's before his death at the battle of oNdini) killing 20, and drove the survivors into the Nkandla forest. The following day, Hlubi went on to attack an uSuthu *impi* of ten *amaviyo* at the Nthaleni stream and killed a further 50.

The British forces in the Reserve Territory reinforced

Despite Hlubi's successes, Lt-Gen H.A. Smyth, the British General Officer Commanding in South Africa, decided to increase the British force in the Reserve Territory to 800 men, of which two companies of the 1st Bn, Princess Louise's (Argyll and Sutherland Highlanders) would be stationed at Fort Chater with

Osborn's levies. By 27 May one squadron of the 6th (Inniskilling) Dragoons was at Fort Curtis with a division of H Battery, 4th Brigade, Royal Field Artillery, two companies of the 1st Bn, The Welsh Regiment and three companies of the 2nd Bn, The Prince of Wales's Volunteers (South Lancashire Regiment).

An uSuthu offensive from the Nkandla forest repulsed and stalemate is reached in the Reserve Territory

Reinforcements were clearly necessary, for the uSuthu in the Nkandla forest were still on the offensive despite their recent setbacks. On 1 June sixteen *amaviyo* under Prince Dabulamanzi, Mehlokazulu kaSihayo of the Qungebe, Ndabankulu of the Ntombela and Sigananda kaSokufa of the Cube attacked Mbuzo and his Ntuli near the Emtanjeni Drift across the Thukela River. Hlubi, supported by Matshana's and Faku's levies, came to Mbuzo's assistance and killed a hundred uSuthu for the loss of two Basutos and two of Mbuzo's Ntuli. Dabulamanzi had a narrow escape and his son Mzikele was killed. The defeated uSuthu scattered, and nine of those who tried to take refuge in Natal were killed by Gayede kaMakedama's Khabela people. Following up this success, Hlubi raided the Nsuze valley on 3 June and captured 1 149 cattle and 150 goats and sheep.

Osborn, assessing his situation on 10 June, estimated that there were still 36 uSuthu *amaviyo*, or 2 160 men, in the Nkandla forest, while he had 135 *amaviyo*, or 8 100 men, available as levies. His intended strategy was that 4 000 levies would be required to operate against the uSuthu in the Nkandla forest, and that the rest should guard the northern borders of the Reserve Territory. British troops from Eshowe and Hlubi's Basutos would back up the levies operating in the Nkandla forest.

The uSuthu in central Zululand driven into their fastnesses by Zibhebhu and Hamu

However, the decisive events were not occurring in the Reserve Territory or along the Zululand coast, but in central Zululand. On 22 April Zibhebhu stationed 35 *amaviyo* at Tokazi Mountain just inside his borders opposite the Ngome forest where Mnyamana was concentrating the Mdlalose and uSuthu refugees from the Reserve Territory, particularly the Qungebe and Magwaza. But on 29 April Hamu forestalled the Mandlakazi when he ambushed and defeated Mnyamana and drove his people back into their fastnesses.

The desperate uSuthu forge an alliance with the Boers and defeat Zibhebhu

A new element now entered the arena. In desperation with their plight, Dinuzulu and the uSuthu leadership decided to throw in their lot with the Boers who for decades had been infiltrating north-western Zululand in search of grazing. By 2 May Dinuzulu was with the Boers in their en-

campment near Hlobane Mountain, and Zibhebhu withdrew to Bangonomo and concentrated some 3 000 of his forces there for fear of the alliance he recognised was being built up against him.

On 21 May the Boers proclaimed Dinuzulu king, and by 28 May their commando was at the Sikhwebezi River summoning Ndabankulu of the Ntombela, as well as Mehlokazulu of the Qungege to join them. Ndabuko, meanwhile, was mustering his forces in the Nhlazatshe region. On 1 June the Boers blockaded Hamu in his caves, and advanced to the Nongoma range where they were joined by the uSuthu. The joint force of about 120 mounted men under Cmdt Lukas Meyer and 20 mounted volunteers under Adolf Schiel, with 6 000 uSuthu under Dinuzulu himself, advanced into Zibhebhu's territory, and on 5 June utterly routed the 3 000 Mandlakazi at Tshaneni, capturing enormous herds of cattle.

> 'It is reported that eight hundred armed Boers are in conference at the Hlobane, Zululand. With them is Dinuzulu, whom they propose to make King in return for territorial cession. The object of the Boers for a long time has been to obtain the uppermost part of Zululand, they will thus eventually make themselves masters of the country, to the great loss of the Zulu people, who will pay heavily for this Usutu compact.'
>
> (Bulwer, 2 May 1884)

The leading Boers of the Committee of Dinuzulu's Volunteers proclaimed Dinuzulu King of the Zulu on 21 May 1884 at their laager at Nyathi Hill. This ceremony was part of a deal whereby the Boers promised the uSuthu military aid against the Mandlakazi in return for land in Zululand. The 'coronation' took place on two wagons arranged to form a platform in the centre of a great multitude. About 350 Boers from the Wakkerstroom and Utrecht Districts of the Transvaal, and from further afield as well, were ranged behind Dinuzulu (as depicted in the engraving) when he faced the Zulu dignitaries who were seated before some 9 000 uSuthu massed behind them. The previous day Dinuzulu's uncles, Ndabuko, Ziwedu and Shingana, had already installed him as king with traditional Zulu ritual.

Pietermaritzburg Archives Repository (C. 4758)

> 'The Chief [Zibhebhu] begs me to say that he blames you [Osborn] very much for not helping him in his trouble. He has fought against his own nation for the British Government, and now that the Boers are coming you will not help him . . . I do not know what I have done wrong to you or the British Government.'
>
> (John Eckersley, Jnr, known to the Zulu as 'Dambuza', or one who walks carefully, trader and mercenary; also secretary to both Hamu and Zibhebhu, 19 May 1884)

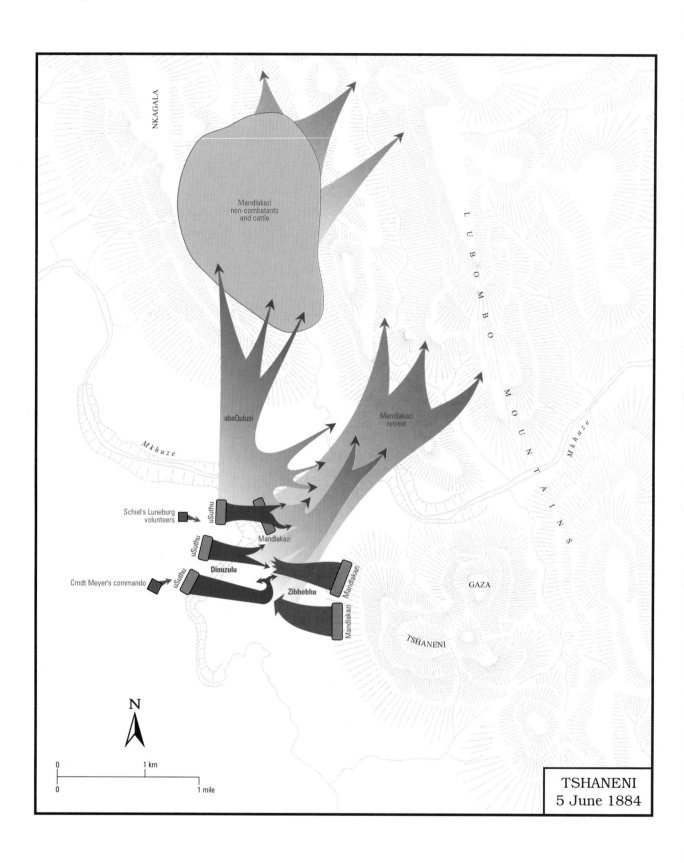

The Battle of Tshaneni

5 June 1884

The Boers and uSuthu mobilise and advance into Mandlakazi territory

On 21 May 1884 the Boers of the Committee of Dinuzulu's Volunteers proclaimed Dinuzulu King of the Zulu, and agreed to assist him militarily against Zibhebhu in return for land. By the beginning of June the uSuthu had gathered an army of more than 6 000 men near Mnyamana's ekuShumayeleni *umuzi*. They were supported by a commando of between 100 and 120 Boers under Cmdt Lukas Meyer, and about 20 mounted volunteers from Luneburg (mainly German settlers) under Adolf Schiel, Dinuzulu's secretary and political adviser.

To avoid falling into one of Zibhebhu's ambushes, as had happened to the uSuthu army at Msebe on 30 March 1883, the uSuthu and Boers scouted ahead thoroughly as they advanced. The invading force reached the Vuna River on 2 June, and camped at Msebe on 3 June. They pressed on past Bangonomo, Zibhebhu's principal *umuzi*, and on the afternoon of 5 June came in sight of the Mkhuze Poort.

Zibhebhu's dispositions

Zibhebhu, who had only been able to muster about 3 000 Mandlakazi and three or four white mercenaries, including John Eckersley (his adviser) and Grosvenor Darke, had fallen back from Bangonomo with his women, children and cattle. Knowing the terrain well, he decided to make his stand at the Mkhuze Poort.

Zibhebhu placed his non-combatants and cattle along a wooded spur north of the Mkhuze River, and positioned his main fighting-force in two divisions to the south of the thickly overgrown river. He believed that the broken country of the plain and the dense thornbush on the slopes of Tshaneni Mountain to his rear would impede the mounted Boers. In advance of the main position, close to the river, he placed a small detachment behind a deep donga running south-east across the track to the Poort. His plan was that the advancing uSuthu would be drawn into an assault on the donga, when the main Mandlakazi force would fall on their right flank and hem them

> 'In making the attack the Boers came first and began firing on my men, they then retired and came on again with the Usutu . . . The Boers were urging on the Usutu, threatening to shoot them if they retreated . . . [My men] gave way, pursued by the Boers, who shot down many in their retreat. The Usutu too pursued. My force ran to the Mkuzi, and while crossing the river very many of my men got killed by the enemy, as the river was deep and the drift not very practicable.'
>
> (Zibhebhu, 13 June 1884)

---

uSuthu forces
About 100 *amaviyo* (some 6 000 men) under King Dinuzulu kaMpande and Mamese.

Boer forces
Commando of 100 to 120 mounted men under Cmdt L.K. Meyer.
About 20 mounted volunteers from Luneburg under A. Schiel.

Mandlakazi forces
About 50 *amaviyo* (some 3 000 men) under Chief Zibhebhu kaMaphitha. Three or four white mercenaries including J.S. Eckersley and G. Darke.

uSuthu and Boer casualties
There were no Boer casualties and the uSuthu losses are unknown.

Mandlakazi casualties
The number is unknown, though it must have been significant, considering that six of Zibhebhu's brothers perished. Besides the fighting-men, hundreds of non-combatants were killed. Between 40 000 and 60 000 cattle (as well as many women and children) were captured.

A photograph taken several decades later of the Tshaneni battlefield of 5 June 1884, still littered with the unburied bones of the routed Mandlakazi. In the background is Mount Gaza, directly in front of which the Mandlakazi deployed, and where they gave way, caught between the advancing uSuthu and flanking fire from the Boer horsemen.
J.Y. Gibson, *The Story of the Zulus*, 1911, opp. p. 272

against the river, thus neutralising their numerical advantage.

The armies engage

The uSuthu circumspectly approached the Mkhuze Poort in the traditional formation of two horns and a chest. The left horn, commanded by Mamese, advanced along the river bank, supported by Schiel's volunteers. The uSuthu chest, led by Dinuzulu, came directly at the donga held by the Mandlakazi advance guard, while the right horn began to cross the donga further to the south. Meyer's commando remained in the rear in support of the uSuthu centre and right.

Mamese's left horn ruined Zibhebhu's strategy by engaging the Mandlakazi at the donga before they could embroil the uSuthu centre. This freed the uSuthu centre and right to face the main Mandlakazi attack, which came on with great determination. The uSuthu wavered and many turned to flee. But Meyer's men behind them shouted at them to stand and fight or risk being shot, and fired a fusillade from their saddles more or less over their heads at the charging Mandlakazi. The Mandlakazi left division had already rolled up the uSuthu right and was forc-

ing it back on the uSuthu centre, but repeated volleys from the Boers into the Mandlakazi flanks steadied the wavering uSuthu and within ten minutes forced the Mandlakazi back.

The Mandlakazi rout

When the Madlakazi gave way, they made for the river and their cattle and families on the north bank. But the abaQulusi contingent reached the ridge on the other side of the Mkhuze ahead of them and cut them off. Retreat turned into rout, and the Mandlakazi were pinned against the river and slaughtered – just as they had intended the uSuthu should be. Zibhebhu and some of his men made good their escape across the river and up the slopes of the Lubombo Mountains. There the survivors were joined by those among the non-combatants who had also managed to out-distance their pursuers. The rest took refuge in the bush and dongas, and the victors spent the day of battle and the two succeeding days winkling them out of their hiding places and rounding up between 40 000 and 60 000 head of cattle (most of which went to the uSuthu leaders and to the Boers).

From the Battle of Tshaneni to the Pacification of the Reserve Territory

June – November 1884

The Boers and uSuthu consolidate their victory over the Mandlakazi

Following the Mandlakazi rout at Tshaneni, those Boers who had stayed back to blockade Hamu induced him to emerge from his stronghold and surrender. Meanwhile, the victorious uSuthu and Boers continued to ravage Mandlakazi territory and to flush out their enemies in the broken, bushy terrain near the Mkhuze River. In mid-July the marauding Boers concentrated in their laager at Hlobane. New arrivals of white adventurers and land-grabbers, attracted by the possibility of sharing in the spoils, swelled their ranks to nearly 800, and a new, larger laager was set up on 20 July at the Mabenge hills.

Zibhebhu and the Mandlakazi seek refuge in the Reserve Territory

The resilient Zibhebhu, defeated but not cowed, returned on 7 August to ekuXedini, the only one of his *imizi* not destroyed in the recent fighting. This the uSuthu–Boer alliance could not permit, and on 25 August 100 Boers arrived at ekuShumayeleni to join 8 000 uSuthu for renewed operations against the Mandlakazi. Completely outnumbered, Zibhebhu did not wait to be attacked, but retreated on 29 August with half his people to the borders of the Reserve Territory, while the uSuthu army swept straight through his already ravaged territory as far as the Lubombo Mountains. On 7 September Osborn permitted Zibhebhu and 6 000 Mandlakazi to cross the Mhlathuze to find sanctuary in the Reserve Territory, and located them in the very south of it along the banks of the Thukela, not far from Middle Drift. For

the time being, Zibhebhu had been eliminated as a player in Zululand north of the Mhlathuze.

The uSuthu in the Nkandla contained

South of the Mhlathuze, however, Osborn was succeeding in containing Dinuzulu's supporters. By 29 June the uSuthu in the Nkandla forest were beginning to disperse, though those remaining were still full of fight. On 3 July eight *amaviyo* attacked Mavumengwana kaNdlela of the Ntuli and seized 300 cattle. The British in the Reserve Territory responded first by marching through Siyunguza's territory to reassure the 'loyal' Mpungose that they would be protected from similar uSuthu raids. Then, on 7 July, the British made a reconnaissance in force towards the Nkandla forest. Colonel Curtis led 120 Dragoons, 59 mounted infantry, 200 Highlanders, two guns and Galloway's levies to a post at eSungelweni commanding the junction of the roads from Eshowe and Middle Drift. There he erected the earthwork Fort Yolland for 250 men. It was connected by patrols along the road to Fort Chater, which held 200 men and was in signalling distance of Eshowe. Reassured by this strong presence, loyalists began to come out of their places of refuge, though there were still sporadic, but minor,

> 'They [the Mandlakazi] numbered 5 or 6,000 souls; the men as lean as greyhounds; sleeping mats and blankets on their heads; all fully armed with assegais and shields, but with few guns; the women with enormous loads on their heads, weary and tired; children of all ages to the infant at the back. they also had a great many cattle.'
>
> (Lt-Col the Hon. Sir L. Smyth, General Officer Commanding in South Africa, 19 September 1884)

> 'Entumeni to be quite 200 strong. Have daily system mounted patrols supported by infantry along advanced road. Firmly entrench and abattis advanced post, which must be within signalling distance of Entumeni, and which must have native scouts in sufficient force.'
>
> (Smyth, 12 June 1884)

Fort Northampton, built on the Zululand bank of the Mzinyathi (Buffalo) River at Rorke's Drift and occupied between June and November 1884 by men of the 2nd Bn, The Northamptonshire Regiment. Note the dry-stone parapet and the mealie-bag traverses to protect the garrison from reverse or enfilading fire. Shiyane Mountain, or the Oskarsberg, looms in the background over the mission station on the Natal side of the river.   Ron Sheeley Collection

uSuthu cattle raids. A reconnaissance from Fort Yolland to Middle Drift on 17 July found all uSuthu-aligned *imizi* deserted, and reports had it that only about 1 200 uSuthu fighting-men were still in the Nkandla forest. Dabulamanzi and other uSuthu leaders had apparently left two days before to join Mnyamana in the Ngome forest.

The coastal uSuthu raid the Reserve Territory

On 24 and 27 July the pro-uSuthu Somhlolo, the regent of the Biyela, raided south with six *amaviyo* across the Mhlathuze against Chief Mgitshwa kaMvu-ndlana, who had moved with the larger part of the Biyela into the safety of the Reserve Territory. The border chiefs of the Reserve were consequently forced to hold themselves in readiness against further raids which, it turned out, were not forthcoming.

The British strengthen Fort Northampton at Rorke's Drift

In June two companies of the 2nd Bn, The Northamptonshire Regiment began the construction of Fort Northampton, on the northern bank of the Mzinyathi River across from the mission station at Rorke's Drift, just within the Reserve Territory. It was very solid with a dry-stone parapet and ditch.

Though reduced in numbers, the uSuthu still in the Nkandla forest remained active, and on 28 July they raided the Tlokwa in the north-western Reserve Territory for cattle. In response, a detachment of the 6th (Inniskilling) Dragoons was sent up on 14 August to camp at Fort Northampton to lend Hlubi moral support. On 9 September Fort Northampton was further strengthened with a company of mounted infantry and two Gatling guns.

'The Rorke's Drift column was only sent as a moral support, and as its early presence there was deemed of importance, its composition depended a good deal on the transport capacity of the moment. My recent visit there showed me that an increase to the infantry is desirable, in view of easing the labour of ordinary camp duties and fatigues, which now press heavily . . . The fort is in a good state of defence, and is safe against any attack by Natives made in the course of a raid.'

(Smyth, 14 August 1884)

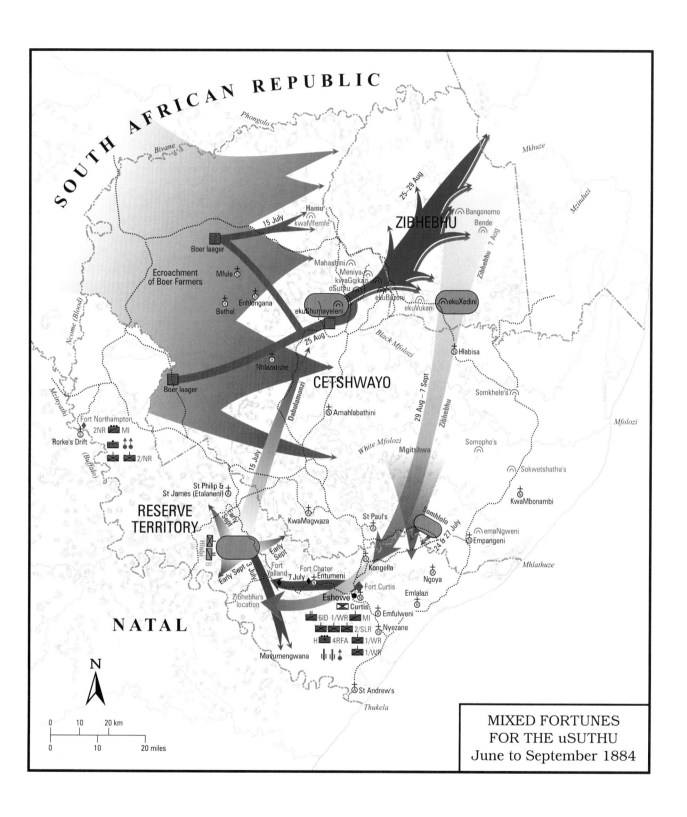

MIXED FORTUNES
FOR THE uSUTHU
June to September 1884

'We heard that many of Nkandhla people had returned with their cattle to their kraals . . . We could not hear of any big force, but companies were in different places, one party being portion of the Ufalaza regiment, formed by the late king [Cetshwayo], since his return from the Cape, was near the place he was buried.'

(Nkonjane and Vundisa, Osborn's agents, 17 August 1884)

The uSuthu in the Nkandla submit

By the middle of August there were less than 1 000 uSuthu men still operating from the Nkandla forest. Except for those of the Cube who had always lived in the area, their families and cattle had been removed north beyond the Mhlathuze. From 11 August Osborn began negotiating for the final submission of the uSuthu remnants in the Nkandla, and by 9 September most had given up hostilities.

The British consolidate their garrison in the Reserve Territory

Conditions in the Reserve Territory were considered by the military sufficiently settled for the British garrison to be withdrawn from Fort Yolland by November, and for it to be replaced by the Reserve Territory Carbineers. British garrisons elsewhere in the Reserve were consolidated to 100 infantry at Fort Chater, 300 infantry and one mounted company at Fort Curtis, and 150 infantry, one mounted company and two Gatlings at Fort Northampton.

PART IV

The Boer Land-Grab
1884–1888

'The price of blood is a hard price; and to encompass the destruction of Usibebu the
Usutu leaders bartered away the best part of the inheritance of the Zulu people, an
inheritance, let it be remembered, which was left untouched by the British
Government after the war of 1879.'

(Bulwer, 6 January 1886)

Pietermaritzburg Archives Repository (C. 1187)

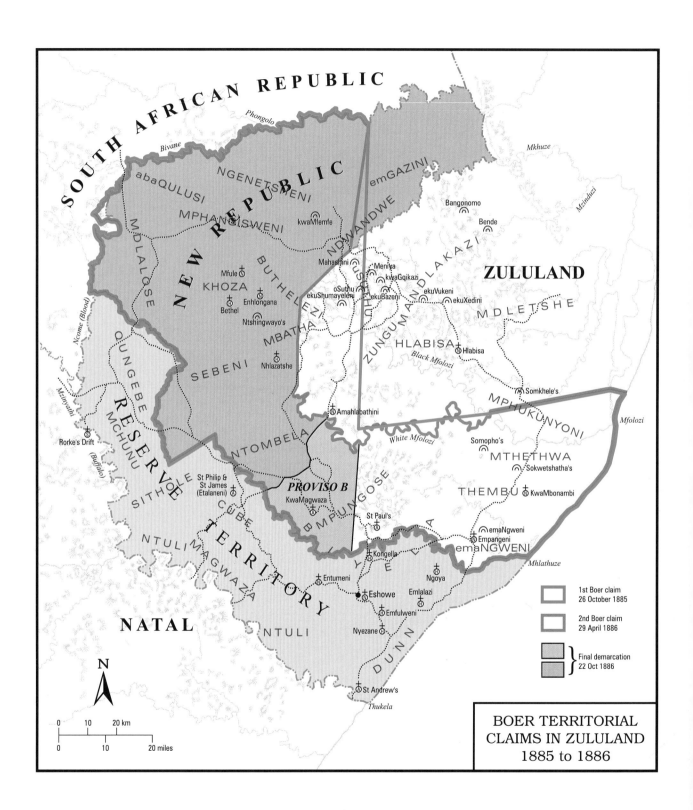

BOER TERRITORIAL
CLAIMS IN ZULULAND
1885 to 1886

The New Republic

The Boers occupy all north-western Zululand

The uSuthu were required to pay a steep price for Boer assistance in their victory over the Mandlakazi at the battle of Tshaneni. On 16 August 1884, at the Boer encampment at Hlobane, Dinuzulu issued a proclamation granting the Boers 1 355 000 morgen for the establishment of the New Republic. Dinuzulu conceded that the New Republic would also extend a protectorate over the rest of Zululand north of the Reserve Territory, thus quite nullifying his authority as Zulu king. Being no more than a nominal ruler in the hands of the Boers, Dinuzulu could not protect his people as the invaders fanned out to occupy the farms they had allocated themselves, even before the new boundaries had been fixed. Driven from their lands, the uSuthu again took refuge in their fastnesses or began to resist, bringing on themselves savage Boer retaliation.

> 'The actual cession that has been made is a cession of land of 802 farms, varying in size, but altogether amounting to 1,355,000 morgen, or 2,710,000 acres. Whether this area of land will cover the whole of the three territories or districts formerly under the Chiefs Seketwayo, Tshingwayo and Uhamu, or whether it will go beyond the limits of these territories will only be known when the farms have been surveyed. In respect of the Zulu country lying beyond the ceded territory, what action the New Republic will take will depend on the construction that they put on their new agreement with the Usutus.'
>
> (Bulwer, 8 September 1884)

The British intervene

Neither the plight of the Zulu, nor the complaints of the Natal settlers who resented the establishment of a Boer republic in their zone of interest, were sufficient to persuade the British government to intervene decisively in the affairs of Zululand. However, wider imperial interests at last

On 13 August 1884 the Volksraad of the New Republic resolved that a town must be laid out as the capital of the state the Boers were carving out for themselves in Zululand. There was initially some controversy about what name it should be given. Many suggestions were made, but on 23 September 1884 the name 'Vryheid' was adopted, since 'Freedom' to be self-governing was the Boers' ultimate aspiration. A site for Vryheid was selected south-west of Zungwini Mountain, and the town was laid out in the typical grid pattern adopted by the Boers wherever they settled. Long, straight streets were connected by cross streets, and the blocks these formed were divided into 300 rectangular *erven*, or plots. A number of *erven* were set aside for the school and church councils, mission societies, government buildings, a church and the market square. The remainder were put up for sale to prospective residents. This engraving of the aspirant capital, which appeared in the Graphic *of 17 April 1886, shows most of the plots yet to be taken up, and the scattering of buildings to be of the simplest construction. Note the typical* sluit *(or furrow) down the side of the main street which brought water to the* erven *for drinking, washing and irrigation.*   Graphic, 17 April 1886

The tall, powerfully built Lukas Johannes Meyer is shown in this photograph of 1899 in the robes of the Chairman of the Volksraad of the South African Republic, of which he had been the Member for Utrecht since 1893. Meyer was both a leading Boer political figure and soldier. A field cornet in the Utrecht District from 1872, he was wounded in the First Anglo-Boer War (1880–1881). In 1882 he went on to become Landdrost of the Utrecht District once the South African Republic regained its independence from Britain. In April 1884 he joined the Committee of Dinuzulu's Volunteers, and was present when the Boers proclaimed Dinuzulu king on 21 May. The following day he was elected commandant of the Boer commando which played the decisive role at the battle of Tshaneni on 5 June. He was elected President and Commandant-General of the New Republic when it was proclaimed on 16 August 1884, and retained that position until 20 July 1888 when the unviable little state became the Vryheid District of the South African Republic. During the Second Anglo-Boer War Meyer was a not particularly successful commander of the southern Transvaal commandos invading northern Natal in 1899, and was partially incapacitated through illness. After the British occupation of Pretoria in June 1900 he took no part in the guerrilla phase of hostilities, but instead worked for a negotiated peace. He was one of the signatories of the Treaty of Vereeniging which ended the war on 31 May 1902.

L.S. Amery (ed.), *The Times History of the War in South Africa 1899–1902*, London, 1902, vol. II, opp. p. 158

drove Britain to take a series of decisive steps.

Imperial Germany's growing interest in the coast of Zululand, and consequent fears of a potential German link-up with the land-locked Boers of the South African Republic by way of the nascent New Republic, caused Gladstone's Liberal administration reluctantly to assert British claims to St Lucia Bay on 21 December 1884. Next, the New Republic's subsequent proclamation of its boundaries on 26 October 1885, which thrust provocatively eastwards towards the Zululand coast, elicited a sharp British reaction and prompted it to modify its boundary line on 29 April 1886. Yet it took the return to power in August 1886 of Lord Salisbury's Conservative administration (with its greater commitment to safeguarding imperial interests in south-east Africa than had been evinced by the Liberals) finally to ensure direct British action over Zululand.

British recognition of the short-lived New Republic

In return for British recognition of the New Republic on 22 October 1886, the Boers agreed to limit their territorial pretensions and to drop all claims to a protec-

torate over Dinuzulu. They also ceded control over a block of territory in central Zululand, known as Proviso B, but were allowed to retain ownership of the farms they had already laid out there. A Boundary Commission completed the task of defining the New Republic's boundaries by 25 January 1887.

Lukas Meyer was elected the President of the little New Republic, whose capital was the tiny and newly-established village of Vryheid. However, the New Republic rapidly had to acknowledge it did not possess the capacity to maintain itself as an independent state. On 20 July 1888 it was incorporated as the Vryheid District into its larger and more established Boer neighbour, the South African Republic.

PART V
The uSuthu Rebellion
1887–1888

'Dinuzulu must know, and all the Zulus must know, that the rule of the House of
Chaka is a thing of the past. It is dead. It is like water spilt on the ground. The
Queen now rules in Zululand and no one else. The Queen who conquered Cetywayo
has now taken the government of the country into her own hands.'

(Havelock, 14 November 1887)

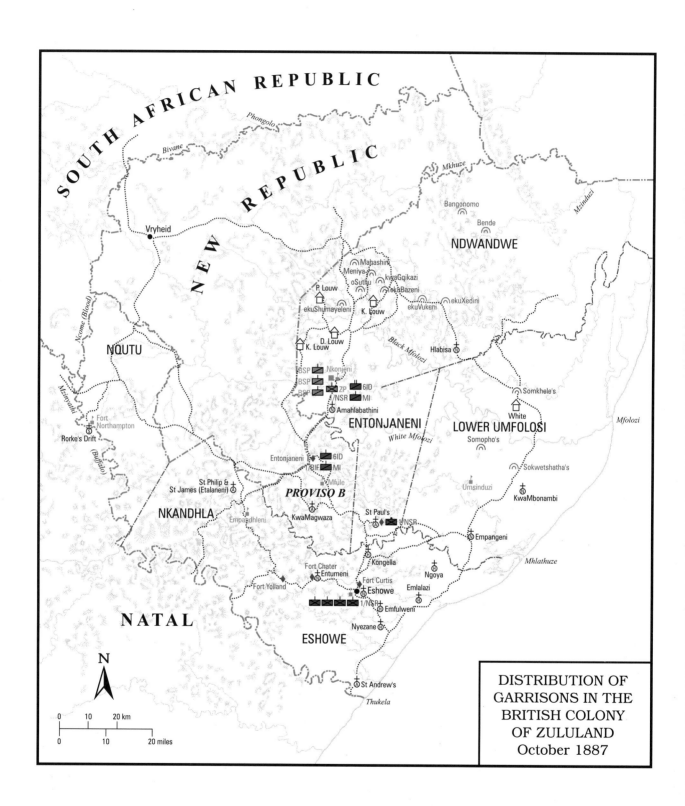

SOUTH AFRICAN REPUBLIC

NEW REPUBLIC

Phongolo

Bivane

Mkhuze

Mzinduzi

Vryheid

Bangonomo

Bende

NDWANDWE

Ncome (Blood)

Mzinyathi

NQUTU

Mahashini

Meniya

oSuthu

kwaGqikazi

P. Louw

ekuShumayeleni

K. Louw

TekaBazeni

ekuVukeni

ekuXedini

D. Louw

K. Louw

Black Mfolozi

Hlabisa

BSP

BSP Nkonjeni

BSP ZP 6ID

/NSR MI

Amahlabathini

ENTONJANENI

White Mfolozi

Somkhele's

White

LOWER UMFOLOSI

Mfolozi

Somopho's

Fort Northampton

Rorke's Drift

(Buffalo)

Entonjaneni 6ID

1/8IF MI

Mfule

Sokwetshatha's

Umsinduzi

PROVISO B

KwaMbonambi

St Philip & St James (Etalaneni)

NKANDHLA

Empandhleni

KwaMagwaza

St Paul's

1/NSR

Empangeni

Kongella

Fort Chater

Entumeni

Fort Curtis

Ngoya

Mhlathuze

Fort Yolland

Eshowe

Emlalazi

NATAL

1/NSR Emfulweni

Nyezane

ESHOWE

N

St Andrew's

Thukela

0 10 20 km

0 10 20 miles

DISTRIBUTION OF
GARRISONS IN THE
BRITISH COLONY
OF ZULULAND
October 1887

The British Colony of Zululand

The British annexation of Zululand

Dinuzulu protested at the British recognition of the New Republic on 22 October 1886 because it regularised the alienations of all north-western Zululand to Boer farmers, and reduced the Zulu living on their farms to the status of labour tenants. Many Zulu who found themselves in this unwelcome situation were resistant to the demands of their new masters, and flocked into the Reserve Territory as refugees.

To his distress, Dinuzulu was powerless to help his former subjects in the New Republic. Indeed, his position was extremely weak. He felt himself vulnerable not only to continued Boer expansionism, but also to plans by Natal colonists to incorporate his remaining territory and throw it open to white settlement. Moreover, he was apprehensive about Zibhebhu's vociferous demands to be allowed to return from his place of exile in the Reserve Territory to his old lands in north-eastern Zululand.

Alarmed by this turbulent and deteriorating situation, the Resident Commissioner of the Reserve Territory, Melmoth Osborn, took the initiative and notified the uSuthu leadership on 5 February 1887 that British protection had been extended over what he termed Eastern Zululand. With no alternative left to them, Dinuzulu and his advisers accepted Osborn's action. The British government, faced with the accomplished fact, duly agreed to the annexation of both Eastern Zululand (including Proviso B) and of the Reserve Territory. The two were brought together under one administration, and from 19 May 1887 became the British Colony of Zululand. Although white traders and missionaries were permitted in the new colony, the land (except that already laid out as farms in Proviso B) was not thrown open to white settlement, but was reserved for sole Zulu occupation.

> 'Umnyamana and the other Zulu Chiefs in their communication . . . anxiously pray that the British Government will protect them against the aggressive proceedings of the Boers. They ask that the Zulu people be taken, with the country they inhabit, under the protection of the British Government and beg that this may be done soon.'
>
> (Osborn, 28 January 1886)

The Zululand administration

In the interests of economy, the British government made the Governor of the Colony of Natal, Sir Arthur Havelock, Governor of Zululand as well. In turn, Havelock appointed Melmoth Osborn Resident Commissioner and Chief Magistrate of Zululand with his seat at Eshowe. The new colony was divided into six administrative districts, each under a white assistant commissioner and resident magistrate. These officials were expected to enforce their authority through a small paramilitary force recruited from among the Zulu. Styled the Zululand Police (or Nongqai), it had originally been raised in 1883 as the Reserve Territory Carbineers, and remained under the command of Cmdt George Mansel with its headquarters at Eshowe. This skeleton administrative machinery was to be financed by a hut tax. The permanent British garrison of Natal, with its headquarters at Fort Napier in Pietermaritzburg, was available if necessary to reinforce the Zululand Police in ensuring order, and from the outset maintained small detachments in garrison in the fledgling colony.

> 'The Queen's Government is free to administer Zululand just as it likes. It has not to consider the shadowy but troublesome claims of kingship on the part of Dinuzulu or anybody else.'
>
> (*Natal Mercury*, 8 July 1887)

The uSuthu withhold their co-operation

Not unsurprisingly, many of the uSuthu

> 'Dinuzulu says, he does not understand this placing of white Magistrates all over the country . . . that they have not been used to Magistrate's offices and do not know how to get on with them, and that they are afraid that they will not be able to do so.'
>
> (Siziba and Pagade kaNgonela, messengers of Dinuzulu, Mnyamana, Ndabuko and the Heads of the Zulu People, 11 October 1887)

leadership, who had accepted the annexation of the rump of Zululand as a British colony only for fear of worse, resented their loss of status and were reluctant to accept in practice the curtailment of their own authority which was a natural consequence of the functioning of the new colonial administration.

Anticipating such resistance, Havelock had instructed the Zululand officials to adopt a conciliatory approach during the delicate time of transition to British rule. Their forbearance was rewarded, for in most parts of the new colony the Zulu and their chiefs soon fell in with the new order, even when, as in the case of Chief Mnya-

R 461/8?

PROCLAMATION,

By His Excellency Sir ARTHUR ELIBANK HAVELOCK, Knight Commander of the Most Distinguished Order of Saint Michael and Saint George, Governor and Commander-in-Chief in and over the Colony of Natal, Vice-Admiral of the same, Supreme Chief over the Native Population, and Her Majesty's Special Commissioner for Zulu Affairs.

WHEREAS Zululand came under the Paramount Authority of Her Majesty the Queen as a consequence of the war of 1879:

AND WHEREAS, in the interests of peace, order, and good government, it has been deemed expedient that Her Majesty's Sovereignty should be proclaimed over Zululand as is hereinafter defined:

AND WHEREAS, Her Majesty has been pleased to authorize me to take the necessary steps for giving effect to Her pleasure in the matter:

Now, THEREFORE, I do hereby proclaim, declare, and make known, that from and after the Nineteenth day of May next the whole of Zululand, including the territory known as the Zulu Reserve Territory, but excluding the territory known as the New Republic, and bounded as follows:—On the South and South-west by the Colony of Natal; on the West and North-west by the New Republic; on the North by Amatongaland; and on the East by the Indian Ocean, shall be and shall be taken to be a British possession under the name of Zululand:

And I hereby require all Her Majesty's subjects in South Africa to take notice of this my Proclamation, and to guide themselves accordingly,

GOD SAVE THE QUEEN!

Given under my Hand and Seal at Government House, Pietermaritzburg, this Fourteenth day of May, One Thousand Eight Hundred and Eighty-seven.

A.E. Havelock

Governor and Special Commissioner

By command of His Excellency the Governor of Natal and Special Commissioner for Zulu Affairs,

Gerald Browne

Private Secretary.

Proclamation of the Annexation of Zululand, 14 May 1887. Pietermaritzburg Archives Repository (Zululand Archives 5, no. R461/87)

mana and the Buthelezi, they had been pillars of the uSuthu cause. But the Resident Magistrate of Ndwandwe, R.H. (Dick) Addison, in whose district Dinuzulu, his uncle Ndabuko and most of the committed uSuthu leadership had their *imizi*, showed himself unsuited to deal successfully with uSuthu defiance. Not even the intervention of Osborn, and then of Havelock himself, proved any more efficacious in winning the compliance of Dinuzulu and his uncles. The impolitic levying of cattle fines as an assertion of British authority only hardened the uSuthu resolve to withhold their co-operation from the new regime.

British troops move up in support of the civil authorities

Havelock was reluctant to send the regular troops of the Natal garrison against his new subjects in Zululand. It should have been up to the civil authorities and the Zululand Police to bring the uSuthu to heel. But since they were not managing to do so, Havelock was compelled to redeploy and augment the troops already in Zululand in their support. On 22 August 1887 the troops in Eshowe were marched northwards to camps at Entonjaneni and Nkonjeni, closer to where the uSuthu were concentrated in the Ndwandwe District. Further increases were made preparatory to likely action against the uSuthu, so that by October infantry of the 1st Bn, The Prince of Wales's (North Staffordshire Regiment) were stationed at Eshowe in Fort Curtis, as well as at St Paul's. Mounted infantry from the 1st Bn, The Royal Inniskilling Fusiliers were at Entonjaneni with a troop of the 6th (Inniskilling) Dragoons. More Dragoons were posted forward at Nkonjeni with mounted infantry drawn from the North Staffordshires, and supported by the Mounted Basuto Special Police (Hlubi's men) and the Zululand Police.

Sir Arthur Elibank Havelock, KCMG, came to Natal as Governor in February 1886 after being Governor of West African Settlements (1881) and Governor of Trinidad (1884). On 19 May 1887, as an economy measure on the part of the Colonial Office, he was appointed Governor of the freshly annexed Colony of Zululand in addition to Natal. He left Natal and Zululand in 1889 to become the Governor successively of Ceylon, Madras and Tasmania. An experienced administrator of proven humanity and sense, it was nevertheless Havelock's mistake to accept the proffered advice of Sir Theophilus Shepstone and the other 'old Zulu hands' of his school. It led him down the road of confrontation with the uSuthu, and by the time Havelock understood that the policies of his Zululand officials were both flawed and biased, it was already too late. Havelock was loath to admit that the rebellion of 1888 proved that his civil administration had failed, which was why he was reluctant to call in the aid of the military, and why he clashed with General Smyth over the conduct of operations. His instinct was ever to negotiate and employ diplomacy in preference to force.
Pietermaritzburg Archives Repository (C. 275/1)

'Our authority being entirely ignored by Dinuzulu, there is great danger of its being defied throughout the country unless vindicated at once.'
(Osborn, 19 August 1887)

'Go and tell Dinuzulu I am coming in a hostile manner and tomorrow morning if the cattle are not handed over you will be old people.'
(R.H. Addison, Assistant Commissioner and Resident Magistrate, Ndwandwe District of Zululand, 9 September 1887)

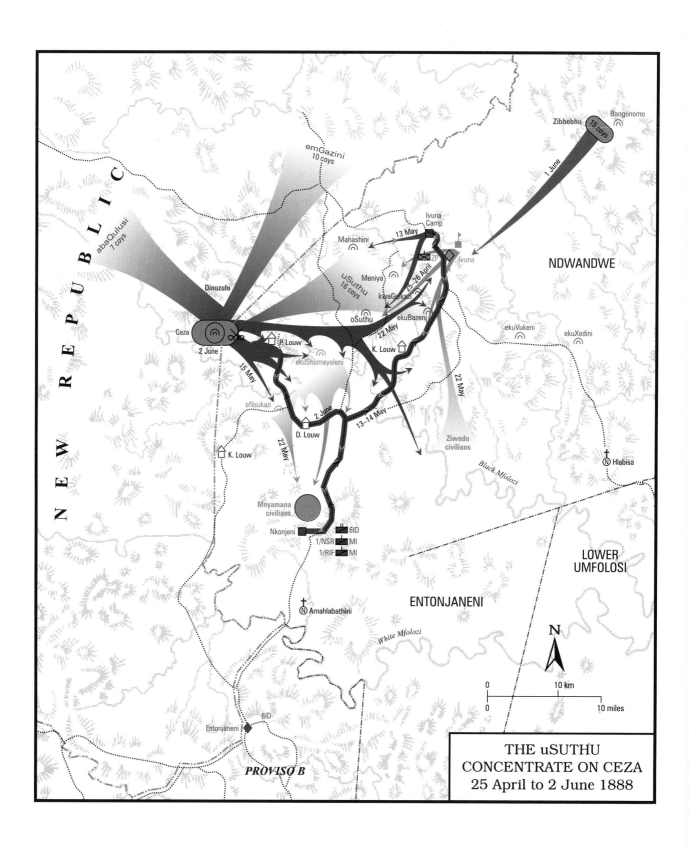

Zibhebhu
15 coys
Bangonomo

1 June

NDWANDWE

emGazini
10 coys

abaQulusi
7 coys

Ivuna
Camp
13 May
Mahashini

Dinuzulu

uSuthu
16 coys
Meniya

25-26 April
Ivuna

kwaGenkazi

Ceza
2 June

P. Louw

oSuthu
22 May

ekuBazeni

ekuVukeni

ekuXedini

ekuShumayeleni

K. Louw

15 May

eNsukazi

22 May

K. Louw

13-14 May

Ziwedu
civilians

Black Mfolozi

Hlabisa

2 June
D. Louw

LOWER
UMFOLOSI

Mnyamana
civilians

Nkonjeni
1/NSR
1/RIF
6ID
MI
MI

ENTONJANENI

N

Amahlabathini

White Mfolozi

0   10 km
0   10 miles

Entonjaneni
6ID

PROVISO B

THE uSUTHU
CONCENTRATE ON CEZA
25 April to 2 June 1888

Raid and Counter-Raid

Mid-April – 2 June 1888

The return of Zibhebhu

In November 1887 the British authorities decided on a fateful means of cowing the uncooperative uSuthu without having to resort to employing British troops to assist the Zululand Police. They turned to Zibhebhu, their old ally and scourge of the uSuthu. The Mandlakazi had been refugees near Middle Drift since their defeat in the battle of Tshaneni in 1884. Now they were to be sent back to their old territory in the Ndwandwe District where, it was calculated, their near and hostile presence would assist Addison, the Resident Magistrate, in finally overawing the uSuthu.

Predictably, though, far from normalising the situation as intended, Zibhebhu's arrival in Ndwandwe only inflamed it. The uSuthu were filled with alarm, especially since the Mandlakazi insisted on the ruthless expulsion of those uSuthu who had settled on their lands during their exile. Addison added to the unrest by blatantly taking Zibhebhu's part in every dispute, and by demarcating an unjustifiably large location for the Mandlakazi from which (with the magistrate's connivance) they proceeded to evict all uSuthu falling within its confines.

The uSuthu resort to arms

During January 1888, with the uSuthu in Ndwandwe in turmoil and in increasingly open defiance of the British, mounted patrols under Lt-Col R.G.R. Martin, 6th (Inniskilling) Dragoons, proceeded from the camp at Nkonjeni to a camp near Ivuna, the seat of Addison's magistracy. The main uSuthu *imizi* were clustered nearby, and Martin's presence temporarily reasserted British sway over them. But coming to the conclusion that the uSuthu would never receive any redress from the partisan Zululand administration save through recourse to arms, Dinuzulu

crossed over the border to the New Republic on 15 February to have discussions with Field Cornet Paul Bester concerning possible Boer assistance. The Boers proved unwilling to commit themselves but, while in the New Republic, Dinuzulu did succeed in rallying to his cause the ardently royalist abaQulusi who had been cut off from the rest of Zululand by the boundary of 1886. The abaQulusi began to muster on Ceza Mountain, a traditional fastness now bisected by the boundary line. Having raised this support, Dinuzulu returned home, and during March his oSuthu homestead became a place of sanctuary for all those defying British authority and that of their collaborator, Zibhebhu.

Between 5 April and 13 May Dinuzulu was once more in the New Republic, and in the South African Republic as well, with the object of raising support from Zulu living north of the Phongolo River. In his absence, on 25 April, Addison with the Zululand Police raided the ekuBazeni and Meniya *imizi* to collect cattle fines levied against the uSuthu for their lack of compliance with his orders. On 26 April the attempt by 80 Zululand Police to arrest four uSuthu ringleaders at Dinuzulu's oSuthu *umuzi* was thwarted by a thousand uSuthu in battle-order under the command of Prince Ndabuko.

As the situation threatened to slip out of control, Zibhebhu assembled ten *amaviyo* at Bangonomo, his principal *umuzi*, and a

> 'Allowance should be made for the ignorance and suspicion of the Chiefs, and for the not unnatural difficulty they experience in accommodating themselves to a new order of things and to circumstances which are, in some respects, disappointing and distasteful to them.'
>
> (Havelock, 12 January 1888)

> 'Dinuzulu complains that the magistrate (Mr Addison) did not abide by the Governor's orders, which were that Usibebu and his people were to re-occupy their old tribal sites. The magistrate has gone beyond these orders, by including in the location a large number of kraals which were never occupied by Usibebu's tribe. This action is causing a hardship on the people affected.'
>
> (King Dinuzulu kaCetshwayo, 3 March 1888)

'Dinizulu and Usibepu are like chained dogs, only anxious to fly at one another, and it must require the utmost skill to prevent an outbreak.'

(*Natal Mercury*, 22 February 1888)

mounted force under Capt E.G. Pennefather moved up from Nkonjeni to the camp near Ivuna, which Colonel Martin had temporarily occupied during January. On 13 May Pennefather made a reconnaissance to the oSuthu and Mahashini *imizi*, which he found evacuated. Pennefather retired the next day to Nkonjeni.

While Pennefather was withdrawing, the uSuthu under Dinuzulu and Ndabuko concentrated on Ceza. They consisted of sixteen *amaviyo* Ndabuko had collected from the cluster of uSuthu *imizi* west of the Ivuna magistracy: namely, Meniya, Mahashini, oSuthu, kwaGqikazi and eku-Bazeni; ten *amaviyo* which Dinuzulu had

recruited mainly from the emGazini living north of the Mkhuze River in the New Republic; and the seven *amaviyo* of abaQulusi already camped on the mountain.

During the latter part of May, the uSuthu on Ceza raided for supplies those they considered guilty of collaborating with the British, as well as white trading-stores in the vicinity, striking as far away as beyond the Black Mfolozi and the Nongoma range. Being the prime victims of these raids, Mnyamana and the Buthelezi abandoned their *imizi* and moved close to the Nkonjeni camp for protection; while Prince Ziwedu and his adherents likewise

Dinuzulu's oSuthu umuzi *was built on a gentle slope between rocky outcrops below a wide, open plain at the upper reaches of the steep-banked and sluggish Vuna River. Close by was his uncle Ndabuko's Meniya* umuzi. *On 26 April 1888 oSuthu witnessed a remarkable standoff when 1 000 uSuthu* amabutho *intimidated a force of 80 Zululand Police, and dissuaded them from attempting to execute warrants of arrest against four uSuthu fugitives from the Resident Magistrate's justice who were sheltering there. Although this photograph of 1907 shows the new oSuthu which Dinuzulu constructed in 1898 on his return from exile on St Helena, and which consisted of traditional huts as well as European-style dwellings, it nevertheless serves to give an impression of the* umuzi *in 1888, and the thornveld terrain where it was situated.*

Pietermaritzburg Archives Repository (C. 556)

took shelter in the lee of the Ivuna magistracy.

The British repulsed on Ceza Mountain

In an attempt to regain control of the situation, Addison with an escort of Zululand Police rendezvoused on 2 June with British troops from Nkonjeni under Pennefather (augmented by auxiliaries drawn from Mnyamana's Buthelezi) to effect the arrest of the uSuthu leaders on Ceza. In order to protect his post at Ivuna, stripped during his absence at Ceza of most of its garrison, Addison ordered up fifteen *amaviyo* of Mandlakazi under Zibhebhu to camp on Ndunu hill close by.

On Ceza the uSuthu resisted Addison and the Zululand Police with determination, and succeeded in a running skirmish

'On the arrival of the troops [on 12 May 1888 at Ivuna] it was found that both the Usutu and Mahashine Royal kraals had been vacated, and that Dinuzulu and N'dabuko had retired, with their followers, to the Ceza Bush. The troops accordingly returned to N'konjeni . . . The valleys of the Isquibesi [Sikhwebezi River] and Umubullwane [Bulwane River], which intervened between the Ivuna and Ceza Bush, being perfectly impracticable for military operations, N'konjeni was considered a preferable position to operate against the latter.'

(Stabb, 19 October 1888)

in driving them and the British troops who had moved up to support them ignominiously down the mountain and back the whole way across the Black Mfolozi. Dinuzulu's success in this armed encounter was the last achieved by the Zulu over British regular troops.

The Battle of Ceza

2 June 1888

> 'In addition to the natural strength of the position of the Keza stronghold the ground immediately below the lower edge of the bush consists of broken rocky terraces which have been further strengthened by the Usutu with stone breastworks. Upon these terraces were erected the kraals in which the impi lived.'
>
> (Capt R.S.S. Baden-Powell, August 1888)

The attempted arrest of the uSuthu leaders

Fearing the disruptive effects on their administration of the rebellious uSuthu concentrated under Dinuzulu and Ndabuko on Ceza Mountain, the Zululand officials resolved on 28 May 1888 to arrest the ringleaders. Since the fiction was being maintained that the execution of the civil warrants, drawn up by Addison, was a police matter, the troops supporting the operation could only take action if he called upon them to do so.

At 04h30 on 2 June Addison, 67 Zululand Police under Commandant Mansel, supported by 84 6th (Inniskilling) Dragoons and 80 mounted infantry under Captain Pennefather, left David Louw's store on the Mfabeni hills for Ceza. On the way they picked up some 600 of Mnyama-

British forces
Capt E.G. Pennefather commanding:
One squadron of the 6th (Inniskilling) Dragoons (three officers, 81 men).
One company of mounted infantry: 1st Bn, The Royal Inniskilling Fusiliers (one officer, 43 men).
One company of mounted infantry: 1st Bn, The Prince of Wales's (North Staffordshire Regiment) (one officer, 35 men).
Thirteen men at eNsukazi under Lt R.B. Briscoe.
Total: Seven officers and 172 men

Cmdt G. Mansel commanding:
One company of Zululand Police (50 men).
Seventeen mounted Zululand Police under Sub-Inspector C.E. Pierce.
Total: Two officers and 67 men

Tshanibezwe kaMnyamana commanding:
Mnyamana's Auxiliaries.
Total: Approximately 600 men

uSuthu forces
King Dinuzulu kaCetshwayo, Prince Ndabuko kaMpande and Hemulana kaMbangezeli commanding:
Sixteen *amaviyo* of uSuthu from the Colony of Zululand (including *amaviyo* from the uFalaza and imBokodwebomvu *amabutho*).
Ten *amaviyo* of emGazini and other uSuthu irregulars from north of the Mkhuze River in the New Republic.
Seven *amaviyo* of abaQulusi irregulars from the New Republic.
Total: Approximately 2 000 men

British casualties
Killed: Two British regulars.
Wounded: Two British regulars and one Zululand Policeman.

uSuthu casualties
The British estimated at least 100 uSuthu killed, though this was probably a considerable exaggeration.

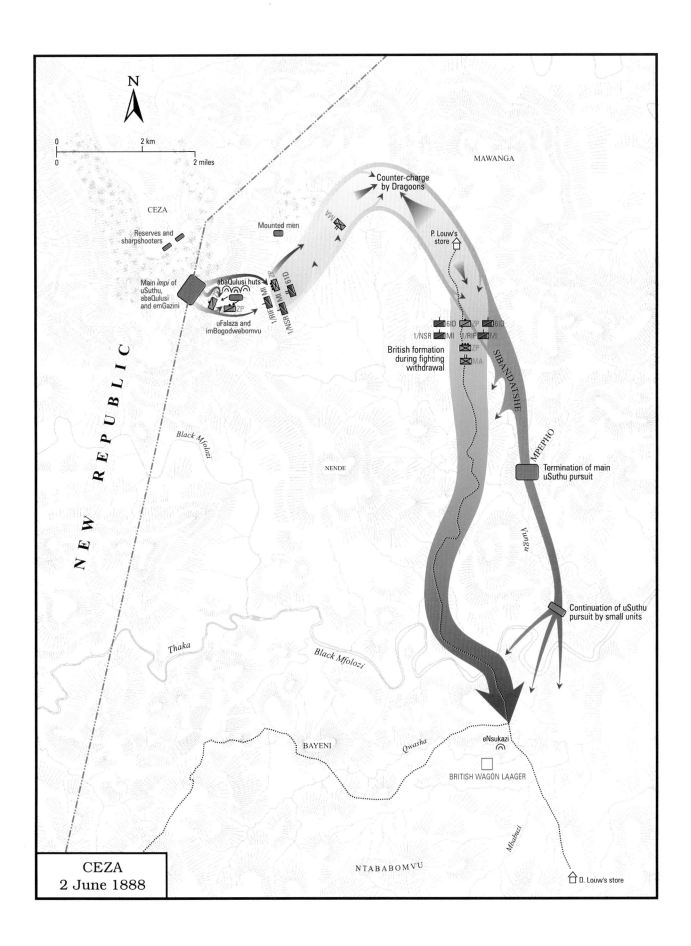

N

0 ___ 2 km
0 ___ 2 miles

MAWANGA

CEZA

Reserves and
sharpshooters

Mounted men

Counter-charge
by Dragoons

P. Louw's
store

Main *impi* of
uSuthu,
abaQulusi
and emGazini

abaQulusi huts

1/RIF MI ZP
1/NSR MI 61D

uFalaza and
imBogodwebomvu

NEW REPUBLIC

Black *Mfolozi*

61D ZP 61D
1/NSR MI 1/RIF MI
ZP

British formation
during fighting
withdrawal

SIBANDATSHE

MPEPHO

NENDE

Termination of main
uSuthu pursuit

Vungu

Continuation of uSuthu
pursuit by small units

Thaka

Black *Mfolozi*

BAYENI   *Qwasha*   eNsukazi

BRITISH WAGON LAAGER

Mhobozi

CEZA
2 June 1888

NTABABOMVU

D. Louw's store

> 'He is the expeller of the rock-rabbit from Ceza,
> And he takes up the whole place.'
>
> (*From* Dinuzulu's praises)

na's Buthelezi who, under the command of his son, Tshanibezwe, were to act as auxiliaries. The combined force halted soon after 10h30 for breakfast at Piet Louw's store about 6 km (3.7 miles) east of Ceza, which the uSuthu had looted on 15 May. While they were eating, they spotted the uSuthu force of 33 *amaviyo* forming up into a semi-circle on the slopes of the mountain to be addressed by its leaders. The uSuthu then began to march towards the flat summit of Ceza which lay just across the border in the New Republic. Fearing that the uSuthu would soon be out of his jurisdiction, Addison decided to execute his warrants without further delay.

The Zululand Police repulsed

Seventeen Zululand Police under Commandant Mansel and Sub-Inspector C.E. Pierce pushed ahead of the main body of troops. As they entered the bush they collided with an *iviyo* of the uFalaza and two *amaviyo* of the imBokodwebomvu (150 men) who were in the huts of the abaQulusi bivouac to their right. Mansel opened fire, which was returned. The main uSuthu force of 20 *amaviyo* or more (approximately 1 200 men), on hearing the shooting, came streaming back down the mountain

in traditional battle formation, led by Dinuzulu himself. The encircling horns were soon threatening to cut off Mansel's detachment. Addison, realising that the menaced Zululand Police were in no position to execute the warrants, called on Pennefather to take charge and extricate them from their dangerous situation.

The British forced to withdraw

With some difficulty the regular troops covered Mansel's retreat. Mnyamana's Auxiliaries had declined to advance up the mountain, but were now caught up in the retreat. The uSuthu pursued their retiring adversaries in two bodies, skirmishing along their flanks. Four *amaviyo* posted on the very edge of the summit of Ceza also kept up a fire. At one stage, when the terrain proved suitable, Pennefather charged the pursuers with the Dragoons and police formed into two ranks. This counter-attack was effective in that the uSuthu gave up their attempts to surround and cut off the British, and their main body halted halfway between Piet Louw's store and the Black Mfolozi. However, four *amaviyo* continued the whole way to the banks of the river and a few even crossed in token pursuit. The retiring British made for

> 'We stopped until they, the Government force, could come up, so that we could fight with them. The order was that we [were] to go up to the Dutch territory . . . We were told to stop, as soon as we had crossed the line. It was said that the Government force would not cross the line. We were told not to fire first . . . by Dinuzulu himself.'
>
> (Umhlalo, son of Npaiye, 5 April 1889)

> 'We were firing from the other side of our horses, which the Usutus had killed: we were firing over them . . . we did not pass beyond the horses. I cannot remember accurately everything which happened: we were blind: I mean by *that*, that we could not see as there were clouds of smoke, and we were quite close. The firing was rapid on both sides . . . We would not be alive today, if the soldiers who were behind, with the Magistrate, had not become engaged then and shot the Zulus.'
>
> (Sergeant-Major Sodoyi, Zululand Police, 26 March 1889)

Mnyamana's eNsukazi homestead south of the Black Mfolozi where Lt R.B. Briscoe and thirteen men had formed a laager of seven wagons and an ambulance cart.

Being short of both food and ammunition the British did not halt, but pressed on beyond their camp of the previous night at David Louw's store, and fell back the whole way to Nkonjeni, which they reached at 10h00 on 3 June.

This reverse and ignominious retreat were devastating blows to British prestige in Zululand, and greatly encouraged the uSuthu in their resistance to British rule.

'Having retired for about a mile from the bush, we came to a fairly level piece of ground . . . The leading Usutus were now within 200 yards of us . . . I therefore dismounted the infantry on the rising ground in rear of my flanks, and charged with the two troops of Dragoons, formed as two single rank squadrons.

Owing to the long day which the horses had already gone through . . . the effect of the charge was not as great as I could have wished, the first squadron rode down and sabred several men, but the second squadron did not come into contact at all . . . The Usutu did not wait to receive our charge, but scattered right and left into the deep valleys, where the fire of the mounted infantry took good effect on them.'

(Capt E.G. Pennefather, 3 June 1888)

The Ceza Aftermath
3 – 23 June 1888

British control compromised

The British débâcle at Ceza on 2 June was followed by an instant collapse of their authority in many parts of Zululand, and a concomitant rise in uSuthu confidence. The jubilant uSuthu forces on the mountain swelled by a third to nearly 3 000. Taking advantage of the British withdrawal south of the Black Mfolozi, small groups of free-booting Boers from the New Republic joined the uSuthu in raiding Mnyamana's and Ziwedu's unprotected cattle. White storekeepers also fell victim to uSuthu raids from Ceza, and on 4 June David Louw was shot at his store at the Mfabeni hills, and on 6 June Klaas Louw was likewise killed at his store near the Vuna River. Alfred Moor's store on the Mahlabathini plain was plundered by uSuthu concentrating on Hlophekhulu Mountain under Dinuzulu's uncle, Prince Shingana kaMpande. By the middle of June the uSuthu on Hlophekhulu numbered between 400 and 1 000 men and were further bolstered when Somhlolo, the Biyela regent, joined them with his followers. Like the uSuthu on Ceza, those on Hlophekhulu provisioned themselves by raiding the 'loyal' Zulu living in the vicinity.

By the second week of June tracks in central Zululand were unsafe for unescorted wagons from attacks by concentrations of uSuthu, some operating out of

Col Henry Sparke Stabb fought in the Indian Mutiny of 1857 and in the Anglo-Zulu War. Between 1881 and 1885 he served with his regiment, formerly the 32nd Foot and now the 1st Bn, Duke of Cornwall's Light Infantry, retiring with the rank of Colonel. In September 1886 he was appointed Colonel on the Staff in Natal, and in 1887 became Officer Commanding Troops, Natal and Zululand. He died in Pietermaritzburg on 22 October 1888 of a heart attack at the early age of 53, worn out by his exertions during the uSuthu Rebellion. The photograph was taken in March 1880 at the site where the Prince Imperial of France had been killed by the Zulu on 1 June 1879. Stabb was in command of the party which, in accordance with Queen Victoria's wishes, had erected a memorial cross at the site. Stabb stands within the white-washed enclosure to the left of the cross, right hand on hip.

Killie Campbell Africana Library (C75/055)

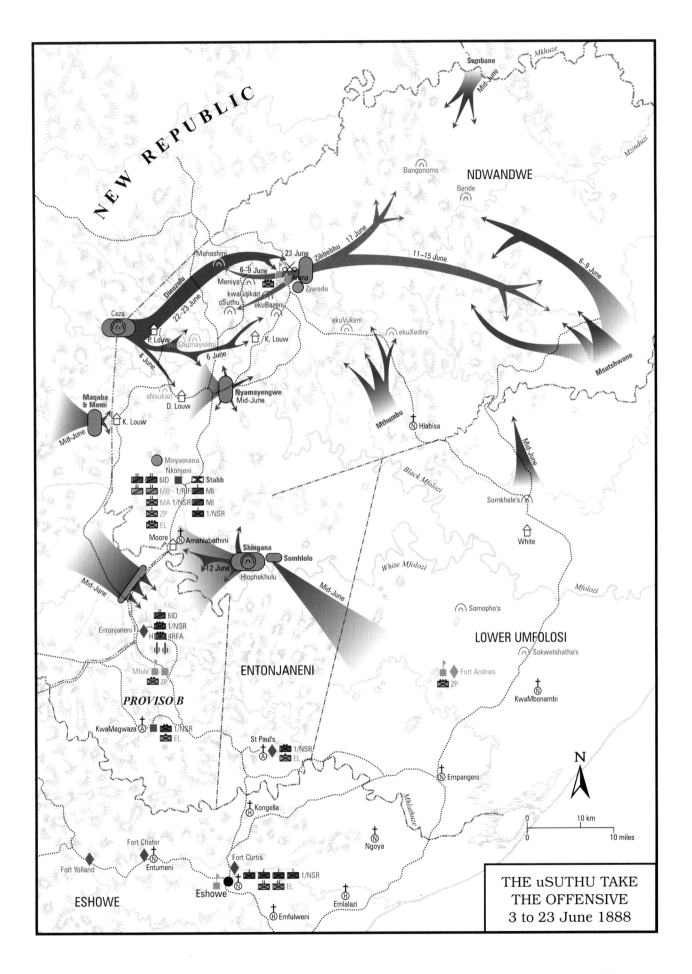

THE uSUTHU TAKE
THE OFFENSIVE
3 to 23 June 1888

> 'Early next morning [11 June 1888] a [Mandlakazi] *impi* came and surrounded the kraal . . . I heard Um-sutsh-wana [the Mdletshe chief] when he was shot, say "My father! here I am dying! what have I done?" I heard Zibebu's men who were killing him cry, "jee!" [an expression of victory over the animal or person killed]. Then Zibebu rode up . . . coming up fast on horse-back, at the time "jee" was cried, and jumped over Um-sutsh-wana and back again [as a sign of victory], being then on foot, and then he went away. Then the impi went off . . . driving cattle with them . . . The impi took away women and children.'
>
> (Nobafo, an old woman, 12 April 1889)

the New Republic. The strategic Eshowe–Entonjaneni line was only kept open through the deployment of military escorts.

British reinforcements

In these deteriorating circumstances, additional regular troops were despatched on 6 June to Zululand from the Natal garrison. By the middle of the month, British regulars were distributed between the main posts at Eshowe, Entonjaneni and Nkonjeni with smaller detachments being stationed at St Paul's and Kwamagwaza. They numbered 22 officers, 515 foot and 455 mounted men, all under the command of the Colonel on the Staff, Commanding Troops, Natal and Zululand, Col Henry Sparke Stabb. Maj A.C. McKean, 6th (Inniskilling) Dragoons and the Resident Magistrate of Nqutu, was meanwhile busy recruiting 200 Mounted Basutos in his District with the assistance of Chief Hlubi of the Tlokwa; while Melmoth Osborn, the Resident Commissioner of Zululand, busied himself raising contingents of some 1 500 to 2 000 Zulu auxiliaries in the Eshowe and Nkandhla Districts.

Zibhebhu raids the uSuthu

Zibhebhu was also active, and between 6 and 9 June from his camp on Ndunu hill (close by the Ivuna magistracy which he was supposed to help protect) plundered uSuthu *imizi* in his vicinity including Dinuzulu's oSuthu and Ndabuko's Mahashini. But while he was thus engaged, the uSuthu-aligned faction of the Mdletshe under Nkhowana kaMfuzi, as well as the Hlabisa of Chief Mthumbu kaMbopha (all of whom lived to the south-east of Zibhebhu's location) took the opportunity to raid the Mandlakazi. Inevitably, Zibhebhu retaliated and, between 11 and 15 June, six Mandlakazi *amaviyo* hit back at the Mdletshe. Then, believing that the now thoroughly provoked uSuthu intended to attack Bangonomo, his principal *umuzi*, on 17 June Zibhebhu and eight *amaviyo* patrolled north-eastwards in its defence. After a few days Zibhebhu became convinced that Bangonomo was not, after all, under threat, and returned to his camp on Ndunu hill.

The uSuthu crush the Mandlakazi at Ivuna

Zibhebhu was barely back at Ndunu hill before the uSuthu on Ceza decided to strike a daring blow against him. On the night of 22–23 June, 88 uSuthu *amaviyo* and 30 to 40 horsemen under Dinuzulu himself marched against the 15 to 18 Mandlakazi *amaviyo* in Zibhebhu's camp and utterly routed them under the very guns of Addison's fort at Ivuna.

The Battle of Ivuna (Ndunu Hill)

23 June 1888

The Ivuna post and its garrison

The post at Ivuna of the Resident Magistrate of Ndwandwe, R.H. Addison, consisted of a heliograph station manned by three British soldiers, and a circular earthwork fort with a diameter of 14 m (15 yards). The fort's parapet was sandbagged and loopholed. Around the fort ran a wide, deep ditch. About 46 m (50 yards) from the fort, and surrounding it, was a strong zariba of thornbushes. Within the enclosure were huts for the garrison of 50 Zululand Police under Sub-Inspector Jack Osborn, and a thatched mess house for the white officers, soldiers and Zululand officials (Addison and his clerk, Cuthbert Foxon). There was also a house where Addison hoped his family (who were living in Eshowe) would one day join him. Outside the zariba were a magistrate's office and a stone cattle kraal.

Below the fort, on the lower slopes of the Ndunu hill next to the Mbile stream, Prince Ziwedu kaMpande's adherents were encamped with large herds of cattle. Having been raided during May 1888 by the uSuthu concentrated on Ceza Mountain, they believed they would be safer close to Addison's post and its garrison. On 31 May Addison ordered up Chief Zibhebhu and his fighting-men to reinforce Ivuna against possible uSuthu attack. Zibhebhu's supporting force of fifteen to eighteen under-strength Mandlakazi *amaviyo* (700 to 800 men) were bivouacked in temporary shelters in the scrub bush on the slopes of Ndunu hill, 830 m (908 yards) from the fort across the marshy Mbile stream. With them were numbers of their women and children.

The uSuthu advance on Ivuna

Learning that Zibhebhu had taken no

> 'He who fought bald-headed with the assegai at Dick's.
> The wreath of smoke being the smoke of cartridges,
> Fired off by the Nongqais,
> At the Fort at Nongoma . . .
> The swift one like lightning,
> On the occasion he went to Ndunu.
> He who anticipated the sun before it rose
> At Nongoma.'
>
> (*From* Dinuzulu's praises)

special precautions against attack, King Dinuzulu and the uSuthu leaders on Ceza resolved to deliver a decisive blow against their mortal foe. Just after dusk on 22 June the entire uSuthu force on Ceza, comprising 88 *amaviyo* (or close to 4 000 men), as well as three or four Boer 'advisers' from the New Republic, set off towards Ndunu hill under Dinuzulu's personal command. In the early hours of 23 June, the uSuthu halted to rest 6 km (3.7 miles) to the north of Ivuna in the valley of the Vuna River.

During the uSuthu rebellion against British rule in 1888, Dinuzulu assumed an active and prominent part in the planning and execution of military operations, courageously fighting in the front line at both the battles of Ceza and Ivuna. In this photograph taken at the time, he is wearing an amulet necklace (or isiqu) to ward off the ritually polluting effects of killing a man in battle, and to demonstrate that he had performed deeds of valour in hand-to-hand combat.
Pietermaritzburg Archives Repository (C. 6477)

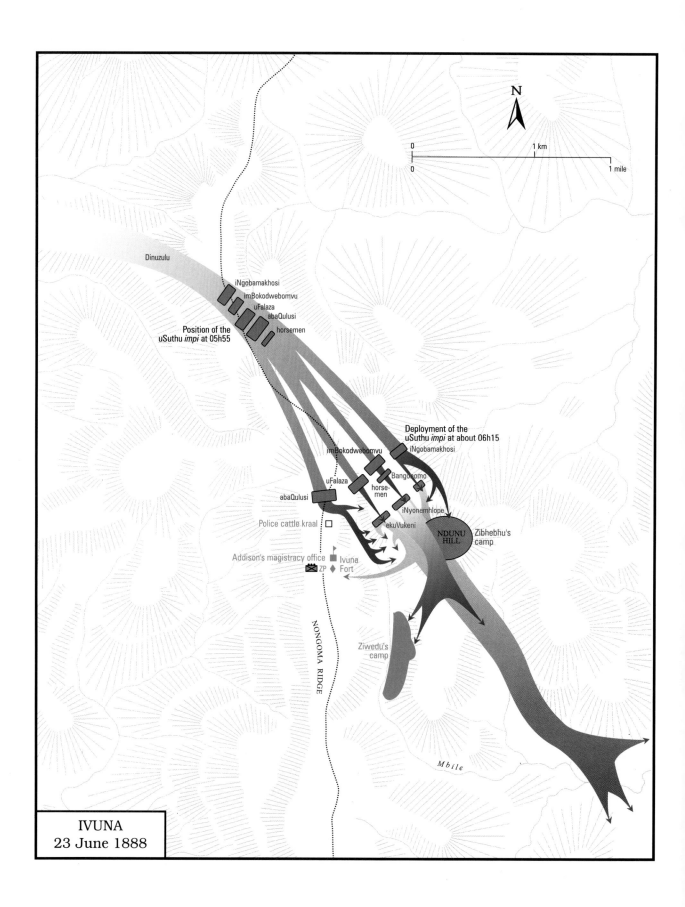

Dinuzulu

iNgobamakhosi
imBokodwebomvu
uFalaza
abaQulusi
horsemen

Position of the
uSuthu *impi* at 05h55

Deployment of the
uSuthu *impi* at about 06h15
iNgobamakhosi

imBokodwebomvu

Bangonomo

uFalaza

horse-
men

abaQulusi

iNyonemhlope

Police cattle kraal

ekuVukeni

NDUNU
HILL

Zibhebhu's
camp

Addison's magistracy office

Ivuna
Fort

ZP

Ziwedu's
camp

NONGOMA RIDGE

Mbile

IVUNA
23 June 1888

At 05h55, just before daybreak, the sentries at the fort gave the alarm that the uSuthu were approaching from the north. The officials, Zululand Police, African court messengers and a few traders and transport-riders, who had been sheltering from uSuthu depredations at the magistracy, all took refuge in the fort.

Within ten minutes of being sighted, the uSuthu force was within 1 100 m (1 203 yards) of the camp and sweeping towards it in traditional formation with skirmishers to the front of the chest and curving horns, and reserves in support. Hemulana, the Buthelezi *induna* who was Dinuzulu's councillor and a veteran of the battle of Tshaneni, had devised the strategy. While the left horn and chest wheeled to the south-east and advanced on Zibhebhu's camp, the right horn, comprising about 1 000 abaQulusi, came straight at the fort.

The Mandlakazi routed

On Ndunu hill the Mandlakazi had been taken entirely by surprise. A number ran away, but the majority rallied to face the uSuthu who outnumbered them nearly three to one. At 320 m (350 yards) the uSuthu charged, Dinuzulu leading his crack force of 30 or 40 horsemen (most of whom had firearms) at the Mandlakazi centre where Zibhebhu had deployed his best fighting-men, the iNyonemhlope. These threw back Dinuzulu's horsemen in confusion, but the uSuthu on foot were in close support and, though they wavered for a moment, their numbers soon told. The Mandlakazi flanks began to crumble

> 'When Zibepu's men were driven back, we, the policemen, fired at the other wing of the Usutus, which was near the Magistrate's house, and that wing ran down to the spruit, went down it, following the other wing which was pursuing Zibepu's men: they pursued them until they crossed the Mona, a river, and so on to the Mangwaza hill where they stopped: then they returned towards the fort, capturing Ziwedu's cattle and those of the Mandhlakazi, which were lower down in the valley of the spruit.'
>
> (Matuta, son of Ketagili, Zululand Police, 31 January 1889)

British forces
R.H. Addison, Resident Magistrate, Ndwandwe District, commanding:
Fifty Zululand Police under Sub-Inspector J.H. Osborn.
Three British troops at the heliograph station.
A few traders and transport-riders.
Total: Two officers and 53 men and a few civilians who would also have been armed

Chief Zibhebhu kaMaphitha, commanding:
Fifteen to eighteen *amaviyo* of Mandlakazi of the ekuVukeni, iNyonemhlope and Bangonomo *amabutho*.
Total: Between 700 and 800 men

uSuthu forces
King Dinuzulu kaCetshwayo, Prince Ndabuko kaMpande and Hemulana kaMbangezeli commanding:
Eighty-eight *amaviyo* of the iNgobamakhosi, uFalaza and imBokodwebomvu *amabutho*. abaQulusi and emGazini irregulars.
Some 30 to 40 horsemen, mostly with firearms.
Three or four mounted Boers 'advisers'.
Total: Approximately 4 000 men

British casualties
Killed: Nearly 300 Mandlakazi and seven of Ziwedu's adherents.
Wounded: Between 50 and 60 Mandlakazi and one of Ziwedu's people.

uSuthu casualties
Killed: Between 25 and 30, some by fire from the fort.

'I inspected the field of the fight . . . Away down the hill, towards the fort and towards the spruit, there was a tract of dead bodies, evidently where the retreating men had gone. On the hill towards the fort, out of the spruit, I saw many dead bodies . . . Most were Zibepu's men, wearing black feathers: their regiment is the Inyoni-Mhlope ("the white bird").'

(Cmdt George Mansel, Zululand Police, 25 March 1889)

and the imBokodwebomvu of the uSuthu left horn outflanked the Bangonomo on the Mandlakazi right. Taken in the rear and in fear of being surrounded, the Mandlakazi disintegrated in flight.

Meanwhile, the abaQulusi right horn came on straight at the fort. Their intention was not to attack the whites behind their impregnable defences, but to cut off the Mandlakazi line of retreat to the Ivuna camp. So, at about 550 m (601 yards) short of the fort, the abaQulusi accordingly wheeled suddenly to their left in the direction of the battle on Ndunu hill. Osborn, to prevent the abaQulusi joining the fray, ordered the Zululand Police to fire on them as they changed front. The abaQulusi rushed towards the cover offered by the steep, narrow valley of the Mbile stream. There they still succeeded in their objective of intercepting those Mandlakazi fleeing to the sanctuary of the fort and killed large numbers of them. Unable to escape across the Mbile, Zibhebhu and most of his surviving adherents fled south-east towards the Mona River 8 km (5 miles) away. The pursuing uSuthu only gave up the chase some way beyond the Mona.

The victorious uSuthu retire

Having routed the Mandlakazi and burned their huts, the uSuthu rounded up nearly 1 000 cattle grazing in the Mbile valley which belonged to Ziwedu's people who were cowering in caves and holes along the stream's banks. The uSuthu also cleaned out the Zululand Police cattle kraal of its livestock. While this was going on, the uSuthu horsemen kept up an inaccurate fire from Ndunu hill on the fort, both to dissuade any hostile intervention and to drive back a small party of mounted Zululand Police who were finishing off the wounded abaQulusi.

Once they had secured the cattle and their Mandlakazi prisoners, the uSuthu regrouped and retired. To avoid fire from the fort, they kept to the east of Ndunu hill and only turned back in the direction of Ceza 1.5 km (0.9 miles) to the north of the post. A patrol of eight Zululand Police under Corporal Mathutha followed the retiring uSuthu for some way and, after a lively skirmish with uSuthu stragglers, succeeded in recapturing about 200 cattle.

Believing Ivuna now to be untenable, the military effected the evacuation of the post on 24 June.

The Situation between the Battles of Ivuna and Hlophekhulu

24 June – 2 July 1888

'I found the country [between Ivuna and Rorke's Drift] in a complete confusion, cattle being driven in all directions, women labouring with heavy burdens of food on their heads and their children on their backs making for their strongholds.'

(Correspondent, *Times of Natal*, 12 July 1888)

The British abandon northern Zululand

On 23 June 1888, on hearing of the successful uSuthu attack on Zibhebhu at Ndunu hill, a column of 516 British troops, Mounted Basutos and Zululand Police, all under the command of Colonel Stabb, and supported by eight *amaviyo* of Mnyamana's Auxiliaries, left Nkonjeni for Ivuna to evacuate the magistrate, Dick Addison, the garrison of Zululand Police, and the survivors of Zibhebhu's forces. The column returned from Ivuna on 25 June without interference from the uSuthu. Some 200 of Zibhebhu's fighting men were allowed to remain at Nkonjeni, but 1 580 Mandlakazi women and children were sent on to the south of the colony.

While the troops were evacuating Ivuna and abandoning all the country north of

General Smyth was photographed with his staff at the British camp at Nkonjeni, having 'cast off' a telegraph to keep him in communication with his base at Eshowe and – less desirably as far as Smyth was concerned – with Havelock in Pietermaritzburg. Smyth stands slightly in front of his staff, seventh from the left. Just behind his left shoulder is his nephew, Capt R.S.S. Baden-Powell, 13th Hussars (the future hero of Mafeking and founder of the Boy Scout movement, but then celebrated as an authority on polo and pig-sticking). Since January 1888 he had been his uncle's aide-de-camp. Assistant Commissary-General E.T. Christie, the Senior Commissariat Officer in South Africa, is on the far left, and Colonel Curtis second from the right. Deputy Surgeon General J.G. Faught, the Principal Medical Officer, wearing a sun helmet, stands to the right of the line.

South African Library (INIL 930)

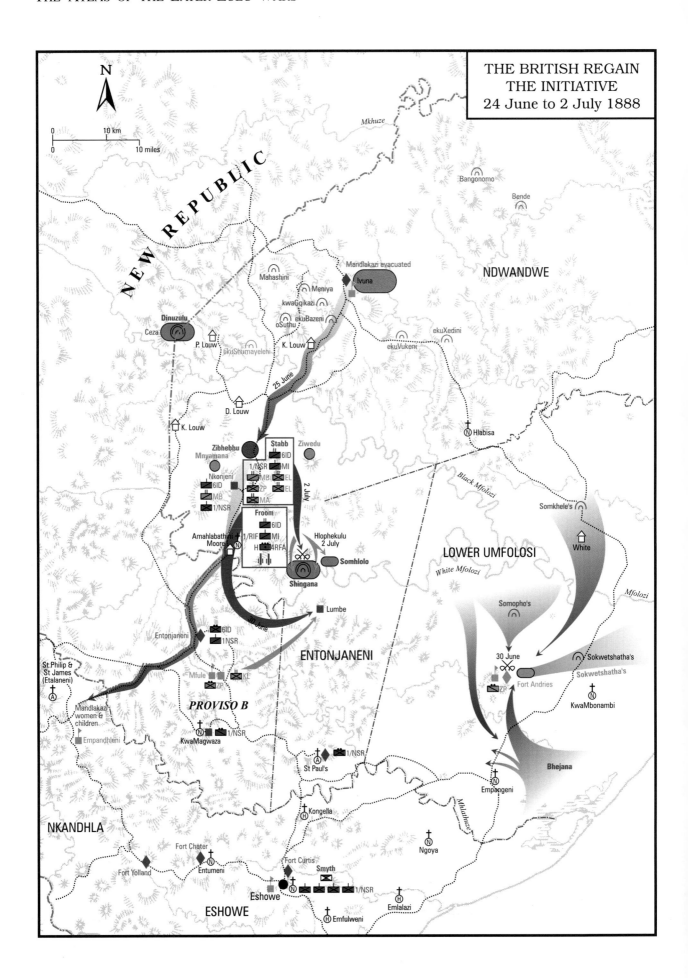

THE BRITISH REGAIN
THE INITIATIVE
24 June to 2 July 1888

N

0   10 km
0   10 miles

NEW REPUBLIC

Mkhuze

Bangonomo

Bende

NDWANDWE

Mahashini

Mandlakazi evacuated
Ivuna

Meniya

kwaGqikazi

ekuBazeni

oSuthu

ekuXedini

Dinuzulu

Ceza

P. Louw

ekuShumayeleni

K. Louw

ekuVukeni

Hlabisa

25 June

D. Louw

K. Louw

Black Mfolozi

Zibhebhu   Stabb
Mnyamana   6ID
                  1/NSR   MI
Nkonjeni   MB   EL
6ID   ZP   EL
MB   MA
1/NSR

Somkhele's

2 July

Ziwedu

Froom
             6ID
Amahlabathini 1/RIF   MI
Moore   H   4RFA

Hlophekulu
2 July

Somhlolo

LOWER UMFOLOSI

White

White Mfolozi

Shingana

Mfolozi

Lumbe

Somopho's

Entonjaneni
             6ID
             1NSR

ENTONJANENI

30 June

Sokwetshatha's

St Philip &
St James
(Etalaneni)

Mfule
        KL
        ZP

Fort Andries

Sokwetshatha's

KwaMbonambi

Mandlakazi
women &
children

Empandhleni

PROVISO B

1/NSR
KwaMagwaza

Bhejana

1/NSR
St Paul's

Empangeni

Kongella

NKANDHLA

Ngoya

Fort Chater

Fort Yolland

Entumeni

Fort Curtis

Smyth
        1/NSR

Eshowe

ESHOWE

Emlalazi

Mhlathuze

Emfulweni

the Black Mfolozi to the uSuthu, Shingana took advantage of their absence to mount an unsuccessful raid on 24 June from his fastness on Hlophekhulu against Mnyamana's cattle in the vicinity of Nkonjeni.

The parameters of civil and military authority defined

Sir Arthur Havelock, the Governor of Natal and Zululand, was forced by this general breakdown of British authority to accept that a military solution was required. However, to hand over the suppression of the revolt entirely to the military would be an admission that his civil administration had failed. He therefore desired that the troops act entirely in support of the civil authorities, and then only at their request. Lt-Gen H.A. Smyth, the General Officer Commanding in South Africa, strenuously objected to this subordination of the military to the civil authorities since he believed such an arrangement would hamper effective operations and endanger his troops. By the beginning of July, Havelock and Smyth had hammered out a compromise, though not before involving the Secretaries of State for the Colonies and for War in their acrimonious exchanges.

The General, in addition to the regular British troops of the garrison, would have command over Major McKean's Mounted Basutos and any African levies organised along military lines which the civil authorities succeeded in raising in Zululand and Natal. Osborn, the Resident Commissioner, would retain control over the Zululand Police and any chiefs and their adherents employed as auxiliaries – provided they were deployed in close co-operation with Smyth's forces. The civil authorities would remain responsible for enforcing the law and arresting the rebels, but could call on the military if necessary to provide support.

The uSuthu cleared off Hlophekhulu and the British position in central Zululand restored

General Smyth arrived in Durban from

> 'It is the duty of a governor to determine the objects with which and the extent to which HM's Troops are to be employed . . . On the other hand, the Officer in Command of the Forces will determine all Military details respecting the Distribution and Movement of Troops in conformity with the general direction issued to him by the Governor . . . And in the event of the Colony . . . becoming the scene of active Military operations, the Officer in Command of HM's Land forces assumes the entire military authority over the Troops.'
>
> (*Colonial Office List 1888: Rules and Regulations*)

Cape Town on 26 June and proceeded straight to Eshowe where, on 28 June, he assumed command of the troops in Zululand. He immediately determined to clear the uSuthu off Hlophekhulu where Shingana was reinforced on the night of 29–30 June by some of Ngobozana's Mpungose. Wet and misty weather, however, delayed the planned assualt for a few days.

On 2 July 198 British troops, 141 Mounted Basutos and 87 Zululand Police, all stationed at Nkonjeni, with 400 of Mnyamana's Auxiliaries and about 1 000 men of the Eshowe Levy, successfully stormed Hlophekhulu under the command of Colonel Stabb and drove the uSuthu off. Stabb's forces were supported from a distance by 205 British regulars with two mountain guns and the 500 men of the Entonjaneni Levy under Lt-Col A. Froom stationed on Lumbe Mountain, south of Hlophekhulu across the White Mfolozi. Froom's men had been encamped there since 30 June with the object of deterring any uSuthu movements in that direction.

The coastal uSuthu in the ascendant

While these operations were restoring the British position in central Zululand, the situation along the coast remained (from their viewpoint) less satisfactory. Between 28 June and 3 July several white traders were killed, and others had to take refuge with the Resident Magistrate of the Lower Umfolosi District, Andries Pretorius, at his post at the Ntondotha hills. Somopho and Bhejana of the emaNgweni proceeded to cut off Pretorius's communications to the south with Eshowe, and the magistrate felt constrained to seek the assistance of a local collaborator, just as Addison at Ivuna had called on Zibhebhu. Accordingly, the anti-uSuthu Mthethwa chief, Sokwetshatha, arrived with his warriors to protect the fortified post (known as Fort Andries), which consisted of two small earthworks flanking the magistracy office.

Meanwhile, the pro-uSuthu Somkhele of the Mphukunyoni, feeling threatened between the collaborationist Mandlakazi to the north and Mthethwa to the south, took refuge in the Dukuduku swamps and forests.

On 30 June 1 500 to 2 000 of Somkhele's men, plus a few hundred of Somopho's and Bhejana's, attacked Fort Andries to get at Sokwetshatha and his Mthethwa. Their assault was inept and was easily driven off by Sub-Inspector Marshall and his small force of Zululand Police. Nevertheless, the coastal uSuthu (of whom less than 2 000 remained active in the field) continued to interrupt Pretorius's communications with Eshowe, and the magistrate called for reinforcements for fear of a further attack on his post.

The uSuthu in the south contained

In the Nqutu District the staunch uSuthu leader, Mehlokazulu kaSihayo of the Qungebe, who had been supplanted by the Tlokwa in the 1879 settlement, took advantage during late June of the absence of Hlubi's Mounted Basutos at Nkonjeni to unsettle the region and to throw 'loyalists' into a state of alarm. To forestall a possible repetition of the uSuthu resistance of 1884 which had been centred in the Nkandla forest, the authorities took into preventative custody Chief Sigananda ka-Sokufa of the Cube and Chief Qethuka kaManqondo of the Magwaza, both of them uSuthu stalwarts.

'The spirit of rebellion is widespread and growing; the country is generally uneasy and astir with rumours, intrigues, and alarms, and even the well-disposed natives are afraid to show pronounced loyalty.'

(Smyth, 2 July 1888)

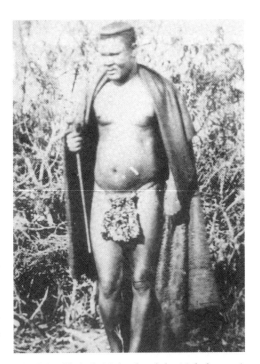

Chief Somkhele kaMalanda of the Mphukunyoni, a first cousin of Cetshwayo, dominated the Zululand northern coastal plain and lived in semi-royal style in his great umuzi *with a double row of huts and a central parade ground at least 183 m (200 yards) wide. He was appointed one of the thirteen chiefs in 1879, but rallied firmly in 1883 to Cetshwayo on his restoration. He continued to play an active part in the uSuthu cause after Cetshwayo's death, though forced on occasion to take refuge in his fastness in the Dukuduku forest. On the British annexation of Zululand in 1887 he found himself in the Lower Umfolosi District, and during the rebellion his followers joined in the unsuccessful attack of 30 June 1888 on the magistrate's fortified post. Somkhele swiftly surrendered in late July 1888 when the British sent columns of troops through his district. He was fined 1 800 cattle by Pretorius, the Magistrate of Lower Umfolosi, and the Court of the Special Commissioners sentenced him to five years' imprisonment. He was released in 1890 and the cattle fine was reduced.*

S.B. Bourquin Collection

British dispositions and lines of communication

Throughout this phase of the campaign, Fort Curtis at Eshowe remained the British base for operations in Zululand, though the greatest concentration of troops continued in a forward position at Nkonjeni. Smaller detachments continued to be stationed at Entonjaneni, Kwamagwaza and

St Paul's to ensure the security of the lines of communications and to reassure nervous wagon-drivers. These posts remained in contact with each other and headquarters at Eshowe through heliograph and limelight signalling. In turn, Eshowe was in telegraphic communication with Pietermaritzburg and Durban, keeping Havelock (on the Governor's own insistence and to General Smyth's extreme annoyance) fully appraised of operations and thus in a position to intervene daily.

The safe transport of supplies to the forward posts remained potentially hazardous because escorts of African levies, which Osborn had undertaken to raise for the purpose, had not yet materialised.

> 'At Eshowe, where I have temporarily established my headquarters, is the base of supplies, which are stored in and adjacent to Fort Curtis . . . There is much difficulty in maintaining the communications between this base and the front posts, on account of the unwillingness and alarm of the native ox drivers . . . The heliograph and limelight signalling have been generally effectively employed, but there have been interruptions by unfavourable weather of two or three days at a time.'
>
> (Smyth, 2 July 1888)

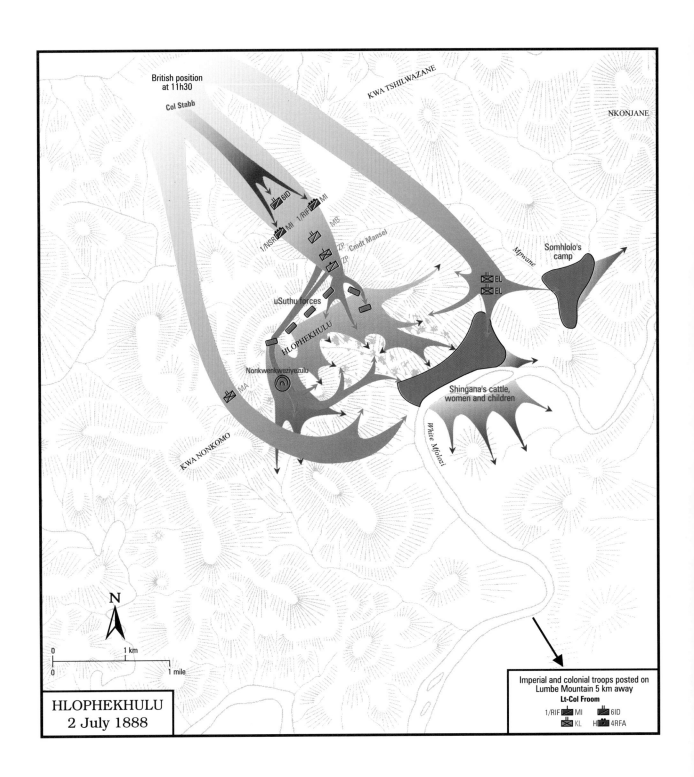

British position
at 11h30

Col Stabb

KWA TSHILWAZANE

NKONJANE

6ID

1/RIF MI

1/NSR MI

MB

ZP Cmdt Mansel

ZP

Mpwane

Somhlolo's
camp

EL

EL

uSuthu forces

HLOPHEKHULU

Nonkwenkweziyezulu

MA

Shingana's cattle,
women and children

KWA NONKOMO

White Mfolozi

N

0   1 km

0   1 mile

**HLOPHEKHULU
2 July 1888**

Imperial and colonial troops posted on
Lumbe Mountain 5 km away
Lt-Col Froom
1/RIF MI   6ID
KL   H 4RFA

The Battle of Hlophekhulu

2 July 1888

The uSuthu concentrate on Hlophekhulu Mountain

On 4 June Prince Shingana began assembling a force of about 1 000 uSuthu on Hlophekhulu Mountain in support of Dinuzulu's army on Ceza. Shingana's stronghold on Hlophekhulu, known as Nonkwenkweziyezulu, overlooked a narrow strip of land between the mountain and the White Mfolozi River where his women and children were encamped with his cattle. In mid-June the pro-uSuthu Biyela regent, Somhlolo, bivouacked south-east of Hlophekhulu with a number of his adherents, and on the night of 29–30 June Shingana was further reinforced by some of Ngobozana's Mpungose.

The British civil and military authorities march on Hlophekhulu

At 06h00 on 2 July, Dick Addison, in his capacity as the representative of the civil government of Zululand, set out from the British base at Nkonjeni for Hlophekhulu escorted by Commandant Mansel and 87 Zululand Police. He carried with him a warrant for Shingana's arrest which was, however, only a judicial fiction. For Addison wished to avoid a repetition of the earlier débâcle on Ceza on 2 June when he attempted unsuccessfully to arrest Dinuzulu. This time, he intended from the outset to request the troops accompanying him and his escort to support the Zululand Police in dispersing the uSuthu on Hlophekhulu and in seizing the cattle they had raided from 'loyal' Zulu.

Colonel Stabb was in command of the troops marching with the civil authorities. He had at his disposal 198 Dragoons and mounted infantry, 141 Mounted Basutos and about 1 400 Africans of the Eshowe Levy and Mnyamana's Auxiliaries.

British forces (under military authority)
Col H. Sparke Stabb commanding:
One squadron 6th (Inniskilling) Dragoons (5 officers and 129 men) under Capt E.G. Pennefather.
One company mounted infantry drawn from the 1st Bn, The Royal Inniskilling Fusiliers and the 1st Bn, The Prince of Wales's (North Staffordshire Regiment) (three officers, 61 men) under Capt H.G. Purdon.
One squadron Mounted Basutos (one white officer and 140 Tlokwa) under Maj A.C. McKean.
Eshowe Levy (1 000 men and five white levy leaders) under Induna Yamela and M.S. Gielink.
Total: Nine officers, five levy leaders, 330 mounted troops, and approximately 1 000 levies on foot

British forces (under civil authority)
R.H. Addison, Resident Magistrate of Ndwandwe commanding:
Zululand Police under Cmdt G. Mansel: Seventeen mounted under Sub-Inspector J.H. Osborn and 70 on foot.
Mnyamana's Auxiliaries (400 men and four white levy leaders).
Total: Two officers, four levy leaders, 87 policemen and approximately 400 auxiliaries

Supporting British force posted on Lumbe Mountain
Lt-Col A. Froom commanding:
One squadron 6th (Inniskilling) Dragoons.
One company mounted infantry drawn from the 1st Bn, The Royal Inniskilling Fusiliers.
Two mountain guns of H Battery, 4th Brigade, Royal Field Artillery.
Knight's (Entonjaneni Levy) under John Locke Knight.
Total: Two hundred and five British regulars and approximately 500 levies

uSuthu forces
Prince Shingana kaMpande commanding:
About 1 000 uSuthu fighting-men on Hlophekhulu and a number of Mpungose under Ngobozana. Some Biyela under their regent, Somhlolo, encamped to the south-east of the mountain.
Total: Approximately 1 100

British casualties
Killed: One officer of mounted infantry, two Mounted Basutos, three Zululand Police; 40 men of the Eshowe Levy and fifteen of Mnyamana's Auxiliaries.
Died: One levy leader (heart attack).
Wounded: One Zululand Policeman and three Mounted Basutos.

Zulu casualties
Killed: Between 200 and 300.

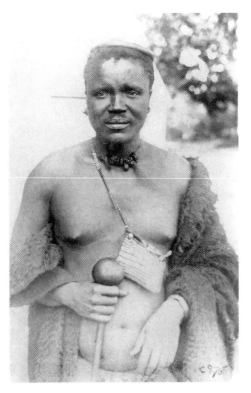

Prince Shingana kaMpande was consistently one of the leaders of the uSuthu cause during the 1880s and took up arms in 1888 in support of his nephew, Dinuzulu. He defied the British from Hlophekhulu Mountain from which he was driven on 2 July 1888. Found guilty of treason in 1889, he joined Dinuzulu and Ndabuko in exile on St Helena. Pietermaritzburg Archives Repository (C. 875)

The supporting British force on Lumbe Mountain

Stabb's men were to co-operate against Shingana with a second British force made up of a squadron of Dragoons, a company of mounted infantry and two mountain guns under the command of Colonel Froom. Froom's force had left Nkonjeni on 30 June and rendezvoused on Lumbe Mountain with the 500-strong Levy raised by John Knight, the Resident Magistrate of Entonjaneni. Lumbe Mountain faced Hlophekhulu from across the White Mfolozi, and Froom's orders were to prevent any of Shingana's men retreating across the river when attacked by Stabb. However, Froom's force lost contact with

Stabb's during the course of the action on Hlophekhulu, and played no active part in the fighting.

The British disperse the uSuthu from Hlophekhulu

Froom's arrival on Lumbe two days ahead of Addison and Stabb's advance had led Shingana to anticipate an attack from that quarter, so that on 2 July many of his men were lying in ambush south of the river. They had to be brought back hurriedly to face the fresh and unexpected British advance from the north-west which halted at about 11h30, 1.5 km (0.9 miles) from Hlophekhulu.

Stabb's first action was to despatch his African levies in two flanking movements around Hlophekhulu, the Eshowe Levy to the east and Mnyamana's Auxiliaries to the west. Once sufficient time had elapsed to allow them to take up their positions in the valleys below the mountain, the Zululand Police, supported by the Mounted Basutos, advanced over the open, narrow neck leading directly to the crest of the mountain which was held by the uSuthu. The mounted infantry stayed back on either side of the neck to prevent the uSuthu outflanking the Police and Basutos, while the Dragoons remained to the rear of the mounted infantry in support.

As they approached the uSuthu positions in the dense bush of the mountain's summit, Mansel's police deployed into a firing-line. The uSuthu could only respond inadequately to their fire with their inferior fire-arms, and soon began to waver. Mansel decided to put a swift end to the fire-fight by turning the uSuthu position. A knoll in advance of the extreme right of the firing line commanded the kloof where Shingana had his stronghold, and Mansel accordingly sent the seventeen mounted police under Sub-Inspector Jack Osborn to seize it. Some 30 uSuthu defended the knoll stoutly, and after two attempts Osborn had to retire with casualties. Mansel thereupon stormed the position with the unmounted Police and carried it with the bayonet. The dislodged uSuthu scrambled down the deep kloofs harried by the Police.

'After 10 minutes' firing the enemy's fire being silenced, Sub-Inspector Osborn with the mounted portion of the Zululand Police in ascending a high point, was fired upon by the enemy from behind stones, and had to retire with the loss of one man killed, and after two attempts to dislodge the Usutus, Commandant Mansel, moved the foot police in their support, and carried the position at the point of the bayonet, with heavy loss to the enemy, who were shot and pursued by the police down into a deep kloof, where further heavy loss was inflicted on them by both the police and the native contingents.'

(Addison, 5 July 1888)

> 'The operation on Hlopekulu was in my opinion judiciously conceived, and for the most part vigorously carried out; it inflicted a severe blow on the rebel gathering, but it did not reap absolute and conclusive success, owing, in a large measure, to the unmanageable character of the native levies.'
>
> (Smyth, 7 July 1888)

Forced down to the strip of land between the mountain and the river where they had their camp, the uSuthu fought hand-to-hand with their pursuers among the stampeding cattle.

Meanwhile, the Basutos advanced to the top of Hlophekhulu to support the Police, and the Dragoons moved up the neck to their former position. Daunted, the remainder of the uSuthu along the crest began to disperse in every direction. The fugitives collided with the black levies and auxiliaries already positioned in the valleys either side of the mountain. Though the Eshowe Levy was at first repulsed with losses, it rallied and completed the rout of the uSuthu, including Somhlolo's people who were encamped to the east of Hlophekhulu.

The victorious British retire

Since it was now afternoon, and Stabb's objective of driving the uSuthu off Hlophekhulu had been achieved with complete success, he rallied his troops and withdrew towards Nkonjeni. The retiring levies and auxiliaries drove 1 000 or more captured cattle with them. During the night the last uSuthu abandoned their boltholes on Hlophekhulu, and Shingana himself fled to sanctuary in the New Republic.

> 'The native levies from Eshowe District, who were under the general command of Chief Yamela and European leaders, rendered good service on the north-eastern side of Hlopekulu, where they encountered the main portion of Tshingana's men, a hand-to-hand fight ensued in which the Eshowe men compelled the retreat of their opponents with very great loss.'
>
> (Osborn, 11 July 1888)

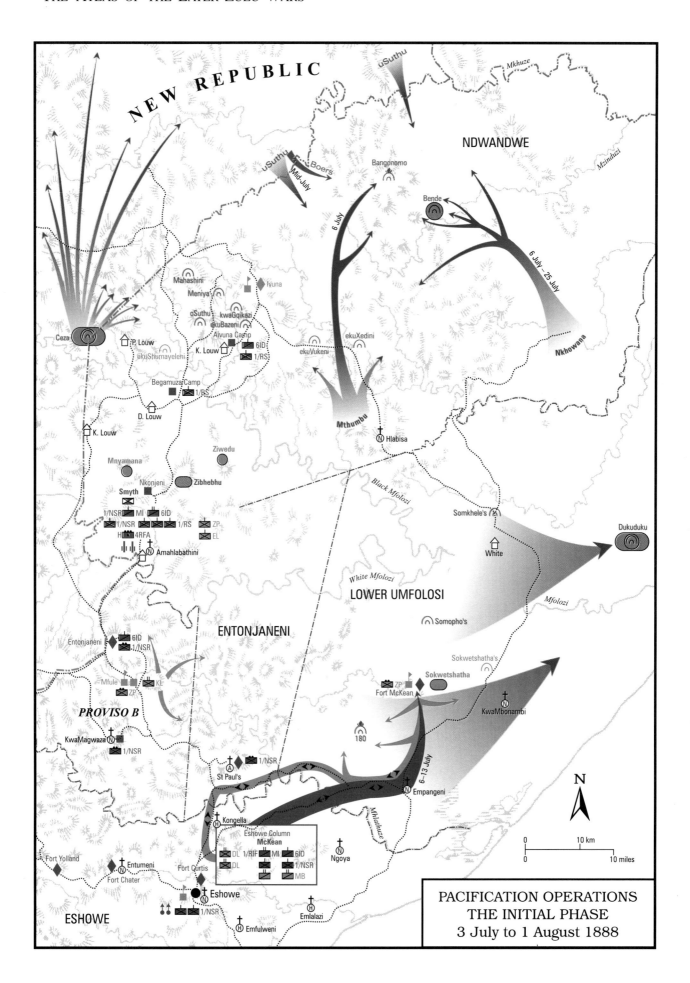

PACIFICATION OPERATIONS
THE INITIAL PHASE
3 July to 1 August 1888

Pacification Operations (1)

3 July – 1 August 1888

Operational options

The battle of Hlophekhulu on 2 July 1888 was the last engagement of any significance during the uSuthu Rebellion. Henceforth, British operations had the objectives of dispersing the rebels still in the field, pacifying the Colony of Zululand and re-establishing the civil administration. Although it made political sense to strike immediately at Dinuzulu on Ceza Mountain, the precarious position of Andries Pretorius, the Resident Magistrate of Lower Umfolosi, who was beleaguered by the uSuthu, made it necessary first to march to his relief. The evident earlier mistake of withdrawing Addison from Ivuna, and thus abandoning all of northern Zululand to the uSuthu, was not to be repeated. The relieving force would bring with it additional arms and ammunition, and would help to ensure that Pretorius remained at his post.

Operations of the Eshowe Column

On 6 July Major McKean accordingly formed the Eshowe Column at Camp Kongella to relieve Fort Andries at Pretorius's magistracy, which was garrisoned by 40 Zululand Police and 300 of Sokwetshatha's Mthethwa. The column was made up of troops drawn from both Eshowe and Nkonjeni, and consisted of 251 British regulars, 180 Mounted Basutos and about 2 000 of John Dunn's Native Levy (500 of whom remained south of the Mhlathuze as border guards). The various elements of the column set off on 7 July and rendezvoused the next day, when six uSuthu *amaviyo* were encountered and easily thrown back. The column relieved Pretorius's post on 9 July and replaced Fort Andries with a military earthwork, named Fort McKean, garrisoned temporarily by the 180 Mounted Basutos. About 1 000 of Dunn's Levy raided the

'A little forward action and I am quite prepared to see the whole thing burst like a pricked bubble. You [General Smyth] seem to find it impossible to make a movement from Nkonjeni until the movement to Mr Pretorius's station has been completed . . . Hope former will follow immediately on latter.'
(Havelock, 9 July 1888)

Officers and British regulars of the Eshowe Column photographed in the field. They marched in early July 1888 to relieve Andries Pretorius, the Resident Magistrate of the Lower Umfolosi District, who was blockaded in his post by uSuthu forces. Seated in foreground, third from the left: Capt C.T. Breton of the 6th (Inniskilling) Dragoons; Major McKean of the same regiment who was in command of the column; Captain Baden-Powell; and Lt J.H.R. Cox, 6th (Inniskilling) Dragoons. Note the variety and casualness of dress typical on campaign, and the sun helmets stained brown.

South African Library (INIL 931)

'I request you [Osborn] to forbid, as a general rule, the practice of burning kraals . . . I do not consider it a judicious means of inflicting punishment for offences committed by British subjects living within British territory. I think recourse to it should be limited to cases in which it appears necessary for the safety of the troops or of the police.'
(Havelock, 7 August 1888)

hills to the south-east and destroyed deserted *imizi*.

On 11 July the column commenced its return to Eshowe in three divisions. The British regulars kept to the main road while the Basutos scoured the country to the south-west and Dunn's Levies moved between the two detachments. The column returned to Eshowe on 13 July having encountered no opposition on the way, and having burned 180 deserted *imizi* as they went. All the uSuthu in their path had done their best to remove their cattle and families to Somkhele's stronghold at Dukuduku.

The uSuthu attack the Mandlakazi in north-eastern Zululand

Meanwhile, in north-eastern Zululand, on 6 July the pro-uSuthu Mdletshe under Nkhowana and the Hlabisa under Mthumbu seized the opportunity to burn Bangonomo, the absent Zibhebhu's main *umuzi*, and to threaten Bende, his fastness. Unchecked by the scattered and demoralised Mandlakazi, they roamed Zibhebhu's location until early August, lifting cattle. Opportunistic Boers from over the Transvaal border encouraged them and joined in their activities.

Nqutu pacified

The Nqutu District, where the pro-uSuthu Mehlokazulu of the Qungebe had been active, was quiet once more.

The levies lose discipline

The British began to experience difficulties with the African levies they had raised on account of inadequate rations, poor pay, their failure to receive their promised share of the cattle confiscated from the uSuthu, and a dearth of white levy leaders qualified to instil military discipline. By 14 July all but 150 of the Eshowe Levy had deserted from Nkonjeni; while the levy which had been raised by John Knight, the Resident Magistrate of Entonjaneni, went out of control on 18 July at his magisterial post at Mfule, burning *imizi* of 'loyal' Zulu all about and rustling 300 cattle. Even the Mounted Basutos were showing

signs of disaffection on account of lack of supplies for themselves and forage for their horses now that the winter grazing had run out at Nkonjeni.

The uSuthu in central Zululand begin to disperse

The uSuthu in central Zululand, meanwhile, especially those from across the Phongolo, were beginning to disperse, and it was mainly the abaQulusi who remained on Ceza with Dinuzulu.

The British prepare for conclusive joint operations

Now that Pretorius's post had been secured, the next British objective was to re-establish civil authority in Ndwandwe, which required a forward movement by the military. During late July reinforcements of British regulars continued to move up to Nkonjeni. By 25 July there were a total of 73 British officers, 1 937 men and 560 horses deployed in central Zululand and at the coast in support of the Zululand Police, Mounted Basutos and various African levies raised by the civil authorities. Preparatory to establishing advanced posts which would need to be supplied, on 15 July Colonel Stabb began sending out reconnaissances and work gangs to repair the roads. On 25 July Stabb established a post across the Black Mfolozi from Nkonjeni called the Aivuna Camp, and on 29 July an intermediate post (the Begamuza Camp). Aivuna was intended as a base for mounted reconnaissances beyond the Black Mfolozi, and for future joint operations with McKean's forces at the coast. With the intention of co-ordinating such operations, on 1 August General Smyth moved his headquarters forward from Eshowe to Nkonjeni. He was now increasingly beyond the reach of the telegraph wire and, with it, Havelock's regular instruction on how to conduct the campaign.

Pacification Operations (2)
23 July – 10 September 1888

The Coastal Column advances to Ivuna

On 23 July 1888 Major McKean formed a new column of 312 British regulars and 180 Mounted Basutos at the Umlalazi Camp on the Zululand coast. The purpose of the Coastal Column was to sweep north along the coastal plain, accepting uSuthu submissions as it went. General Smyth intended that this movement would also prevent Dinuzulu from leaving Ceza to join Somkhele in his Dukuduku stronghold. Once it had pacified the coast, McKean's column was to swing north-west to co-operate with Smyth in an attack on Ceza.

On 25 July the column joined with Dunn's Native Levy of 48 *amaviyo* (or 2 400 men) which had mustered at the lower Mhlathuze drift. The levies were accompanied by C.R. Saunders, Resident Magistrate of Eshowe, who represented the civil authorities.

The flooding of the Mfolozi River held up McKean's Coastal Column for a couple of days, but on 28 July it finally crossed and encamped on the northern bank at Camp Umfolosi, sending out the call for surrenders. McKean reinforced his summonses with the ruthless burning down of *imizi* of uSuthu accused of trying to cut his lines of communications. Havelock strongly deprecated this practice, but it had its desired effect. At the approach of the British the cowed emaNgweni and Mphukunyoni abandoned their stronghold at Dukuduku, much to the relief of McKean who had not believed that his column was strong enough to attack it without the support of gunboats on Lake St Lucia and along the coast.

Somkhele and various Mphukunyoni *izinduna* duly surrendered on 30 July at Camp Umfolosi and were sent to the Res-

ident Magistrate, Andries Pretorius. The next day he fined Somkhele and his people 2 000 cattle and five individual *izinduna* 100 head each for their participation in the insurrection. Many of the emaNgweni and their leaders, however, took refuge with their cattle in the broken terrain of the Hlabisa district: Somopho in the Nhlati hills; Lokothwayo in the Mpembe hills; and Bhejana in the Yome bush.

On 1 August General Smyth ordered the Coastal Column to proceed to Ndwandwe except for Dunn's Levy, who were left to collect the cattle fines. (Dunn's men completed this assignment by 6 August and returned to the Eshowe District on 8 August.) On 2 August the Coastal Column resumed its march, living off captured cattle and looted grain pits. Mounted abaQulusi, Boers and emaNgweni were seen scavenging in the area, but did not interfere with McKean's forces. The Hlabisa and Mdletshe people were returning to their homes after their recent depredations in Mandlakazi territory, but fled again on the approach of the column. The squadron of Dragoons, whose presence was not proving necessary, left the column on 3 August and returned directly to the Entonjaneni Camp.

> 'The surrender of Somkeli was most fortunate, as on our arrival in his district the officer commanding the column [Major McKean] found the force at his disposal was not sufficient to attack the stronghold [Dukuduku], and had Somkeli not given himself up, the troops were to move on to N'dwandwe . . . This course would have been attended with the most disastrous results, as all the people would have been more convinced than ever that their stronghold was impregnable, and the district [Lower Umfolosi] would have been in a more disturbed state than ever.'
>
> (C.R. Saunders, Resident Magistrate of Eshowe, 9 August 1888)

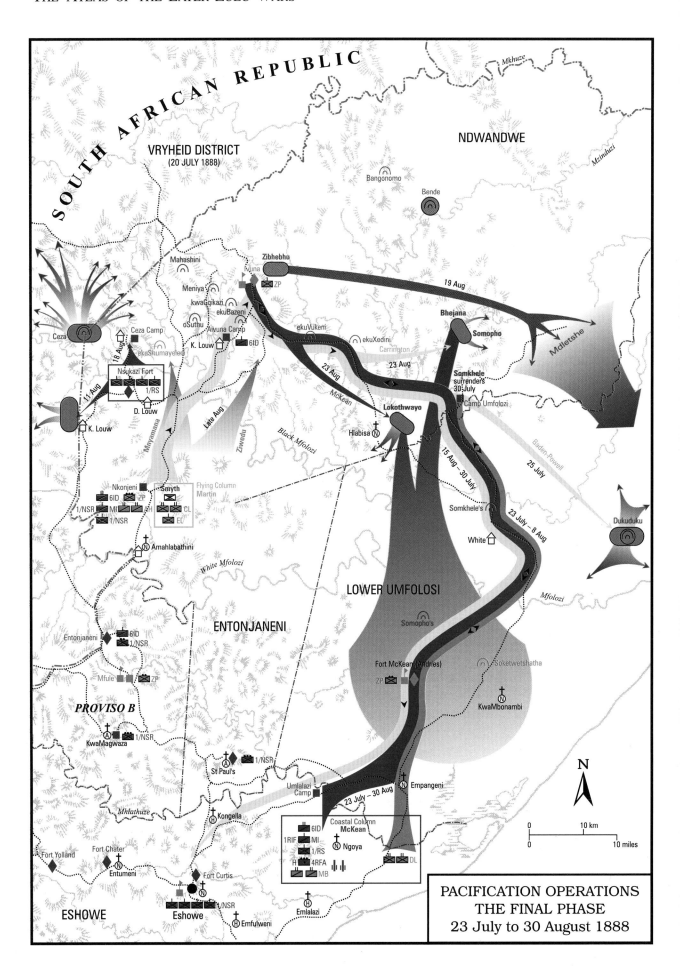

PACIFICATION OPERATIONS
THE FINAL PHASE
23 July to 30 August 1888

The Coastal Column joined at Ivuna by the Flying Column

The reduced Coastal Column reached the Ivuna magistracy on 6 August when McKean immediately made epaulements for the guns at the fort and laagered the wagons for defence. The following day Colonel Martin's Flying Column arrived at Ivuna from Nkonjeni. It consisted of 1 760 levies under Col Sir Frederick Carrington, KCMG (including Zibhebhu and 200 of his Mandlakazi who had taken refuge at Nkonjeni after the battle of Ivuna, and 150 of Yamela's men who had not deserted on 14 July from Nkonjeni with the rest of the Eshowe Levy). Carrington had been in command of the Bechuanaland Police since August 1885, and on account of this experience, and his previous commands in South Africa as a dashing leader of mounted infantry, had been recruited by General Smyth to bring some organisation and discipline to the demoralised levies.

Discipline was nevertheless not of the best at Ivuna, and between 8 and 20 August the Mounted Basutos, who had been short of rations and forage for weeks, raided all around for food, their victims including 'loyal' Africans, such as Ziwedu's people. The Nkonjeni garrison also acted against its African allies, though by mistake. On 11 August scouts and uSuthu clashed at Dlebe Mountain, and the next day Capt R.S.S. Baden-Powell (General Smyth's nephew and Acting Assistant Military Secretary) led a punitive expedition inadvertently over the border into the territory of the South African Republic, killing twelve 'loyal' Buthelezi and taking fifteen prisoner.

The uSuthu on Ceza disperse

During 6–7 August, believing that their situation on Ceza had been rendered untenable by the greatly increased British presence in Ndwandwe, Dinuzulu and Ndabuko disbanded the remnants of the

St Paul's Anglican mission, situated on the great Nkwenkwe spur overlooking the plains to the south through which the Mhlathuze and Mfule rivers meander, was a strategic point on the dangerous and winding track between Eshowe and the heart of Zululand. On 28 July 1879 the Royal Engineers began a small redoubt on the hill adjacent to the mission building, which men of the 90th Light Infantry garrisoned until the end of September 1879. On Zululand becoming a British colony in 1887, the post was again garrisoned by various detachments of British troops stationed in Zululand in order to secure this main route from Eshowe to the Ndwandwe District. Troops moving north to the epicentre of the uSuthu disturbances during 1887 and 1888 would regularly halt at St Paul's after the toilsome ascent. The photograph shows the 6th (Inniskilling) Dragoons in camp there in 1888. The Dragoons had formed part of the Natal garrison since January 1881, and played an active part in operations and garrison duty in Zululand from September 1883 until they sailed back to England in November 1890 . Pietermaritzburg Archives Repository (C. 253)

'I had a report from Dinizulu last night, from which I understand that his army is altogether broken. They no longer have any intention to take up arms against the English Government. And he begs me to settle the matter for him . . . My answer to Dinizulu is that he is a British subject, that I have nothing to do with him, and that I defy him to come or trespass over the boundary line of the Transvaal.'

(P.M. Bester, Field-Cornet, Ward [No. 3], South African Republic, 2 August 1888)

uSuthu forces still on the mountain. They themselves and some 22 of their followers made for hoped-for sanctuary in the South African Republic, evading the Border Guard which, under the command of Border Commissioner Lukas Meyer (the former President of the New Republic), had been engaged since late July in co-operating with the British in preventing the uSuthu from crossing the frontier. The rest of the uSuthu on Ceza dispersed to their homes in British Zululand.

The British consolidate their hold on Ndwandwe

The British increased their hold on north-western Zululand with the establishment of the Nsukazi Fort on 9 August between Ceza and Ivuna (despite the site being unsuitable because of the thick bush), and with the reinforcement of the Nkonjeni garrison on 12 August by the 150 men of Addison's Horse under the command of Capt Charles B. Addison, the younger brother of Dick Addison.

The joint Coastal and Flying Columns march back to Eshowe

On 15 August General Smyth and his staff left Nkonjeni for Ivuna preparatory to the joint march of the Coastal Column and the Flying Column through the still disaffected regions north of the Black Mfolozi, and then on through the Lower Umfolosi District to Eshowe. With the joint columns' departure from Ivuna on 18 August, the Nsukazi Fort and the Begamuza Camp were abandoned in favour of Peter Louw's store nearer Ceza Mountain. Commandant Mansel and the Zululand Police left Ivuna for Nkonjeni, and those levies and Mounted Basutos not required during the march to the coast were disbanded by 23 August.

The joint column left Ivuna on 18 August and reached Eshowe on 30 August, when the levies still embodied were disbanded. During the course of the march the few remaining centres of uSuthu resistance were eliminated. On 23 August Colonel Carrington left on a night march to the Nhlati hills to capture Somopho's

imizi. The chief had fled a few days previously, and his adherents, after firing harmlessly on Carrington's force, dispersed. During the same night Major McKean marched to the Mpembe hills where he too was fired on by Lokothwayo's people. In the skirmish the uSuthu were dispersed and Lokothwayo killed. Captain Baden-Powell reconnoitred the Dukuduku fastness, but found it deserted.

Since the countryside he had traversed was clearly pacified, Smyth withdrew the posts still at Fort McKean (Andries) and at the middle drift across the Mhlathuze. On 27 August Addison reoccupied his post at Ivuna with 100 Zululand Police under Sub-Inspector Pierce. Since all the uSuthu in Ndwandwe had left their refuges and submitted by the end of August, the loyalists Mnyamana and Ziwedu now felt it sufficiently safe to return with their adherents to their imizi north of the Black Mfolozi.

Zibhebhu's last fling

The indefatigable Zibhebhu, whose levies were officially disbanded on 23 August, continued to create disturbances. On 19 August he and ten amaviyo of Mandlakazi attacked Nkhowana of the Mdletshe and Mthumbu of the Hlabisa (who had burned his Bangonomo umuzi and had been harrying the Mandlakazi around his stronghold at Bende) killing up to 50 people. The survivors withdrew towards St Lucia, and retaliated on 10 September with a raid against the Mandlakazi. Havelock, seeing that Zibhebhu was bringing the settlement of Zululand into jeopardy, had him arrested on 17 November. Finally, on 1 August 1889, the exasperated Governor decreed that in the interests of the future harmony of Zululand, Zibhebhu could not be allowed to return to Ndwandwe.

The Distribution of the Zululand Garrison

September – December 1888

The Zululand garrison reduced to its normal level

Military operations in Zululand were over by the end of August 1888 and, since the situation seemed settled north of the Black Mfolozi, General Smyth could find no justification for the expense of maintaining his troops at their advanced posts, especially since he was concerned about their health in the coming rainy season. He therefore ordered that all advanced posts in Ndwandwe be given up by 30 September, and the men redistributed to the garrisons of regular troops at Entonjaneni and Eshowe. Moreover, those troops no longer required in Zululand were instructed to return to their regular garrisons in Natal.

By 2 November the Zululand garrison was reduced to its 'normal' level of one squadron of the 6th (Inniskilling) Dragoons and two companies of mounted infantry drawn from the 1st Bn, The Royal Scots (Lothian Regiment). The 250 Zululand Police, seven sub-inspectors and commandants were distributed by December to the magisterial posts of the Eshowe, Ndwandwe, Lower Umfolosi and Entonjaneni Districts, as well as to the posts at Nkonjeni and Mahashini (Ndabuko's *umuzi* near Ivuna). Their headquarters remained at the Nongqai Fort in Eshowe. On 7 September General Smyth and his staff sailed for Cape Town, their mission accomplished.

The surrender and sentencing of the uSuthu leadership and the punishment of their followers

The role of the soldiers being over, the capture and punishment of Dinuzulu and the uSuthu leadership was a matter for the civil authorities. It was not a difficult

> 'Dinuzulu, we find you guilty of high treason. After a patient hearing of your case we are justified in saying to you that we are convinced. . . . you were endeavouring to regain that power to which the annexation by Her Majesty had put an end and that your intention was to overthrow the existing form of government in Zululand. You are sentenced by this Court to imprisonment for ten years.'
>
> (Mr Justice Walter T. Wragg, President of the Court of the Special Commissioners for Zululand, 27 April 1889)

undertaking. With their defeated supporters scattered back to their homes, the leaders of the uSuthu Rebellion gave themselves up to the civil authorities: Ndabuko on 17 September; Shingana on 6 November; and Dinuzulu on 15 November. They, and other uSuthu prominently implicated in the late rebellion, stood trial in Eshowe between 13 February and 27 April 1889. The Special Court of Commission found Dinuzulu, Ndabuko and Shingana guilty of high treason and public violence, and sentenced them respectively to ten, fifteen and twelve years' imprisonment, to be served on the Atlantic island of St Helena.

Their followers paid the price in lost lives and destroyed *imizi*, as well as in cattle fines which, between May 1887 and May 1889, amounted to 3 376 seized (though 799 were returned to Somkhele). Most of the confiscated cattle were issued as rations to the African levies in the field, with the remainder being sold by public auction for the benefit of the Zululand treasury.

The uSuthu Rebellion thus suppressed, the Zululand officials were left with the difficult task of restoring Zulu confidence in their administration.

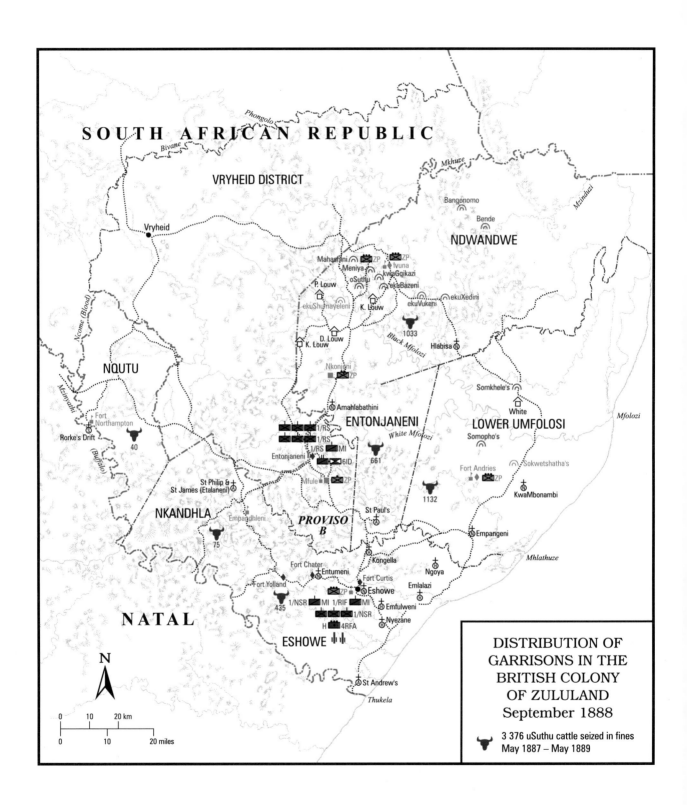

SOUTH AFRICAN REPUBLIC

VRYHEID DISTRICT

NDWANDWE

NQUTU

ENTONJANENI

LOWER UMFOLOSI

NKANDHLA

PROVISO
B

NATAL

ESHOWE

N

0   10   20 km

0   10   20 miles

DISTRIBUTION OF
GARRISONS IN THE
BRITISH COLONY
OF ZULULAND
September 1888

3 376 uSuthu cattle seized in fines
May 1887 – May 1889

With the failure of the uSuthu Rebellion, Dinuzulu initially sought sanctuary in the South African Republic. Learning he was to be handed over to the British, he fled back to Zululand. Evading the attempts the authorities made to apprehend him, he crossed into Natal at Rorke's Drift and then took the train at Elandslaagte for Pietermaritzburg, thus submitting to Harriette Colenso's advice to surrender. In the early hours of 15 November 1888 he arrived at Bishopstowe, the Colenso's house outside the city. Taken into police custody, he was sent to Eshowe to stand trail for high treason. The Court of the Special Commissioners for Zululand duly found him and other uSuthu ringleaders guilty in April 1889. With the confirmation of their sentences on 18 December 1889, Dinuzulu and his uncles were removed to St Helena to serve their sentences. Each was allowed one male attendant, and Ndabuko and Shingana, as married men, were permitted the company of one wife each. The unmarried Dinuzulu was conceded two women from his household. The illustration from the Graphic *shows them and their accompanying women leaving the Eshowe jail under guard by the Zululand Police. They are all attired in European dress for their journey into exile. In January 1898 Dinuzulu was returned to Zululand as part of a general settlement to restore stability to the region. However, he came back not as a king, but simply as a 'Government Induna'. He was nevertheless still perceived by many Zulu as their legitimate ruler, and the British were reluctantly forced to exploit his continuing standing during the Anglo-Boer War of 1899–1902 to raise Zulu levies to defend Zululand against Boer incursions. Dinuzulu was controversially charged with being implicated in the 1906 Rebellion, and was imprisoned and stripped of all his remaining powers by the Natal authorities. In 1910, with the Union of South Africa, Prime Minister Louis Botha commuted Dinuzulu's sentence to exile on the farm Rietfontein in the Middelburg District of the Transvaal. There Dinuzulu died on 18 October 1913, and his body was carried to the emaKhosini, the valley of kings in the very heart of the old Zulu kingdom, to lie among his royal ancestors.*

Graphic, 29 March 1890

On 10 December 1907 Dinuzulu was formally arraigned at the Court House in Nongoma for his alleged involvement in the recent 1906 Rebellion and in continuing unrest in the Province of Zululand. Nothing was calculated better to demonstrate the powerlessness to which the heir of the Zulu royal house had been reduced when confronted with the authority of the colonial state. News of Dinuzulu's arrest spread quickly among his followers, and many leading Zulu from the surrounding district congregated at Nongoma to find out what the colonial officials intended doing with the man they forlornly still regarded as their king. The photograph shows several small groups of men disconsolately waiting for information of the proceedings. Note that they are all wearing various forms of European clothing and headgear for, only 20 years after the annexation of Zululand, it had already become inappropriate – even in the remote uSuthu Location No. 1 created in 1891 to separate Dinuzulu's closest adherents from the Mandlakazi – to appear in the proximity of the magistrate's office wearing traditional dress. Pietermaritzburg Archives Repository (C. 25/5)

PART VI
Conclusion

'A period of peace ensued, during which the house of Zulu had no share in the
direction of affairs.'
(J.Y. Gibson, magistrate in Zululand and historian, 1911)

The Significance of the Zulu Wars of 1883–1888

The military implications

The Anglo-Zulu War of 1879 continues to commandeer considerable academic and popular attention. Nevertheless, it is in itself incomplete, for its true significance can only be assessed in conjunction with the after-shocks of the lesser wars of 1883–1888. Certainly, the campaigns of the 1880s were not on the scale of that of 1879, but in their diversity and intensity they are of interest in themselves to military historians. They are, moreover, of key importance in completing and rendering irreversible the political, social and economic processes the Anglo-Zulu War had begun.

It is true, though, that the pivotal consequences of the Zulu wars of the 1880s were not entirely matched by similarly key military implications. In none of the engagements in Zululand during the 1880s – whether between Zulu factions (with or without the involvement of Boers or white mercenaries), or between the Zulu and British regulars and auxiliaries – is there much indication of military innovation. Zulu military culture was too deeply ingrained ideologically and socially, and the suddenness and disruptive impact of the British invasion of 1879 too severe and recent, for the Zulu to have embarked on the steep and rapid learning-curve necessary to adjust a style of warfare previously effective in pre-colonial African conditions to meet the new Western challenge. Typical of nineteenth century colonial campaigns, military encounters between the Zulu and British remained crucially asymmetrical with marked differences in weapons, weapon systems (the means of delivering and sustaining force), organisation and tactics. Where some Zulu commanders did begin to make somewhat better use of modern firearms and horses (often in conjunction with white mercenaries or Boer allies oper-

ating as mounted infantry), this made an appreciable difference only in encounters with other, even more conventionally composed and led Zulu forces. Limited innovations of this nature simply were not sufficient even to dent the overwhelming British military ascendancy in the Zululand theatre, and the occasional, limited success the Zulu enjoyed was more at the expense of African police and levies than against British regulars. Nothing in the nature of operations in Zululand during the 1880s caused the British to deviate from or improve upon the standard and well-tried procedures for waging colonial 'small wars'.

Not that the wars of the 1880s were that small. While it is estimated that in excess of 6 000 Zulu died in battle during the Anglo-Zulu War of 1879, about a half to two-thirds of that number were killed during the military engagements of the 1880s, mainly during the civil war. Moreover, in these later wars, considerably more men of status lost their lives than in 1879, which caused much greater disruption to the continuity and effectiveness of Zulu political structures. The casualties suffered by the British, Boers and African police and levies were negligible, however, especially when compared with those of 1879.

Civilian sufferings were far worse in the wars of the 1880s than during the British invasion of 1879. In 1879, even though the British destroyed Zulu crops and *imizi* and drove off livestock in order to induce civilians to submit, there were exceedingly few occasions when the British committed atrocities against the non-combatant population. Besides which, British operations were limited through logistical difficulties and lack of mounted troops to relatively confined theatres, so that much of the country was spared their depredations. In

> 'The destruction of old men which occurred on this occasion [the battle of oNdini] rendered it difficult afterwards to find those in the country who could supply from memory accounts of the incidents of the nation's progress.'
>
> (Gibson, 1911)

contrast, the campaigns of the 1880s, which were waged intermittently over several years (and not confined to a concentrated period of several months, as in 1879), ranged over every corner of Zululand. Since it was the deliberate policy of the Zulu belligerents to drive their opponents' civilian population from their homes, to devastate their fields, empty their grain stores and capture their livestock, the extent of destruction and the total number of civilian deaths (though unknowable) would certainly have enormously exceeded those of the Anglo-Zulu War. During the 1880s civilians and their livestock had to take sanctuary for months on end in their mountain or forest fastnesses, suffering terrible privations while their enemies systematically ravaged their lands; whereas in 1879 civilians were usually able to return to their homes only days or weeks after the advancing British columns had passed. Indeed, there can be no doubt that the immediate impact of the wars of the 1880s on the fabric of Zulu society was considerably more damaging than that of the campaign of 1879.

The consequences of collaboration and resistance

After the initial large-scale military engagements of 1879 and the political settlement that followed the violence, the British (whether they confined themselves to the role of a practically absentee overseer, or intervened more directly administratively and militarily) had to deal with a Zulu population that remained entirely in place. There had been no substantial, or even partial extirpation or expulsion in 1879 of the indigenous people; nor was there the immediate introduction of a large settler population and infrastructure. Indeed, the British initially prohibited the opening of Zululand to white settlement. This meant that for the British to assert any political influence over the affairs of Zululand, or to exercise any effective military control in a situation where, for reasons of economy, the prolonged presence of regular troops or the maintenance of a large para-military police force could

never be entertained, much rested on the ability to create co-operative indigenous structures of authority, and to win and retain local support as a military resource.

Yet the problem with collaborators (necessary as they might seem) is that by influencing the pattern of pacification, they determine the response of the colonial administration. So whether when dealing with uSuthu resistance to the thirteen appointed chiefs, with a restive and resentful Cetshwayo after his restoration, or with Dinuzulu withholding co-operation in British Zululand, all the British and colonial officials involved in Zulu affairs between 1879 and 1888 were liable to have their judgement warped by viewing the problems of the country through the eyes of self-serving collaborators whose survival depended on thwarting uSuthu aspirations. Officials were concomitantly blind to the fact that the good fortune of their cosseted agents rankled bitterly with less adaptable or less fortunate traditionalist leaders, who naturally extended their antagonism to the colonial administration as a whole.

The 1880s in Zululand consequently make for a fascinating study in the politics of collaboration and resistance. An unusually extended time-span elapsed between initial Zulu defeat in 1879 and the ultimate division of the former kingdom in 1887 between the Boers of the New Republic and the British. When the latter did finally take responsibility for the rump of Zululand, it was thus over a polity long acquainted with the destructive colonial presence and the excision of territory, yet unprepared for a fully-fledged colonial administration's intrusive intervention in the lives of its subjects.

The instinctive reaction of those affected by colonial rule was a traditionalist yearning towards familiar patterns of authority, rather than a striving for novel means of extruding the unwelcome colonial presence. The revolt of 1888 was consequently a last, futile attempt to assert Zulu independence. It also took the form of what is now known as a colonial 'post-pacification revolt' in that it was typically

'Today Zululand is no longer Zululand, it is Natal, ruled by the English, the original government having passed away and a new one taking its place. The rule of Zulu has disappeared.'

(Magema M. Fuze, the first Zulu to write a history of his people, 1902)

haphazard, uncoordinated and subject to the vagaries of fragmented local leadership, and because it collapsed at the first concerted show of real force by the British.

What gave a peculiarly bitter edge to hostilities in 1888 was the unreserved reliance of the Zululand officials on Zibhebhu and other collaborators who had been the bane of the royalists during the recent civil war, and whom they naturally regarded with the deepest resentment, suspicion and fear. The Zululand administration was eventually compelled through force of evidence to admit that employing such collaborators had been nothing less than an unfortunate mistake, and that they had been a major contributing cause, rather than the solution, to persistent unrest in Zululand.

A significant consequence of the 1888 revolt was therefore the removal of Zibhebhu as an active player in Zulu affairs (despite the continuing personal support of many of the Zululand officials whose cause he had served), and the search for a genuine solution to the interminable uSuthu–Mandlakazi strife. A new boundary delimitation of 1891 succeeded in physically separating the two factions, and this territorial settlement received the necessary political underpinning in 1898 with the superficially amicable return of both Dinuzulu and Zibhebhu to their respective re-delimited locations.

The political effects

That Zululand did not go the preferable route of some neighbouring African kingdoms, and become a British protectorate like Basutoland in 1884 and Swaziland in 1907, but was instead incorporated into white-ruled South Africa, was a direct consequence of the war of 1879 and the related developments of the 1880s.

Since the settlement which Wolseley imposed in September 1879 permitted the traditional Zulu homestead economy to continue functioning as before, as well as the existing patriarchal social order under its chiefs, the short-term effects of the Anglo-Zulu War were essentially political. The abolished Zulu monarchy and the *ibutho* sytem which sustained it were not

Harriette Colenso was the eldest daughter of John Colenso, the first Anglican Bishop of Natal, and called 'Dlwedlwe', or 'the staff of her father' by the Zulu. Bishop Colenso, or 'Sobantu', 'father of the people', antagonised many colonists and officials by his championing of the indigenous people, his protests against the injustice of the Anglo-Zulu War and his efforts to have the exiled Cetshwayo restored to his kingdom. Colenso died in 1883 and his mantle fell on Harriette, who for many years had collaborated closely with him. Harriette was best known for her unstinting advocacy of Dinuzulu's cause as Cetshwayo's successor, and her excoriation of the colonial officials and their Zulu collaborators whom she blamed for Zululand's descent into bloodshed. She played a prominent part in organising the defence of Dinuzulu and other accused at the treason trials that followed the uSuthu Rebellion of 1888, and spent many subsequent years in Britain actively campaigning and pamphleteering to secure Dinuzulu's pardon. When Dinuzulu, who had returned to Zululand in 1898, was arrested for his role in the 1906 Rebellion, Harriette once again rallied his legal defence. She was held in both abhorrence and fear by the Zululand officials whose policies she so trenchantly criticised, and whose bias and mismanagement she relentlessly exposed. In contrast, she was looked upon with admiration and gratitude by many Zulu, just as her father had been, for her part in resisting the forces of imperialism. In her frail, but obsessively determined person she embodied many of the tensions and contradictions of those troubled times in Zululand, though in the longer term a subsequent age has come to recognise the truth in many of her didactically expressed opinions.

Pietermaritzburg Archives Repository (C. 776)

replaced by a viable alternative system of authority. Indeed, it was Wolseley's objective to leave Zululand divided, weak and no threat to its colonial neighbours. However, the nominal but disruptive supervision which Britain continued to exercise over the affairs of Zululand predictably failed to dowse the inflammable situation its policies had created. The former kingdom was wracked by the vicious civil wars Wolseley's settlement had spawned, and was then partially devoured by land-hungry Boers who seized their opportunity in the prevailing chaos. It was more to thwart the territorial aspirations of the Boer New Republic and also of its colonial rival, Germany, than to remedy its disastrous mishandling of Zululand since 1879 that, in 1887, Britain finally annexed the remnants as a colony.

The failed rebellion of 1888 against the new colonial administration left the Colony of Zululand in a very uneasy state. On 20 December 1897 the British government permitted its incorporation into the Colony of Natal as the Province of Zululand. This was part of a general settlement to pacify Zululand, and also to accommodate the Natal settlers who, for decades past, had been coveting the territory's mineral and agricultural potential. When on 31 May 1910 the British Colony of Natal became one of the four provinces of the new Union of South Africa, it consequently brought with it into the Union not only the Province of Zululand, but also the former Zulu territory of the Vryheid District of the former South African Republic, which had been annexed to Natal on 27 January 1903 following the Anglo-Boer War.

Thus all the lands ruled over on the eve of the Anglo-Zulu War by the Zulu kings were drawn in as part of a single South Africa. However, they were now governed by the representatives of a series of white administrations who, for many decades to come, ensured that the Zulu royal house remained in political eclipse.

Labourers photographed with bread on trolleys at the De Beers compound in 1905. In that same year, 7 083 passes were issued to men from the twelve magisterial districts of the Colony of Natal formerly comprising the Zulu kingdom to work as migrant labourers outside the boundaries of Natal, mainly on the mines. Although records were not similarly kept of those Zulu living within the Province of Zululand who were employed in Natal itself (particularly in Durban and Pietermaritzburg), magistrates reckoned that they amounted to some ten per cent of the estimated total population of about a quarter of a million. This estimate did not include the thousands more, particularly women, who went into domestic service in white households. Less than 20 years after falling under colonial rule, therefore, the majority of Zulu adults were already regularly integrated as labour into the economy of an industrialising southern Africa. Pietermaritzburg Archives Repository (C. 1232/96)

Social and economic repercussions

If Dinuzulu and his heirs chafed at their lost political status, their former subjects laboured under increasing disabilities. The settlement of 1882 had placed the southern part of Zululand (the Reserve Territory) under colonial officials who funded their administration through the imposition of a hut tax, as already levied in Natal. With the proclamation of the Colony of Zululand in 1887, the hut tax was extended to the rest of Zululand outside the New Republic, and continued to be levied (with additional taxes) once Zululand was incorporated into Natal in 1897. To pay these taxes, the young men of Zululand, who before 1879 had served their king in their *amabutho*, were forced to seek work as migrant labourers in the mines, factories and harbours and on the railways of an industrialising South Africa. Already, by 1904, 17 000 Zulu were employed outside the Province of Zululand. Migrant labour and the introduction of a money economy upset traditional domestic and kinship relationships and modified cultural patterns and practices.

Traditional structures of authority were also eroded. As Zululand was brought under British administration during the 1880s, white colonial officials usurped and overlaid the age-old functions of chiefs which had initially been left untouched by the 1879 settlement. By the late 1880s chiefs had been reduced to nothing more than salaried and subordinate officials of the colonial state, and this caused them progressively (as was the intention) to forfeit the respect and obedience of their people, who turned instead to their real masters, the white magistrates.

And the Zulu also lost much of their land. The British victory in 1879 was not followed by white settlement in Zululand. Nor was it permitted in terms of the settlement of 1882. Nevertheless, a major consequence of the civil wars was Dinuzulu's alienation in 1884 of a third of Zululand in return for Boer aid against Zibhebhu. At one stroke, all the Zulu living in what became the New Republic found themselves expropriated and trans-formed into tenants of white farmers since no land was set aside as reserves for their exclusive occupation. As landless tenants, they were required to pay substantial rents to the new landowners, or to render labour services. In the British Colony of Zululand, except for a limited number of mission stations and trading stores, no white settlement was allowed, and the Zulu remained in occupation of the land. But as part of the deal the British struck with the settler government of Natal in 1897 in return for the incorporation of Zululand as a province, the territory was at last thrown open to white settlement. In October 1904 the Zululand Lands Delimitation Commission set aside 40.2 per cent of the Province of Zululand for white purchase. Some of the Zulu living on this land were permitted to remain as tenants on the new farms, but the rest were removed to the African reserves made up of the remaining (and less agriculturally valuable) 59.8 per cent of land in Zululand.

Conclusion

The Zulu wars of the 1880s, of military interest in themselves, crucially accelerated and consummated the processes of political, social and economic change set in motion by the Anglo-Zulu War. Inexorably, the bitter conflicts and rivalries of these years led to the further fragmentation and weakness of Zululand, which in turn invited growing intervention by its colonial neighbours and by Britain, the paramount power of the region. The fundamental and long-lasting consequences were devastating for the Zulu in every way, for they lost their political independence, most of their land and much of their traditional way of life, and were reduced to wage-earners or tenants in a white-controlled South Africa. The wars of the 1880s are thus epochal, marking for Zululand the definitive transition from the pre-colonial to the modern world. That a strong, living sense of Zulu national and cultural identity has nevertheless survived into the twenty-first century is all the more remarkable for that.

Quotation References

PART I

p. 1 (top) Webb and Wright, *Stuart Archive*, vol. 5, p. 272; (bottom) Webb and Wright, *Stuart Archive*, vol. 5, p. 198.

p. 4 *British Parliamentary Papers* [*BPP*] (C. 3466), enc. in no. 79.

p. 6 *BPP* (C. 4191), enc. in no. 70.

p. 7 (top) *Court of the Special Commissioners for Zululand* [*CSCZ*], p. 260; (bottom) *CSCZ*, p. 290.

p. 8 Government House Zululand, papers in the Pietermaritzburg Archives Repository [GHZ] 685, no. 142.

p. 10 *Natal Witness*, 11 August 1887.

p. 12 War Office, *Précis*, p. 27.

p. 16 *CSCZ*, p. 264.

p. 17 War Office, *Précis*, pp. 40–1.

p. 20 *BPP* (C. 4191), enc. 2 in no. 16.

p. 22 *BPP* (C. 4191), enc. in no. 70.

p. 23 *BPP* (C. 5522), enc. in no. 53.

p. 24 *BPP* (C. 5522), no. 49.

p. 26 *BPP* (C. 6684), enc. 1 in no. 1.

p. 27 *BPP* (C. 5331), enc. 3 in no. 2.

p. 29 *BPP* (C. 5331), enc. 2 in no. 9.

PART II

p. 31 Campbell, *With Cetywayo*, p. 11.

p. 34 Preston, *Wolseley's Journal*, pp. 104–5.

p. 38 (top) Colonial Office correspondence, microfilms in the Pietermaritzburg Archives Repository, [CO] 179/138, no. 15682; (bottom) Colenso, *Digest*, series no. 2, p. 409.

PART III

p. 41 *Natal Mercury*, 1 April 1883.

p. 43 Pridmore, 'Diary of Fynn', vol. II, p. 24.

p. 45 Pridmore, 'Diary of Fynn', vol. II, p. 64.

p. 49 (top) Pridmore, 'Diary of Fynn', vol. II, pp. 73–4 ; (bottom) Pridmore, 'Diary of Fynn', vol. II, pp. 74–5.

p. 50 (top) *BPP* (C. 3705), enc. in no. 39; (bottom) Pridmore, 'Diary of Fynn', vol. II, p. 110.

p. 53 Pridmore, 'Diary of Fynn', vol. II, p. 128.

p. 55 Cope and Malcolm, *Izibongo*, p. 206.

p. 57 (top) Colenso, *Digest*, series no. 2, p. 819; (bottom) *BPP* (C. 3864), enc. 2 in no. 51.

p. 58 (top) *BPP* (C. 3864), enc. 3 in no. 49; (bottom) Pridmore, 'Diary of Fynn', vol. II, pp. 150–1.

p. 59 *BPP* (C. 3864), enc. 2 in no. 59.

p. 60 (top) *BPP* (C. 3864), enc. 4 in no. 66; (bottom) Pridmore, 'Diary of Fynn', vol. II, p. 175.

p. 62 (top) *BPP* (C. 3864), enc. 9 in no. 81; (bottom) *BPP* (C. 3864), enc. 12 in no. 98.

p. 64 *BPP* (C. 4037), enc. 1 in no. 44.

p. 65 *BPP* (C. 4037), enc. 1 in no. 104.

p. 69 (top) *BPP* (C. 4037), no. 79; (bottom) *BPP* (C. 4191), enc. 3 in no. 46.

p. 71 *BPP* (C. 4191), enc. in no. 70.

p. 73 (top) *BPP* (C. 4272), enc. in no. 10; (bottom) *BPP* (C. 4191), enc. 10 in no. 81.

p. 74 *BPP* (C. 4214), enc. 3 in no. 54.

p. 76 *BPP* (C. 4214), enc. 1A in no. 43.

PART IV

p. 77 *BPP* (C. 4913), no. 1.

p. 79 *BPP* (C. 4214), no. 60.

PART V

p. 81 *BPP* (C. 5331), enc. 2 in no. 37.

p. 83 (top) *BPP* (C. 4913), enc. 7 in no. 13; (bottom) *Natal Mercury*, 8 July 1887.

p. 84 Colenso Collection (Pietermaritzburg Archives Repository), box 101: 11 October 1887.

p. 85 (top) GHZ 845: 19 August 1887; (bottom) Colenso Collection, box 106: evidence given on 22 December 1888.

p. 87 (top) Zululand Archives, papers in the Pietermaritzburg Archives Repository [ZA] 5, no. R105/88; (bottom) *BPP* (C. 5522), enc. 1 in no. 6.

p. 88 *Natal Mercury*, 22 February 1888.

p. 89 GHZ 716, no. Z767/88: 19 October 1888.

p. 90 War Office, *Précis*, p. 15.

p. 92 (top) Samuelson, *Long, Long Ago*, p. 286; (middle) *CSCZ*, p. 761; (bottom) *CSCZ*, p. 676.

p. 93 *BPP* (C. 5522), enc. 2 in no. 38.

p. 96 *CSCZ*, pp. 801–2.

p. 97 Samuelson, *Long, Long Ago*, p. 285.

p. 99 *CSCZ*, p. 262;

p. 100 *CSCZ*, pp. 667–8.

p. 101 *Times of Natal*, 12 July 1888.

p. 103 *Colonial Office List 1888*, pp. 304–5.

p. 104 *BPP* (C. 5522), enc. 1 in no. 60.

p. 105 *BPP* (C. 5522), enc. 1 in no. 60.

p. 108 *BPP* (C. 5522), enc. 1 in no. 66.

p. 109 (left) *BPP* (C. 5522), enc. in no. 75; (right) *BPP* (C. 5522), enc. 4 in no. 66.

p. 111 War Office, papers in the Public Record Office [WO] 32/7838, file 079/6962.

p. 112 *BPP* (C. 5892), enc. 4 in no. 4.

p. 113 *BPP* (C. 5892), enc. 3 in no. 9.

p. 116 *BPP* (C. 5892), enc. in no. 10.

p. 117 *BPP* (C. 5892), enc. 1 in no. 170.

PART VI

p. 121 Gibson, *Story of the Zulus*, p. 316.

p. 122 Gibson, *Story of the Zulus*, p. 258.

p. 124 Fuze, *Black People*, p. 146.

Section References

The references to the text and/or map in each section into which this atlas has been divided are restricted to the major printed primary and secondary sources. These alone are considerable, with the pertinent dispatches and enclosures in the *British Parliamentary Papers (BPP)*, for example, taking up several thousand pages. Readers wishing to delve into the large collections of germane unpublished private and official sources (many of them fortunately printed in the *BPP*) should consult the bibliographies and the footnotes to the relevant pages of the theses (published and unpublished) cited below, as well as the footnotes to the scholarly articles and chapters in books. The references to those sections describing a military engagement have been recorded more completely than is otherwise the case.

PART I

Introduction
Colenso, *Ruin of Zululand*, vol. II, pp. 384–5; Laband, *Rope of Sand*, pp. 28, 139–40, 168.

Zulu Military Organisation and Fighting Techniques during the 1880s
Although admitting that by 1894 the Zulu military system was 'completely disorganised', the War Office, *Précis*, pp. 80–1, 111–15 detailed how the Zulu army operated before 1879 because, in the event of an uprising, it was expected that the Zulu would 'attempt to re-establish the system as it existed before'. Since then, only Knight in *Zulu Army*, pp. 250–3 and Thompson in 'Isandlwana to Mome', pp. 13–14 have attempted to analyse the Zulu army during the 1880s. This chapter is consequently the product of my reflections on the subject based on the events of the 1880s as detailed in the succeeding sections of this book. For the Zulu military system in 1879 when it was still fully operational, see Laband and Thompson, *Anglo-Zulu War*, pp. 9–19.

British, Colonial and Boer Forces in Zululand during the 1880s
By the 1880s the British and colonial military systems had not developed much since the Anglo-Zulu War, during which campaign they were described in Laband and Thompson, *Anglo-Zulu War*, pp. 21–30. The limited lessons the British military drew from the 1879 campaign for future operations in Zululand are to be found in War Office, *Précis*, pp. 36, 39–41, 47–78, 125–42. The classic treatise on colonial campaigning is Callwell, *Small Wars, passim*. A recent account of changes in the 1880s to uniforms, weapons and the British way of colonial warfare is in Knight, *Go to Your God Like a Soldier*, pp. 131–2, 142–90, 195–200, 204–6. Spiers, 'The Late Victorian Army' remains invaluable, as does Strachan, *European Armies and the Conduct of War*, pp. 76–89: 'Colonial Warfare'. Also see Porch, 'Imperial Wars' for a masterly overview. Otherwise, this section, like the preceding one, is based on my cumulative impressions of how military operations were conducted in Zululand during the 1880s.

Zulu and British Military Strategy in Zululand during the 1880s
Again, my comments are the result of my examination of how the various campaigns of the 1880s unfolded. However, War Office, *Précis*, pp. 7–16, 26–7 should be consulted, as well as Callwell, *Small Wars, passim*.

Boundaries and Colonial Control in Zululand
Correspondence and reports on various boundaries the British assigned to Zibhebhu's location during the 1880s can be found in *BPP* (C. 3705), no. 36 and enc 1–4; *BPP* (C. 6684), no. 1 and encs 1–7. The issue is discussed in detail in Laband, 'British Boundary Adjustments and the uSuthu–Mandlakazi Conflict in Zululand', *passim*. For Boer boundaries imposed on Zululand, see the references below to Part IV, The Boer Land-Grab, 1884–1888.

Collaborators and Colonial Officials
For the role of collaborators in Zululand during the 1880s, see Guy, *Zulu Kingdom*, pp. 80–3; Laband, 'Dick Addison', pp. 2–10, 222–5; Laband, 'Zululand Administration', *passim*; Laband and Thompson, 'Reduction of Zululand', pp. 207–8; Laband, *Rope of Sand*, pp. 380–2.

PART II

The Partition of the Zulu Kingdom
BPP (C. 2482), no. 88 and encs 1–2; nos 93–6 and encs; encs 1–6 in no. 157; no. 187; *BPP* (C. 2505), no. 12 and enc.; no. 16 and enc.; no. 58 and enc.; *BPP* (C. 2584), enc. in no. 66; enc. in no. 75; Colenso, *Ruin of Zululand*, vol. I, pp. 2–10; War Office, *Précis*, pp. 91–2; Gibson, *Story of the Zulus*, pp. 218–22; Binns, *Last Zulu King*, pp. 179–81; Guy, *Zulu Kingdom*, pp. 69–78; Ballard, *John Dunn*, pp. 141–3, 146–57; Laband, 'Cohesion of the Zulu Polity', pp. 58–62; Laband and Thompson, 'Reduction of Zululand', pp. 201–7; Laband, *Rope of Sand*, pp. 334–9.

The Partition of Zululand
BPP (C. 2695), enc. in no. 18; no. 20 and encs 1–2; no. 25; no. 33 and enc. 1; no. 35; no. 43 and enc.; *BPP* (C. 3182), nos 14–17 and encs; nos 28–

31 and encs; nos 34–36 and encs.; no. 41; nos 43–44 and encs; no. 46; enc. in no. 49; nos 52–3 and encs; no. 55; nos 59–60 and encs; no. 63; no. 65; no. 67; enc. in no. 71; nos 75–78 and encs; nos 80–88 and encs; enc. in no. 93; nos 100–109 and encs; *BPP* (C. 3247), no. 1 and enc.; no. 3 and encs 2–3; enc. in no. 10; enc. in no. 17; no. 55 and encs 1–3; no. 58 and encs 1–2; no. 63; no. 68 and enc.; nos 72–74 and encs; nos 78–79 and encs; nos 83–84 and encs; nos 87–91 and encs; *BPP* (C. 3270), no. 1 and encs 1–2; nos 3–5 and encs; no. 7; *BPP* (C. 3293), nos 1–3 and encs; *BPP* (C. 3174), no. 8; *BPP* (C. 3466), enc. 2 in no. 5; no. 7 and enc. 1; no. 16 and encs 1–2; enc. in no. 18; nos 21–22 and encs; no. 25 and encs 1–2; no. 28 and encs 1–4; nos 36–37; nos 41–42 and encs; nos 48–50 and encs; enc. in no. 53; encs 1–2 in no. 58; nos 60–61 and encs; no. 69 and encs 1–3; encs 1–3 in no. 75; nos 79–80 and encs; enc. in no. 84; nos 88–95 and encs; no. 106 and encs 1–2; no. 108; no. 114; no. 117; enc. 2 in no. 122; enc. in no. 126; nos 133–139 and encs; no. 145 and encs 1–27; nos 149–158 and encs; Colenso, *Ruin of Zululand*, vol. I, pp. 12, 17, 28–53, 92–240, 252, 293; vol. II, pp. 2–37, 72–97, 102–258, 264–70, 278–88; War Office, *Précis*, p. 92; Fuze, *Black People*, pp. 115–17; Gibson, *Story of the Zulus*, pp. 222–39; Binns, *Last Zulu King*, pp. 182–99; Guy, *Zulu Kingdom*, pp. 98–118, 124–44, 148–64; Ballard, *John Dunn*, pp. 188–218; Laband and Thompson, 'Reduction of Zululand', pp. 208–9; Laband, *Rope of Sand*, pp. 346–53.

PART III

The Msebe Campaign

BPP (C. 3466), no. 151; encs 1–3 in no. 159; encs 1–2 in no. 161; *BPP* (C. 3616), nos 8–11 and encs; nos 15–19 and encs; nos 22–26 and encs; nos 28–31 and encs; nos 35–37 and encs; nos 41–42 and encs; nos 44–46 and encs; nos 49–50 and encs; nos 52–58 and encs; nos 66–72 and encs; nos 77–79 and encs; no. 86; enc. 4 in no. 87; *BPP* (C. 3705), no. 8 and encs 1–2; no. 13 and enc.; encs 1–2 in no. 22; Pridmore, 'Diary of Fynn', vol. II, pp. 1–64: 29 January – 30 March 1883; Colenso, *Ruin of Zululand*, vol. II, pp. 289–412, 434–72, 493–7; War Office, *Précis*, pp. 92–3; Gibson, *Story of the Zulus*, pp. 239–46; Binns, *Last Zulu King*, pp. 200–6; Guy, *Zulu Kingdom*, pp. 167–79, 183–91; Laband and Thompson, 'Reduction of Zululand', pp. 209–12; Laband, *Rope of Sand*, pp. 355–7.

The Battle of Msebe

Pridmore, 'Diary of Fynn', vol. II, pp. 73–5: 4 April 1883: statement by Ntangweni son of Nobengula; *BPP* (C. 3705), enc. 1 in no. 3: statements by Nsaba, 10 April 1883, and Marwanqa and Matiya, 12 April 1883; enc. in no. 39: statement of Thomas Edwin Peachey, 27 April 1883; *BPP* (C. 3864), enc. in no. 9: statements by Maqondiyana, Lagatyana and Nongai, 14 June 1883; Colenso, *Digest*, series no. 2, pp. 534–5: extract

from the *Natal Mercantile Advertiser*, 7 April 1883; Colenso, *Digest*, series no. 2, pp. 562–8: extract from the *Natal Mercury* by Herbert Nunn, 28 April 1883; pp. 575–6: messenger from Cetshwayo; pp. 630–1: Cetshwayo to Colenso, 6 April 1883; A. Xaba, 'Before and After Umsebe Battle', Dr Killie Campbell's Essay Competition, 1842; Gibson, *Story of the Zulus*, pp. 247–9; Guy, *Zulu Kingdom*, pp. 191–3; Laband, *Rope of Sand*, pp. 357–9.

From Msebe to oNdini

BPP (C. 3616), no. 87 and encs 1, 3; *BPP* (C. 3705), nos 3–4 and encs; no. 6; nos 9–10 and encs; encs 1–6 in no. 12; nos 14–16 and encs; nos 23–26 and encs; nos 28–29 and encs; nos 38–44 and encs; no. 48; no. 51 and encs 1–3; nos 54–61 and encs; *BPP* (C. 3864), enc. 2 in no. 2; no. 5 and encs 1–3; enc. in no. 7; enc. in no. 9; nos 11–13 and encs; nos 17–21 and encs; no. 23; no. 26 and encs 1–2, nos 27–29 and encs; nos 34–37, encs 1–4, 7–10 in no. 38; no. 47 and encs 1–2; no. 71 and enc.; no. 85 and encs 1–6; *BPP* (C. 4037), no. 11; Pridmore, 'Diary of Fynn', vol. II, pp. 66–141: 31 March – 21 July 1883; Colenso, *Ruin of Zululand*, vol. II, pp. 497–500; War Office, *Précis*, p. 93; Gibson, *Story of the Zulus*, pp. 250–4; Binns, *Last Zulu King*, pp. 206–8; Guy, *Zulu Kingdom*, pp. 193–200; Laband, *Rope of Sand*, pp. 359–60.

The Battle of oNdini

Pridmore, 'Diary of Fynn', pp. 140, 146, 148, 150–1, 161–4, 166: 21, 24, 30 July, 2, 23, 27 August 1883; *BPP* (C. 3864), encs 3, 9, 12, 13, 14, 16 in no. 38; enc. in no. 39: Osborn to Bulwer, 25 July 1883; enc. in no. 71: Fynn to Bulwer, 23 August 1883; Colenso, *Digest*, series no. 2, pp. 780–3: Walton; pp. 815–20: Darke; pp. 820–2: uSuthu; pp. 823–5: Cetshwayo; Webb and Wright, *James Stuart Archive*, vol. I, p. 125: Dunjwa kaMabedhla; vol. III, pp. 203–4: Mkebeni kaDabulamanzi; vol. IV, pp. 185–6, 199–9, 193: Ndabazezwe kaQubabanye; Samuelson, *Long, Long Ago*, pp. 120–1; Fuze, *Black People*, pp. 117–18; Gibson, *Story of the Zulus*, pp. 255–8; Guy, *Zulu Kingdom*, pp. 201–4; Laband, *Rope of Sand*, pp. 360–5; Knight, *Great Zulu Battles*, pp. 165–80.

From the Battle of oNdini to the Death of Cetshwayo

BPP (C. 3864), nos 32–33 and encs; encs 5, 11–22 in no. 38; nos 40–42 and encs; no. 44 and encs 1–11; nos 48–54 and encs; nos 59–61 and encs; no. 63; nos 65–69 and encs; nos 68–69 and encs; nos 72–73 and encs; no. 78; nos 80–82 and encs; nos 86–94 and encs; nos 97–99 and encs; nos 101–102 and encs; nos 106–113 and encs; nos 115–117 and encs; no. 121; nos 123–126 and encs; nos 129–130 and encs; no. 132; nos 134–138 and encs; nos 140–142 and encs; nos 145–147 and encs; nos 151–154 and encs; nos 160–166 and encs; *BPP* (C. 4037), no. 3; nos 8–9A and encs; nos 13–17 and encs; no. 20 and enc. 1; nos 24–26 and encs; nos 30–31 and encs; nos 37–40 and encs; no. 43 and encs 1–3; enc. in no. 46; Pridmore, 'Diary of Fynn', vol. II, pp. 144–60, 164–84, 195–214: 22 July – 27 September, 29 October – 22 December 1883; War Office, *Précis*, pp. 93–4; Fuze, *Black People*, pp. 119–21; Gibson, *Story of the Zulus*, pp. 259–66; Binns, *Last Zulu King*, pp. 208–13; Guy, *Zulu Kingdom*, pp. 204–9; Laband and Thompson, 'Reduction of Zululand', p. 212; Laband, *Rope of Sand*, pp. 367–8.

From the Death of Cetshwayo to the Battle of Tshaneni

BPP (C. 4037), nos 44–45 and encs; nos 48–51 and encs; no. 53; nos 55–56; nos 59–63 and encs; nos 65–68 and encs; no. 70; nos 72–76 and encs; nos 84–86 and encs; nos 88–93 and encs; nos 95–99; nos 101–106 and encs; nos 108–114; *BPP* (C. 4191), nos 1–2; enc. in no. 3; nos 7A–14 and encs; nos 16–23 and encs; nos 26–28 and encs; nos 30–32; nos 34–35; nos 37–39; nos 43–48 and encs; nos 52–54 and encs; no. 55A; nos 59–60 and encs; nos 62–65 and encs; enc. 1 in no. 66; nos 67–68 and encs; War Office, *Précis*, pp. 94–5; Fuze, *Black People*, pp. 121–4; Gibson, *Story of the Zulus*, pp. 267–70; Binns, *Dinuzulu*, pp. 7–34; Van Zyl, 'Uitbreiding van Britse Gesag', pp. 119–32; Guy, *Zulu Kingdom*, pp. 217–26; Laband and Thompson, 'Reduction of Zululand', pp. 212–13; Laband, *Rope of Sand*, pp. 369–72.

The Battle of Tshaneni

BPP (C. 4191), enc. in no. 70: Usibebu, 13 June 1888; John Eckersley, 13 June 1888; (C. 4214), no. 13: Bulwer to Derby, 22 July 1888; Fuze, *Black People*, p. 124; Gibson, *Story of the Zulus*, pp. 270–2; Binns, *Dinuzulu*, pp. 34–8; Van Zyl, 'Uitbreiding van Britse Gesag', pp. 132–3; Guy, *Zulu Kingdom*, p. 226; Dominy, 'Etshaneni', pp. 28–31; Laband, *Rope of Sand*, pp. 372–4; Knight, *Great Zulu Battles*, pp. 181–93.

From the Battle of Tshaneni to the Pacification of the Reserve Territory

BPP (C. 4191), no. 66 and encs 2–6; nos 69–70 and encs; nos 73–74 and encs; nos 76–77 and encs; nos 80–82 and encs; *BPP* (C. 4214), nos 2–6 and encs; no. 8 and enc.; nos 11–32 and encs; no. 34; no. 37; nos 39–41 and encs; nos 43–50 and encs; no. 52 and encs 1–3; nos 56–57 and encs; nos 60–64 and encs; nos 66–70 and encs; nos 73–74 and encs; *BPP* (C. 4247), nos 1–4 and encs; nos 6–8 and encs; nos 10–11 and encs; nos 13–16 and encs; nos 18–19 and encs; nos 22–23; no. 30; no. 33 and enc.; no. 36; nos 42–45 and encs; War Office, *Précis*, pp. 95–6; Binns, *Dinuzulu*, pp. 39–43, 45–8, 50, 60–1; Van Zyl, 'Uitbreiding van Britse Gesag', pp. 133–50; Laband, *Rope of Sand*, p. 374.

PART IV

The New Republic

BPP (C. 4214), no. 1; no. 12; no. 33; no. 42 and

encs 1–3; no. 53 and encs 1–2; no. 60; nos 69–70; *BPP* (C. 4274), no. 9 and enc.; no. 20; no. 24 and enc.; no. 27; nos 34–35 and encs; *BPP* (C. 4587), nos 1–16 and encs; nos 21–26 and encs; nos 29–31 and encs; nos 33–36 and encs; nos 39–48 and encs; nos 52–67 and encs; no. 69; nos 72–77 and encs; nos 79–90 and encs; nos 92–94 and encs; nos 97–104 and encs; nos 106–111 and encs; nos 113–114 and encs; no. 117; *BPP* (C. 4645), nos 4–5 and encs; nos 7–9 and encs; nos 11–13; nos 15–16; no. 18; nos 20–25 and encs; no. 27; no. 30 and enc.; no. 32 and enc.; nos 35–40 and encs; enc. 2 in no. 40; no. 45; no. 47; no. 49; nos 50–52 and encs; no. 56 and encs 1–2; nos 59–62 and encs; *BPP* (C. 4913), nos 1–6 and encs; no. 9 and encs 1–2; no. 11 and enc.; nos 13–19 and encs; nos 21–22 and encs; nos 25–26 and encs; nos 29–32 and encs; nos 40–41 and encs; nos 48–51 and encs; nos 54–55 and encs; nos 61–65 and encs; *BPP* (C. 4980), nos 1–4 and encs; no. 6; nos 8–10 and encs; nos 16–17 and encs; no. 22; nos 25–27 and encs; nos 31–47 and encs; nos 58–61 and encs; nos 65–69 and encs; nos 76–77 and encs; nos 85–87 and encs; no. 90; no. 93; encs 1–2 in no. 96; no. 106 and enc.; *BPP* (C. 5143), nos 5–7 and encs; no. 9; no. 14; no. 20; nos 25–26 and encs; no. 36; no. 38 and enc.; nos 41–42; *BPP* (C. 5331), nos 13–14 and encs; no. 19 and enc.; no. 23 and enc.; *BPP* (C. 5892), no. 41 and enc.; no. 51; War Office, *Précis*, pp. 96–7; Gibson, *Story of the Zulus*, pp. 273–82; Binns, *Dinuzulu*, pp. 44, 49, 51–9, 61–93, 98–9; Van Zyl, 'Uitbreiding van Britse Gesag', pp. 150–73; Van Wyk, *Dinuzulu*, pp. 6–11; Laband and Thompson, 'Reduction of Zululand', pp. 213–15; Laband, *Rope of Sand*, pp. 374–6.

PART V

The British Colony of Zululand

BPP (C. 4980), nos 48–50 and encs; nos 62–64 and encs; nos 72–74; no. 78 and enc; nos 80–81 and encs; no. 95 and enc.; nos 97–98 and encs; nos 100–104; no. 107; *BPP* (C. 5143), nos 2–3 and encs; no. 8 and enc.; nos 10–13 and encs; nos 15–16 and encs; nos 18–19; nos 21–24 and encs; nos 27–33 and encs; no. 39; nos 43–45 and encs; *BPP* (C. 5331), nos 1–4 and encs; nos 7–12 and encs; nos 15–18 and encs; nos 20–22 and encs; nos 24–31 and encs; War Office, *Précis*, pp. 97–9, 107; Gibson, *Story of the Zulus*, pp. 282–91; Binns, *Dinuzulu*, pp. 93–105; Van Zyl, 'Uitbreiding van Britse Gesag', pp. 73–8; Van Wyk, *Dinuzulu*, pp. 11–19; 21–43; Laband, 'Dick Addison', pp. 1–2, 16–18, 40–2, 45–53; Laband and Thompson, 'Reduction of Zululand', pp. 215–17; Laband, *Rope of Sand*, pp. 376–80, 382–5; Nicholls, 'Colenso Endeavour', pp. 49–59.

Raid and Counter-Raid

BPP (C. 5331), nos 38–41 and encs; nos 43–53 and encs; nos 55–56 and encs; *BPP* (C. 5522), nos 1–4 and encs; nos 6–8 and encs; nos 10–11 and encs; nos 13–28 and encs; nos 33–35 and encs;

no. 38 and encs 1–2; *BPP* (C. 5892), no. 66 and enc.; no. 119 and enc.; no. 122 and enc.; War Office, *Précis*, p. 99; Gibson, *Story of the Zulus*, pp. 292–303; Binns, *Dinuzulu*, pp. 106–25; Van Wyk, *Dinuzulu*, pp. 43–61, 63–9; Laband, 'Dick Addison', pp. 53–131; Laband and Thompson, 'Reduction of Zululand', pp. 217–18; Laband, *Rope of Sand*, pp. 385–404; Nicholls, 'Colenso Endeavour', pp. 59–64, 98–105.

The Battle of Ceza

GHZ 712, no. Z413/88: statement by Sifo and Soni, 9 July 1888; GHZ 716, no. Z767/88: Stabb to Assistant Military Secretary, Cape Town, 19 October 1888; *BPP* (C. 5522), enc. 1 in no. 38: Addison to Osborn, 3 June 1888; enc. 2 in no. 38: Stabb to Deputy Adjutant General, 7 June 1888; Pennefather to Staff Officer, Eshowe, 3 June 1888; Mansel to Osborn, 3 June 1888; *Court of the Special Commissioners for Zululand*, pp. 191–5, 659–72: Mansel; pp. 289–91, 760–2: Umhlalo; pp. 673–8: Sodoyi; Webb and Wright, *James Stuart Archive*, vol. III, p. 317: Mpatshana; Fuze, *Black People*, p. 127; Gibson, *Story of the Zulus*, pp. 304–5; Van Wyk, *Dinuzulu*, pp. 69–75; Laband, 'Dick Addison', pp. 131–4; Laband, *Rope of Sand*, pp. 404–5.

The Ceza Aftermath

BPP (C. 5331), no. 38; nos 41–43 and encs; encs 1–4 in no. 50; enc. 1 in no. 51; no. 53 and enc.; *BPP* (C. 5892), no. 8 and encs 1–2; no. 66 and enc.; War Office, *Précis*, pp. 99–100; Gibson, *Story of the Zulus*, pp. 305–7; Binns, *Dinuzulu*, pp. 124–7; Van Wyk, *Dinuzulu*, pp. 75–7, 88–9; Laband, 'Dick Addison', pp. 134–9; Laband, *Rope of Sand*, pp. 405–8.

The Battle of Ivuna (Nduna Hill)

BPP (C. 5522) enc. 1 (II) in no. 52: Addison to Osborn, 26 June 1888; Colenso Collection Box 106 (Trials of the Zulu Chiefs 1888–9, no. 1): pp. 33–4: Dinuzulu; pp. 8, 21–2: Ndabuko; *Court of the Special Commissioners for Zululand*, pp. 30, 120–1, 356: Addison; pp. 159–61, 183–4: Foxon; p. 195: Mansel; pp. 262–4, 266: Matuta; pp. 294–5, 298: Umhlahlo; pp. 255, 258–9: Mbusane; pp. 260–1: Mhlupeqi; p. 245: Norris; p. 241: Roberts; pp. 175, 178: Vuzindhlu; *Natal Advertiser*, 23 July 1888; *Natal Mercury*, 7 July and 6 December 1888; *Times of Natal*, 7 and 12 July 1888; M. Mangele, 'Battle of Nongoma', Dr Killie Campbell's Essay Competition, 1942; Fuze, *Black People*, pp. 125–6; Gibson, *Story of the Zulus*, pp. 307–9; Lugg, *Historic Zululand*, pp. 148, 150; Binns, *Dinuzulu*, pp. 126–7; Van Wyk, *Dinuzulu*, pp. 77–82; Laband, 'Dick Addison', pp. 139–48; Laband, 'Battle of Ivuna', pp. 16–22; Laband, *Rope of Sand*, pp. 407–12.

The Situation between the Battles of Ivuna and Hlophekhulu

BPP (C. 5522), nos 29–32 and encs; no. 50; no. 52 and encs 1–2; encs 1–2 in no. 60; no. 66 and encs 1–4; enc. in no. 75; *BPP* (C. 5892), no. 34 and encs 1–5; no. 66 and enc.; War Office, *Précis*, pp. 100–1; Gibson, *Story of the Zulus*, pp. 309–12; Binns, *Dinuzulu*, p. 127; Van Wyk, *Dinuzulu*, pp. 82–6, 88–9; Laband, 'Dick Addison', pp. 148–55; Laband and Thompson, 'Reduction of Zululand', pp. 218–19; Laband, *Rope of Sand*, pp. 413–17.

The Battle of Hlophekhulu

BPP (C. 5522), no. 54: Havelock to Knutsford, 4 July 1888; enc. 1 in no. 66: Addison to Osborn, 5 July 1888; enc. 2 in no. 66: Longden to Knight, 7 July 1888; Knight to Osborn, 7 July 1888; enc. 3 in no. 66: Mansel to Osborn, 6 July 1888; enc. 4 in no. 66: Osborn to Havelock, 11 July 1888; enc. in no. 75: Smyth to Secretary of State for War, 7 July 1888; Stabb to Chief of Staff, Eshowe, 6 July 1888; Minutes I and II, 8 July 1888; Gibson, *Story of the Zulus*, pp. 311–14; Binns, *Dinuzulu*, pp. 128–9; Van Wyk, *Dinuzulu*, pp. 86–8; Laband, 'Dick Addison', pp. 155–6; Laband, *Rope of Sand*, pp. 417–20.

Pacification Operations

BPP (C. 5522), nos 36–37; no. 40 and enc.; no. 45; nos 47–48 and encs; nos 54–55; nos 61–65 and encs; no. 67 and enc.; nos 69–74 and encs; no. 77; *BPP* (C. 5892), nos 1–6 and encs; nos 9–13 and encs; nos 15–19 and encs; no. 23; enc. in no. 25; no. 27 and encs 1–4; no. 36 and enc.; no. 66 and enc.; no. 67; no. 190 and encs 1–19; *BPP* (C. 6070), no. 35; War Office, *Précis*, pp. 101–3; Binns, *Dinuzulu*, pp. 129–32; Van Wyk, *Dinuzulu*, pp. 89–98, 157–61; Laband, 'Dick Addison', pp. 156–72, 181–91; Laband, *Rope of Sand*, pp. 420–3.

The Distribution of the Zululand Garrison

BPP (C. 5892), no. 7; nos 19–21; no. 24 and enc.; no. 26; no. 29 and encs 1–5; nos 31–33 and encs; no. 35 and encs 1–2; nos 37–40 and encs; nos 43–50 and encs; nos 52–53 and encs; nos 59–66 and encs; no. 68; no. 7 and enc.; no. 76 and enc.; no. 80; nos 89–90 and encs; no. 107 and encs 1–2; nos 123–124 and encs; no. 139; no. 147; no. 177; no. 187; *BPP* (C. 5893), nos 1–2 and encs; no. 5; no. 7; *BPP* (C. 6070), no. 4; no. 21; no. 26 and encs 1–2; no. 32 and enc.; War Office, *Précis*, pp. 103–4; Fuze, *Black People*, pp. 127–31; Binns, *Dinuzulu*, pp. 132–49; Van Wyk, *Dinuzulu*, pp. 114–21; 150–7; Laband, 'Dick Addison', pp. 177–81, 191, 198–9; Laband, *Rope of Sand*, pp. 424–8; Nicholls, 'Colenso Endeavour', pp. 69–73, 113–19, 130.

PART VI

The Significance of the Zulu Wars of 1883–1888

For Zululand's fate in the aftermath of the uSuthu rebellion, see Laband and Thompson, 'Reduction of Zululand', pp. 219–24; Laband, *Rope of Sand*, pp. 429–39.

Sources

In comparison to the enormous and still growing literature associated with the Anglo-Zulu War of 1879, there is relatively little published material on the civil wars and rebellion in Zululand during the 1880s. Most of the sources on this period are still in unpublished manuscript collections such as the Colenso and Shepstone papers in the Pietermaritzburg Archives Repository, which also holds the essential Government House (Natal) and Government House (Zululand) papers, the Zululand Archives and the archives of the various Zululand magistracies. The War Office papers in the Public Record Office, Kew, contain vital information on British military operations in Zululand during the 1880s, including contentious correspondence omitted from the *British Parliamentary Papers*. Considerable information is nevertheless to be found printed in sources such as the *British Parliamentary Papers* and contemporary newspapers, as well as in the books and pamphlets published by Bishop Colenso and his daughters, most notably their rambling *Digest of Zulu Affairs*. Much of the recent research into this period is in the form of academic theses.

Official Printed Sources

British Parliamentary Papers: C. 2482, C. 2505, C. 2584, C. 2695, C. 3174, C. 3182, C. 3247, C. 3270, C. 3293, C. 3466, C. 3616, C. 3705, C. 3864, C. 4037, C. 4191, C. 4214, C. 4274, C. 4587, C. 4645, C. 4913, C. 4980, C. 5143, C. 5331, C. 5522, C. 5892, C. 5893, C. 6070, C. 6684.

Callwell, Col C.E. *Small Wars: Their Principles and Practice*, 3rd edition, London, 1906.

The Court of the Special Commissioners for Zululand, 1888–9: Zulu Trials, London, 1889.

Fynney, F.G. *The Zulu Army and Zulu Headmen*, revised edition, Pietermaritzburg, April 1879.

Infantry, Field Exercises and Evolutions of, pocket edition, London, 1877.

Intelligence Division of the War Office, *Précis of Information Concerning Zululand: Corrected to December, 1894*, London, 1895.

War Office, *The Monthly Army List*, London, January to December 1883, 1884, 1887, 1888.

Unofficial Contemporary Printed Sources

Newspapers and serial publications

Graphic
Illustrated London News
Natal Advertiser
Natal Mercury
Natal Witness
Pictorial World
Times of Natal

Books and pamphlets

Campbell, W.Y. *With Cetywayo in the Inkandhla and the Present State of the Zulu Question*, Durban, 1883.

Colenso, F.E. *The Ruin of Zululand: An Account of British Doings in Zululand since the Invasion of 1879*, London, 1884–5, 2 vols.

Anon. [Colenso, H.E.] *The Zulu Impeachment of British Officials 1887–8 Confirmed by Official Records in 1892*, London, 1892.

Colenso, H.E. *Cases of 6 Usutu (Other than the Exiles at St Helena) Punished for Having Taken Part in the Disturbances of 1888*, London, 1893.

Colenso, Bishop J.W. and Colenso, H.E. *Digest of Zulu Affairs Compiled by Bishop Colenso and Continued after his Death by his Daughter Harriette Emily Colenso*, Bishopstowe, 1878–88, series no. 1: December 1878 – April 1881; series no. 2: October 1881 – 16 June 1883; series no. 3: Boers and Zululand 1884; series no. 5: Zulu, British and New Republic, November – June 1887; series nos 6–9: Annexation and 1888 Rebellion.

Dixie, Lady Florence *In the Land of Misfortune*, London, 1882.

Escombe, H. and Dumat, A. *A Remonstrance on Behalf of the Zulu Chiefs*, London, 1889.

Gibson, J.Y. *The Story of the Zulus*, London, 1911.

Richards, W. *Her Majesty's Army: A Descriptive Account of the Various Regiments now Comprising the Queen's Forces, from their First Establishment*, London, n.d. (c. 1885), vols 1–2.

Later Edited, Annotated and Printed Contemporary Sources

Cope, T. (ed.) and Malcolm, D. (tr.) *Izibongo: Zulu Praise–Poems Collected by James Stuart*, Oxford, 1968.

Filter, H. (comp.) and Bourquin, S. (tr. and ed.) *Paulina Dlamini: Servant of Two Kings*, Durban and Pietermaritzburg, 1986; reprinted 1998.

Fuze, M.M. (Lugg, H.C. [tr.] and Cope, A.T. [ed.]) *The Black People and Whence They Came: A Zulu View*, Pietermaritzburg and Durban, 1979; reprinted 1998.

Preston, A. (ed.) *Sir General Wolseley's South African Journal 1839–80*, Cape Town, 1973.

Webb C. de B. and Wright, J.B. (eds) *The James Stuart Archive of Recorded Oral Evidence Relating to the History of the Zulu and Neighbouring Peoples*, Pietermaritzburg and Durban, 1976, 1979, 1982, 1986, 2001, vols 1–5.

Later Printed Sources

Articles

Bailes, H. 'Technology and Imperialism: A Case study of the Victorian Army in Africa', *Victorian Studies*, 24, 1, autumn 1980.

Burroughs, P. 'Imperial Defence and the Victorian Army', *Journal of Imperial and Commonwealth History*, 15, 1, October 1986.

Cloete, D. 'From Warriors to Wage Slaves: The Fate of the Zulu People since 1879', *Reality*, 11, January 1979.

Crossley, R.G. 'The Imperial Garrison of Natal', *Military History Journal*, 2, 5, 1973.

Davenport, T.R.H. 'The Fragmentation of Zululand 1879–1918', *Reality*, 11, 5, 1979.

Dominy, G. 'The New Republicans: A Centennial Reappraisal of the "Nieuwe Republiek", 1884–1888', *Natalia*, 14, 1984.

—. 'In the Aftermath of the Anglo-Zulu War: The Battle of Etshaneni 5 June 1884', *Soldiers of the Queen*, 74, September 1993.

Edgecombe, D.R. 'Sir Marshal Clarke and the Abortive Attempt to "Basutolandise" Zululand', *Journal of Natal and Zulu History*, 3, 1980.

Laband, J.P.C. 'The Battle of Ivuna (or Ndunu Hill)', *Natalia*, 10, 1980.

—. 'The Establishment of the Zululand Administration in 1887: A Study of the Criteria Behind the Selection of British Colonial Officials', *Journal of Natal and Zulu History*, 4, 1981.

—. 'The Cohesion of the Zulu Polity under the Impact of the Anglo-Zulu War: A Reassessment', *Journal of Natal and Zulu History*, 8, 1985.

—. 'British Boundary Adjustments and the uSuthu–Mandlakazi Conflict in Zululand, 1879–1904', *South African Historical Journal*, 30, May 1994.

—. and Thompson, P.S. 'The Reduction of Zululand, 1878–1904' in Duminy, A. and Guest, B. (eds) *Natal and Zululand from Earliest Times to 1910: A New History*, Pietermaritzburg, 1989.

Marks, S. 'Harriette Colenso and the Zulus, 1874–1913', *Journal of African History*, 4, 1963.

Porch, D. 'Imperial Wars: From the Seven Years War to the First World War' in Townshend, C. (ed.) *The Oxford History of Modern War*, Oxford, 2000.

Spiers, E. 'The Late Victorian Army 1868–1914' in Chandler, D. (gen. ed.) and Beckett, I. (assoc. ed.) *The Oxford Illustrated History of the British Army*, Oxford, 1994.

Thompson, P.S. 'Isandlwana to Mome: Zulu Experience in Overt Resistance to Colonial Rule', *Soldiers of the Queen*, 77, June 1994.

Tylen, Maj G. 'Mounted Infantry', *Journal of the Society for Army Historical Research*, 22, 1943–4.

Wesseling, H.L. 'Colonial Wars: An Introduction' in De Moor, J.A. and Wesseling, H.L. (eds) *Imperialism and War: Essays on Colonial War in Asia and Africa*, Leiden, 1989.

Books and pamphlets

Ballard, C. *John Dunn: The White Chief of Zululand*, Craighall, 1985.

Barthorpe, M. *The British Army on Campaign 1816–1902,* London, 1987–8, series of four.

Binns, C.T. *The Last Zulu King: The Life*

and Death of Cetshwayo, London, 1963.

—. Dinuzulu: The Death of the House of Shaka, London, 1968.

Black, J. War Past, Present & Future, Stroud, 2000.

Boyden, P.B., Guy, A.J. and Harding, M. (eds) Ashes and Blood: The British Army in South Africa, 1795–1914, London, 1999.

Braatvedt, H.P. Roaming Zululand with a Native Commissioner, Pietermaritzburg, 1949.

Brookes, E.H. and Webb, C. de B. A History of Natal, Pietermaritzburg, 1965.

Bulpin, T.V. Shaka's Country: A Book of Zululand, 3rd edition, Cape Town, 1956.

Guy, J. The Destruction of the Zulu Kingdom: The Civil War in Zululand, 1879–1884, 3rd edition, Pietermaritzburg, 1998.

—. The Heretic: A Study of the Life of John William Colenso 1814–1883, Johannesburg and Pietermaritzburg, 1983.

—. View Across the River: Harriette Colenso & the Zulu Struggle against Imperialism, Oxford, 2001. [Published too late in 2001 to be consulted for this historical atlas.]

Headrick, D.R. The Tools of Empire: Technology and European Imperialism in the Nineteenth Century, New York, 1981.

Knight, I.J. The Anatomy of the Zulu Army from Shaka to Cetshwayo 1818–1879, London, 1995.

—. Go to Your God Like a Soldier: The British Soldier Fighting for Empire, 1837–1902, London, 1996.

—. Great Zulu Battles 1838–1906, London, 1998.

— Great Zulu Commanders, London, 1999.

Laband, J.P.C. Rope of Sand: The Rise and Fall of the Zulu Kingdom in the Nineteenth Century, Johannesburg, 1995.

—. and Thompson, P.S. The Illustrated Guide to the Anglo-Zulu War, Pietermaritzburg, 2000.

Leverton, B.J.T. and Pringle, J.A. The Pioneers of Vryheid: The Nieuwe Republiek and its Staats Courant, Pietermaritzburg, 1974.

Lugg, H.C. Historic Natal and Zululand, Pietermaritzburg, 1949.

Maddox G. and Welliver, T.K. (eds) Conquest and Resistance to Colonialism in Africa. Vol. 1 of Colonialism and Nationalism in Africa: A Four-Volume Anthology of Scholarly Articles, New York, 1993.

Samuelson, R.C.A. Long, Long Ago, Durban, 1929.

Seegers, A. The Military and the Making of Modern South Africa, New York, 1995.

Spiers, E. The Late Victorian Army, 1868–1902, Manchester, 1992.

Strachan, H. European Armies and the Conduct of War, London, 1983.

Taylor, S. Shaka's Children: A History of the Zulu People, London, 1994.

Van Creveld, M.L. Technology and War from 2000 B.C. to the Present, London, 1989.

Vandervort, B. Wars of Imperial Conquest in Africa 1830–1914, London, 1998.

Van Wyk, A.J. Dinuzulu en die Usutu-Opstand van 1888, Pretoria, 1983.

Van Zyl, M.C. Dinuzulu se Flug na die Suid-Afrikaanse Republiek in 1888, Pretoria, 1961.

—. 'Die Uitbreiding van Britse Gesag oor die Natalse Noordgrensgebiede 1879–1897' Archives Year Book for South African History, Cape Town, 1966, vol. I of 29th year.

Whitehouse, H. Battle in Africa 1879–1914, Mansfield, 1987.

Unpublished theses

Dominy, G.A. 'The Imperial Garrison in Natal with Special Reference to Fort Napier 1843–1914: Its Social, Cultural and Economic Impact', Ph.D. thesis, University of London, 1995.

Harrison, K.A. 'Melmoth Osborn and Events in Zululand, 1879–1883', BA (Hons) thesis, University of Natal, 1967.

Kemp, B.H. 'John William Colenbrander: A History of the Times, People and Events with which he was Associated, 1879–1896, Ph.D. thesis, University of Natal, 1962.

Laband, J.P.C. 'Dick Addison: The Role of a British Official during the Disturbances in the Ndwandwe District of Zululand, 1887–1889', MA thesis, University of Natal, 1980.

Nicholls, B.M. 'The Colenso Endeavour in its Context, 1887–1897', Ph.D. thesis, University of Natal, 1997.

Paterson, H. 'The Military Organisation of the Colony of Natal, 1881–1910', MA thesis, University of Natal, 1985.

Pridmore, J. 'The Diary of Henry Francis Fynn, Jnr: 1883', MA thesis, University of Natal, 1987.

Index

Zulu names are entered under the first letter of the stem, rather than the prefix.